Agamben's Philosophical Trajectory

Agamben's Philosophical Trajectory

Adam Kotsko

EDINBURGH
University Press

Edinburgh University Press is one of the leading university presses in
the UK. We publish academic books and journals in our selected subject
areas across the humanities and social sciences, combining cutting-edge
scholarship with high editorial and production values to produce academic
works of lasting importance. For more information visit our website:
edinburghuniversitypress.com

Edinburgh University Press Ltd
The Tun – Holyrood Road
12(2f) Jackson's Entry
Edinburgh EH8 8PJ

Typeset in 11/13 Bembo by
IDSUK (DataConnection) Ltd

A CIP record for this book is available from the British Library

ISBN 978 1 4744 7600 3 (hardback)
ISBN 978 1 4744 7602 7 (webready PDF)
ISBN 978 1 4744 7601 0 (paperback)
ISBN 978 1 4744 7603 4 (epub)

Contents

Acknowledgements

Before setting out on my investigation, I would like to acknowledge those who have contributed to this project. As ever, I thank Natalie Scoles for pointing me in the direction I was already going, helping convince me it was time to write a study on Agamben (at a time when I imagined I was carrying out my systematic study for my own personal edification and nothing more) and pushing me to apply for funding to meet with him. I am grateful to North Central College for providing a summer research grant to facilitate that visit and to Giorgio for taking the time to reflect with me on the development of his thought. I also had the opportunity to share my preliminary findings at seminars in Toronto (hosted by York University Communication Program and Ryerson University Faculty of Communication and Design) and Prague (hosted by the Faculty of Protestant Theology, Charles University). I would like to thank Virgil Brower and František Štěch for their invitation to Prague and Philippe Theophanidis for his invitation to Toronto and all the participants at both events for their engagement and feedback (especially Kim Berkey, who provided a formal response to my paper in Prague). André Dias provided crucial bibliographical guidance, and both Marika Rose and Colby Dickinson read drafts and provided valuable comments, for which I am grateful. Finally, I would like to thank my two anonymous reviewers, along with Carol Macdonald, Tim Clark, and the rest of the editorial and support staff at Edinburgh University Press.

Abbreviations for Works of Agamben

A   *The Adventure*. Trans. Lorenzo Chiesa. Cambridge, MA: MIT Press, 2018.

ARS   *Autoritratto nello studio*. Milan: Nottetempo, 2017.

CA   *Creation and Anarchy: The Work of Art and the Religion of Capitalism*. Trans. Adam Kotsko. Stanford: Stanford University Press, 2019.

CC   *The Coming Community*. Trans. Michael Hardt. Minneapolis: University of Minnesota Press, 1993.

EP   *The End of the Poem: Studies in Poetics*. Trans. Daniel Heller-Roazen. Stanford: Stanford University Press, 1999.

HP   *The Highest Poverty: Monastic Rules and Form-of-Life*. Trans. Adam Kotsko. Stanford: Stanford University Press, 2013.

HS   *Homo Sacer: Sovereign Power and Bare Life*. Trans. Daniel Heller-Roazen. Stanford: Stanford University Press, 1998.

IH   *Infancy and History: On the Destruction of Experience*. Trans. Liz Heron. New York: Verso, 1993.

IP   *Idea of Prose*. Trans. Michael Sullivan and Sam Whitsitt. Albany: SUNY Press, 1995.

K   *Karman: A Brief Treatise on Action, Guilt, and Gesture*. Trans. Adam Kotsko. Stanford: Stanford University Press, 2018.

KG   *The Kingdom and the Glory: For a Theological Genealogy of Economy and Government*. Trans. Lorenzo Chiesa and Matteo Mandarini. Stanford: Stanford University Press, 2011.

LD   *Language and Death: The Place of Negativity.* Trans. Karen E. Pinkus with Michael Hardt. Minneapolis: University of Minnesota Press, 1991.

MWC   *The Man Without Content.* Trans. Georgia Albert. Stanford: Stanford University Press, 1999.

MWE   *Means Without End: Notes on Politics.* Trans. Vincenzo Binetti and Cesare Casarino. Minneapolis: University of Minnesota Press, 2000.

O   *The Open: Man and Animal.* Trans. Kevin Attell. Stanford: Stanford University Press, 2004.

OD   *Opus Dei: An Archaeology of Duty.* Trans. Adam Kotsko. Stanford: Stanford University Press, 2013.

P   *Potentialities: Collected Essays in Philosophy.* Ed. and trans. Daniel Heller-Roazen. Stanford: Stanford University Press, 1999.

Pr   *Profanations.* Trans. Jeff Fort. Cambridge, MA: Zone Books, 2007.

Pu   *Pulcinella: Or, Entertainment for Children.* Trans. Kevin Attell. New York: Seagull, 2018.

RA   *Remnants of Auschwitz: The Witness and the Archive.* Trans. Daniel Heller-Roazen. Cambridge: Zone Books, 2002.

RG   *Il Regno e il Giardino.* Vicenza: Neri Pozza, 2019.

S   *Stanzas: Word and Phantasm in Western Culture.* Trans. Ronald L. Martinez. Minneapolis: University of Minnesota Press, 1993.

SE   *State of Exception.* Trans. Kevin Attell. Chicago: University of Chicago Press, 2005.

SL   *The Sacrament of Language: An Archaeology of the Oath.* Trans. Adam Kotsko. Stanford: Stanford University Press, 2011.

ST   *The Signature of All Things: On Method.* Trans. Luca D'Isanto with Kevin Attell. New York: Zone, 2009.

STA   *Stasis: Civil War as a Political Paradigm.* Trans. Nicholas Heron. Stanford: Stanford University Press, 2015.

TL   'The Tree of Language'. Trans. Connal Parsley. *Journal of Italian Philosophy* 1 (2018), 12–21.

TTR   *The Time That Remains: A Commentary on the Letter to the Romans.* Trans. Patricia Dailey. Stanford: Stanford University Press, 2005.

UB   *The Use of Bodies.* Trans. Adam Kotsko. Stanford: Stanford
          University Press, 2016.
UG   *The Unspeakable Girl: The Myth and Mystery of Kore.*
          Trans. Leland de la Durantaye and Annie Julia Wyman.
          New York: Seagull, 2014. (With Monica Ferrando.)
WA   *What is an Apparatus? And Other Essays.* Trans. David
          Kishik and Stefan Pedatella. Stanford: Stanford University
          Press, 2009.
WP   *What is Philosophy?* Trans. Lorenzo Chiesa. Stanford:
          Stanford University Press, 2018.
WR   *What is Real?* Trans. Lorenzo Chiesa. Stanford: Stanford
          University Press, 2018.

Introduction: Living With Agamben

For most of the 2000s, there was no thinker more in tune with his historical moment than Giorgio Agamben. His most famous work, *Homo Sacer: Sovereign Power and Bare Life* (1995),[1] had established him as a major political thinker, but world events conspired to make him a prophet. In that pathbreaking work, he argued that Western politics had always been fundamentally about the relationship between sovereign power and bare life – in other words, politics has always been a matter of deciding who is a citizen with rights and who is a non-person. Making this decision is the ultimate function of any sovereign political entity, and the line between person and non-person is the line between where the law applies and where sheer necessity (and therefore limitless violence) reigns. In the mid-1990s, one could perhaps be forgiven for finding this thesis to be provocatively overblown. With the dawn of the War on Terror, however, and especially the revelation of the abuses at Abu Ghraib and Guantánamo Bay, Agamben's idiosyncratic diagnosis seemed disturbingly prescient. And in his sequel to *Homo Sacer*, *State of Exception* (2003), Agamben forcefully asserted the contemporary relevance of his ideas by inscribing the Bush administration in a longer history of modern Western democracies' reliance on exceptional emergency powers.

Already, that insight was enough to make an intellectual career, but he remained astoundingly productive in other areas as well. Shortly before the appearance of *State of Exception*, Agamben put out *The Open: Man and Animal* (2002), an investigation into the relation between humanity and animality that anticipated the rise of animal studies in academic circles and the transformation of animal rights from a fringe concern to a serious moral and ethical issue for increasing numbers of people around the world. Arguably even more remarkable was the timing of Agamben's next major work, *The Kingdom and the Glory: Toward a Theological Genealogy of Economy and Government* (2007),[2] which took the form of a massive study of the theological origins of economic ideas. Arguing against the market triumphalism of the 1990s and 2000s, Agamben claimed that, far from offering the path to freedom and salvation, the nihilistic providential guidance of the invisible hand was leading us down the road to perdition. Published amid the early warning signs of the global financial crisis, *The Kingdom and the Glory* established Agamben as one of the few thinkers to anticipate both of the great calamities of the first decade of our young century.

Almost immediately after the English translation of *Homo Sacer* in 1998, a critical literature sprung up around Agamben (largely, though not exclusively, in English), dedicated to explaining and applying his theories and probing their foundations. And there was much to explain and to probe, as all of Agamben's works featured abstract metaphysical and linguistic speculations and fine-grained philological investigations, whose relation to his provocative political claims was not always immediately clear. The initial stage of scholarship focused all but exclusively on *Homo Sacer* itself, producing critical articles and even an edited volume.[3] Later work, as represented in a special issue of *South Atlantic Quarterly* entitled *The Agamben Effect*,[4] expanded the purview somewhat to include *The Open* and *State of Exception*. After the initial scramble to respond to Agamben's most recent writings – and amid translation delays that would prevent most Anglophone readers from engaging with *The Kingdom and the Glory* until 2011 – scholars turned their attention to the considerable body of work that had preceded them. Especially after the publication of Daniel Heller-Roazen's important collection of Agamben's essays, *Potentialities* (2005), it was impossible to ignore the fact that Agamben's career as a writer was already in its third decade when *Homo Sacer* was published – and that the

earlier works were already exploring the metaphysical and linguistic questions that were so difficult to place within the later
political works.

Hence a new wave of scholarship arose, seeking to contextualise
Agamben's most famous works within the broader perspective of
his entire philosophical output. Often, however, the effect was the
opposite – to present Agamben's earlier work as a kind of prelude
to his great political interventions of the 1990s and 2000s. Most
often, commentators justify this move by claiming a remarkable
degree of consistency in his vast and varied body of work. Catherine Mills, the author of the earliest full monograph on Agamben's
thought, cautiously sets the tone here, claiming that

> if one reads progressively through Agamben's work, it is
> evident that there is very little sense in which it follows
> a straightforward incremental or systematic trajectory.
> Instead, his work over the past several decades is a complex
> recursive exercise that extends and modifies his approach
> to several key questions and issues that reappear in one
> guise or another in almost every text. In this way, there is
> a densely interconnected conceptual web, but no (more or
> less linear) system as such.[5]

Nevertheless she presents the earlier works – particularly *Infancy
and History* (1978) and *Language and Death* (1982) – as a necessary
precondition to understanding *Homo Sacer* (1995). On one level,
this approach makes sense: where else should we turn for guidance
on Agamben's method and position but his own writings? At the
same time, though, if those texts are so crucial for understanding
Homo Sacer, why does Agamben himself never explicitly refer back
to them?

Shortly afterward, Leland de la Durantaye's study, which is
widely regarded as the most thorough and authoritative work on
Agamben to date, goes further than Mills. After complaining at
some length about the *Homo Sacer*-centric literature, Durantaye
declares, 'The interests and issues of the *Homo Sacer* project are,
at least in part, new ones; but alongside this novelty is an equally
striking continuity and a remarkable reformulation of concerns

that have accompanied Agamben's work since his first publications nearly thirty years prior to it.[6] For Durantaye, this principle
of continuity is the concept of potentiality, which is present *in
nuce* from Agamben's very first work, even if it is not explicitly
named as such. Carlo Salzani, the author of the first book-length
study of Agamben's work in Italian, takes a similar position,
arguing that

> if it is unquestionable that, beginning from the '90s, Agam-
> ben's philosophy focuses in a particular way on the question
> of politics and of its contemporary crises (and if it is unques-
> tionable that the influence of Foucault contributes to this
> 'turn'), it is just as certain that these 'political' analyses are
> founded upon, and rearticulate in a more explicitly political
> sense, the critiques of metaphysics, aesthetics, language, and
> history that Agamben had carried out, in a coherent and
> substantially unitary way, from the beginning of the '70s.[7]

Later he underscores the point, claiming that *Homo Sacer* 'was a caesura, but more in Agamben's career – since it gave him international
fame and marked the beginning of a more systematic "project"
that continues for almost twenty years – than in his thought, which
instead shows unity and continuity'.[8] And in their more recent co-
authored study, Claire Colebrook and Jason Maxwell make a similar
point, but stated a bit more baldly: 'Although the many book-length
works he has composed are ostensibly devoted to distinct themes . . .
every book makes a continuing contribution to a long-term project.'[9] Again, questions arise: if all of Agamben's books contribute to
a continuous project, then what sense does it make to designate only
a subset of them, from relatively late in his career, as an explicit series?
And how can *Homo Sacer* represent a starting point for that series
if it is but one volume in the broader series that all of Agamben's
corpus supposedly represents?

Meanwhile, a growing body of literature devoted to specific
topics in Agamben's work has also presupposed the essential unity
of his corpus. For instance, Colby Dickinson, in the introduction to his study of Agamben's use of theology, states, 'On the
whole, [Agamben's] is a remarkably cohesive body of work, one

which links his early writings in near seamless fashion with his later projects . . . This consistency of thought, if it can be labeled as such, means that it is often possible to find the same or similar themes present in varying contexts from publication to publication.'[10] Within the body of his argument, Dickinson relies on this remarkable cohesion, often shifting among works from widely different periods within a single paragraph. In his study of Agamben's relationship to literature, William Watkin claims, somewhat more enigmatically, that 'Agamben is a sporadic and yet profoundly consistent writer',[11] and he follows Dickinson in jumping casually between different periods. In his attempt to reconstruct Agamben's relationship to astrology, Paul Colilli uses a similarly eclectic approach, though without explicitly thematising it.[12] The same is true of Mathew Abbott's 'development and defense' of Agamben's thought centred on the concept of political ontology,[13] which moves freely among works that evince a more positive (as opposed to merely critical) philosophical position from all periods of his thought – something that could equally be said of David Kishik and Arne de Boever's more 'constructive' works on Agamben, as well as Watkins' more comprehensive follow-up study.[14]

Among commentators on Agamben's politics, Jessica Whyte is perhaps more cautious in focusing primarily on texts that deal explicitly with the topic, though she too can point back to even the earliest texts in a way that presupposes continuity – above all her frequent reference to his declaration in *Man Without Content* that 'it is only in the burning house that the fundamental architectural problem becomes visible for the first time' (MWC 115).[15] Most extreme is Sergei Prozorov, who devotes almost half of his study of Agamben's politics to early works with no obvious connection to his theme. In the final chapter of his study, he summarises his approach as follows:

Our discussion of Agamben's politics in the preceding pages has tended to emphasize continuity in Agamben's thought, demonstrating the persistence of the same themes in his work from his earliest writings on aesthetics, language, and ontology to his most recent studies of government and religion. Rather than indicate a discontinuous 'turn' towards politics in the post-Cold War period, the *Homo Sacer* series and subsequent works must be understood as taking explicit stock of Agamben's politics as it has been theorized implicitly or elliptically in the previous decades.[16]

Nevertheless, he detects 'an important discontinuity in Agamben's work' on 'the question of anthropocentrism' – meaning that *The Open*, published at the beginning of the fourth decade of Agamben's writing career, represents the first and only significant change to arise at any point in his intellectual trajectory.[17] Why only *this* particular change, though, after a career of such astonishing uniformity? And why so late?

*   *   *

According to his commentators, then, Giorgio Agamben is one of the most innovative and relevant thinkers of our time, and he has also been saying more or less the same thing since the early 1970s. How can both of these claims be true? Is it really possible for a writer with a career spanning just over half a century to remain as remarkably consistent as Agamben's commentators claim? And, perhaps more importantly – even if it were possible, would it be a good thing?

This book presupposes that the answer to both questions is no. No living, human author can *or should* aspire to the kind of continuity that these studies claim to see in Agamben's body of work. The fantasy of the pure systematician, working out a continuous project with no serious deviations or dead ends, is a particularly tempting one in the context of American continental philosophy, a field that is dominated by commentary on authoritative figures from abroad. Yet it *is* a fantasy – and in Agamben's case, I would argue that it is one that can actively impede our attempts to answer what should be the most important question about his interventions of the 1990s and 2000s: *how did he do it?* How did an erudite theorist of language and aesthetics not only transform himself into one of the world's leading political thinkers, but do so in a way that was so uncannily in step with his times? Surely the answer cannot be that he simply kept repeating the same basic ideas for decades until the times coincidentally matched up with his diagnoses.

Any attempt to answer the question of how Agamben achieved what he did must begin with the recognition that he has lived through tumultuous times, beginning his intellectual career amid the upheaval of the late 1960s, witnessing the collapse of the Soviet bloc and the eruption of genocidal war in Yugoslavia, making his name as a commentator on Bush's War on Terror, and completing his life's work amid the ongoing collapse of the neoliberal economic order. As I will argue in later chapters, all of his work responds in some way to the times in which he finds himself, but seldom in the mode of direct political commentary. Moreover, world events are far from the only source of dynamism in his thought. As he reveals most clearly in his 2017 memoir, *Autoritratto nello studio* (*Self-Portrait in His Studio*), he has lived a life rich in intense intellectual friendships with a startling range of strong personalities. And even aside from personal relationships, a study of his texts shows him taking on new influences even as he deepens and complicates his most familiar ones. No one reading his works of the 1970s would ever guess the central role Foucault would come to play in the *Homo Sacer* series, for instance, nor how critical his position on Heidegger in the later works turns out to be.

As the latter observations indicate, my argument in this book is not based solely on my intuition that he neither could nor should maintain the kind of consistency that his commentators attribute to him. More importantly, it is based on my empirical observation that he in fact *does not*. Shortly after completing my translation of *Creation and Anarchy*, a published lecture series on the paradoxical place of art in the modern world, I was curious how his views expressed there matched up with what he had said on the same topic in his very first book, *The Man Without Content*. That book was one of the first I had read after *Homo Sacer*, and I had not returned to it since.[18] Opening it up, I found it to be almost a foreign country – not only was the prose style very different from most of his works, but (as I will discuss in the first chapter) many of the key reference points seemed skewed or even reversed compared to the 'official' position in his mature works.

This experience led me to undertake a larger project: to read every work by Agamben that I could find, in as close to chronological order as I could discern. While I do not claim to have read every word the man has ever published, I have covered every text that has appeared in book form in Italian or English. At times, this proved quite laborious, as I had to skip back and forth among the three major essay collections – *Potentialities*, *The End of the Poem*, and *Means Without End* – the first two of which in particular bring together texts from widely different periods, arranged thematically rather than chronologically.[19] While I had already read most of the texts at least once before, I spent the better part of a year systematically working my way back through Agamben's entire corpus in this chronological fashion, reading (or rereading) every work word-for-word and taking detailed notes as I went.

When I told fellow scholars of Agamben about this project, they were often sceptical. Many doubted that the date of publication was actually meaningful, since Agamben may well have written a text long before he published it. Sometimes this is clearly the case, as with the short books *Taste* and *Stasis*, both of which appeared in 2015, though they were originally written in 1979 and 2001, respectively. Yet my method of moving between the various essay collections revealed striking parallels between texts that appeared in the same year, even those with seemingly unrelated topics. The same concepts and argumentative moves reappeared, whether he was talking about poetry or ontology, messianism or linguistics. From these patterns, I inferred that, even if he did have some raw materials 'lying around' at any given time, Agamben tends to approach his writing much as most scholars do – namely, by doing some mixture of self-initiated and invited writing, and bending the latter to fit whatever they happen to be exploring at any given moment. I had the opportunity to meet with Agamben at his home in Venice while I was in the process of drafting the present manuscript, and in the course of our conversation, he confirmed this intuition, saying that he seldom waits long to publish texts once he has written them. Hence, except in cases where there is strong evidence to the contrary (as in the cases of *Taste* and *Stasis*), I have tended to assume that pieces that are published close together are also written close together.

The result of this philological investigation has been clear: Agamben's thought does indeed change over time. This is not to say that Agamben's work develops in a linear or progressive fashion. Yet there are clear inflection points. Most notably, politics are virtually absent from his work prior to *The Coming Community* (1990), to the point where no one familiar with the first twenty years of his career would have guessed that he would one day become a world-renowned political theorist. As we have seen, Durantaye, Salzani, and Prozorov all dismiss the idea that some kind of 'turn' is at work here. But clearly *something* has changed, because it was immediately apparent when reading chronologically that he abruptly shifts from virtually never talking about politics to talking about politics a great deal. After that change on the level of content, there is a change on the level of form. The early 2000s – when he set to work constructing the *Homo Sacer* series, on a much larger scale than readers of the first few volumes would have expected – mark the emergence of a new system-building impulse, which stands in some tension with the ever-increasing scope of the project. Finally, the publication of *The Use of Bodies*, which brought the *Homo Sacer* project to a close, marked another shift in focus, as the works that have continued to appear in recent years have all taken on a more explicitly personal and reflective tone.

None of these turning points marks a definitive break. The commentators are right to observe that Agamben keeps returning to familiar ideas and patterns of thought. No theme or concept is ever truly left behind, nor does he ever explicitly repudiate any previous argument – so a 'turn' on the model of Wittgenstein or Heidegger is not in the cards. Indeed, it was clear from our conversation in Venice that he has always been striving toward some kind of consistency, some sense that his body of work adds up to something more than a series of randomly juxtaposed texts. Yet that impulse stands in productive tension with Agamben's responsiveness – to his ever-changing cast of intellectual comrades, to new influences and new ways of understanding old ones, and to the most important historical events that have unfolded around him. He wants to remain faithful to his key insights, but he seldom incorporates passages from much older works directly into

his texts.[20] Instead, he continually reworks and recontextualises
them, sometimes to the point where they come to have a radically
different valence. As he put it during our conversation, when he
returns to his earliest texts, he always finds that his key concepts
were somehow present – 'but I didn't know it at the time'. His
core ideas are not already there in his earlier works as a permanent
deposit, then, but as a perpetual *problem* that he is constantly trying
to work out.

*   *   *

The goal of this book is to give the reader an idea of the varied
ways that Agamben wrestles with the problems that he has set
himself and the problems that the world has imposed upon him.
I resort to periodisation not as a simplistic mnemonic device, but
as a framework for presenting Agamben's thought as a truly living and historical thought – one that strives toward a unity that
is never pre-given but must always be won anew. Each chapter
will take in turn one of the periods of Agamben's work, with an
emphasis on development and change. My conversation and subsequent emails with Agamben will be a major point of reference
here, but their contribution is often indirect. In my experience,
Agamben is happy to talk in general terms about his career, but
tends to be reluctant to go into very fine-grained detail. Hence,
although nothing I say here explicitly contradicts Agamben's own
description of his writing process, my account of his development
and motivations represents my own reconstruction based on a
close, chronological reading of his texts.

The first chapter covers the early stages of Agamben's work,
from the late 1960s until the mid-1980s. While many scholars read
these texts as a kind of prelude to his explicitly political writings,
I argue that we need to realise that their apolitical character is the
result of a conscious choice on the part of an iconoclastic young
thinker who views the political options imposed by the Cold War
as unworthy of serious reflection and has chosen instead to focus
on the realm of personal experience. Read on their own terms,
they represent a series of ambitious, but never quite successful
attempts to establish a truly interdisciplinary 'general science of
the human' grounded in a philosophically articulated linguistics.

In the second chapter, I pick up threads from Agamben's work of the mid-1980s that retrospectively lay the groundwork for his later shift into the realm of politics in his works of the 1990s. Both the debate between Nancy and Blanchot on community and, later, the collapse of the USSR made politics appear potentially fruitful to Agamben at this time, but it is the war in Yugoslavia, with its genocidal violence, that truly shapes his project in *Homo Sacer* (1995). I present this period as one of rapid development and daring experimentation, which in a sense runs aground in *Remnants of Auschwitz* (1999), a work that suffers from his lack of a clearly articulated methodology.

In the 2000s, Agamben's search for a method takes place in the context of a radical expansion of the *Homo Sacer* project into the realms of theology and economics. These two themes come together in *The Kingdom and the Glory* (2007), which in the third chapter I present as an especially problematic text within the existing terms of his project, and therefore as a spur to the development of his distinctive archaeological method. I conclude with a discussion of that method as it is reflected in *The Signature of All Things* (2008).

The fourth chapter brings the *Homo Sacer* project to its completion with *The Use of Bodies* (2014). I trace the ways that the archaeological method shapes the remaining volumes of the series and investigate the continuing challenges of coherence that are inherent in such a long-term writing project. The text of *The Use of Bodies* itself stands as a kind of model in miniature for the whole series, insofar as it brings together texts from a range of periods, and I reflect on the implications of this gesture for Agamben's own sense of the development of his thought.

For Agamben, *The Use of Bodies* was far from a stopping point, as he has continued to publish prolifically in recent years. The fifth chapter examines this series of books, which are by turns boldly experimental and seemingly predictable. I finish up the main body of my argument by reflecting on Agamben's decision to publish all the *Homo Sacer* books together as a single mammoth volume. This leads into a conclusion in which I raise questions about Agamben's contemporaneity and untimeliness, his unique style and its potential for repetitiveness, and the ways we might respond to the works he has offered up to us.

A truly exhaustive critical account of Agamben's exceptionally rich and varied body of work would run to many hundreds of pages. Throughout my writing process, I was vividly aware of how much I was leaving out in the interest of brevity and focus. Aside from the main arcs of development and continuity that I trace out, there are many minor themes whose development I could have followed. At times, I have chosen to address such trends when they reach a critical mass, rather than attempting to track them step-by-step through all the works in which they are mentioned. At other times, I was forced to omit them altogether, or consign them to endnotes.

This book is in one sense an intervention in the literature on Agamben, insofar as it aims to discredit the main trope that has dominated his reception in the English-speaking world after the initial *Homo Sacer*-centric phase: namely, that his body of work as a whole evinces an inhuman level of systematicity from 1970 to the present day. At the same time, I recognise great value in my colleagues' commentaries on Agamben's texts, and I do not intend to nit-pick anyone's exposition of any particular passage or concept.[21] My references to the scholarship will therefore be sparing, mostly limited to comments that bear directly on questions of continuity and systematicity. As a consequence of this focus, I refer less and less to my fellow commentators as the argument progresses – not only because the continuity of his work is more explicitly asserted by Agamben himself in the gesture of presenting the *Homo Sacer* books as a cohesive series, but also because fewer scholars have had an opportunity to address the most recent works.

While I expect that this book will be valuable to readers who have relatively little knowledge of Agamben's thought, it is not meant to be primarily introductory or expository. I do not wish to duplicate the labours of my colleagues who have already provided a great deal of helpful work along those lines. At the same time, my approach will be comprehensive in the sense that I address all of Agamben's book-length publications in some way and give the reader an idea of how they fit into his project and intellectual trajectory. Hence it may serve as an introduction insofar as it provides an orientation for the reader to begin exploring Agamben's works independently.

More than that, though, I hope to present Agamben as an exemplary model of a thinker who lives in the tension between his own creative insights and his responsiveness to the world around him. When we read Agamben as a living human being rather than an Absolute Master who was somehow fully formed from the first moment he set pen to paper, we will realise that the twists and turns of his intellectual career can help us as we reflect on how to respond to our own tumultuous times in our thinking and writing. In other words, I aim not so much to vindicate Agamben as a unique philosophical genius but to prepare the ground for a thousand Agambens to bloom – in their own enigmatic, idiosyncratic, and fascinating ways.

Notes

1. All parenthetical dates refer to the original Italian publication. For the dates of the English translations, as well as the abbreviations used in parenthetical references to Agamben's works, see the list of abbreviations in the preliminary pages or the bibliography.
2. See footnote 8 in Chapter 3 for a discussion of my choice to alter the existing translation of the subtitle.
3. Norris, ed., *Politics, Metaphysics, and Death*.
4. Ross, ed., *The Agamben Effect*.
5. Mills, *Philosophy of Agamben*, 2.
6. Durantaye, *Giorgio Agamben*, 11.
7. Salzani, *Introduzione*, 8 (all translations from this volume are my own).
8. Salzani, *Introduzione*, 54.
9. Colebrook and Maxwell, *Agamben*, 31.
10. Dickinson, *Agamben and Theology*, 4.
11. Watkin, *The Literary Agamben*, 189.
12. See Colilli, *Agamben and the Signature of Astrology*.
13. Abbott, *The Figure of This World*, 1.
14. Kishik, *The Power of Life*; De Boever, *Plastic Sovereignties*; and Watkin, *Agamben and Indifference*.
15. Whyte, *Catastrophe and Redemption*. As will become clear in the chapters that follow, I agree with Whyte that this principle does represent an element of continuity throughout his corpus.
16. Prozorov, *Agamben and Politics*, 150–1.
17. Ibid.

18. Like most Anglophone readers, I was also misled about its original publication date when I first read it. As Durantaye points out, the copyright page places the Italian publication date in 1995 – in other words, at the same time as *Homo Sacer* itself – but that is the date of the second edition. In reality, it was first published in 1970.

19. A further complication was that *Potentialities* was initially published in English, and only later did Agamben bring out an Italian equivalent – adding a handful of essays when he did so, and excluding the Bartleby text (which was already available in book form in Italian).

20. One apparent exception is 'Notes on Gesture', which appears in both *Infancy and History* (1978) and *Means Without End* (1992) – but Durantaye clarifies that it does not appear in any Italian edition of *Infancy and History*, and was added unannounced to the English translation.

21. Nor, though I do sometimes alter translations (including my own!), is it my intention to nit-pick other translations – hence I have cited all works in English translation where available and have not sought to belabour the nuances of the original Italian text.

1
Becoming Agamben

For the first two decades of his career as a writer, no reader of
Agamben's work would have expected him to become a major
political thinker. Indeed, they would be more likely to think of
him as a resolutely *apolitical* thinker, concerned primarily with
aesthetics and abstract questions of linguistics and ontology. As
I note in the introduction, scholars of Agamben are dismissive
of the idea of a 'political turn' in his work, but it is hard for me
to understand 1990 – which marks the appearance of his first
overtly political work, *The Coming Community*, along with the
first of the political essays that would later be gathered under the
title *Means Without End* – as anything but a turning point in his
thought. Even granted that his work always had political 'implications', it surely makes a difference that he decided, apparently
quite abruptly, to stop leaving them implicit and start making
them explicit.

I agree with the scholars of Agamben's work that to understand his shift into a more overtly political mode, one needs to
understand the work that came before it. This is not, however,
because his earlier works 'lay the foundation' for his political theory, as though he always consciously intended to address political
questions but somehow only got around to it beginning in the
1990s. My position is somewhat different: in order to understand
why Agamben felt he needed to start addressing the political, at
the time and in the way that he did, we need to understand why
he *chose* not to address the political directly in his previous works.
For it is my contention that the apparently apolitical nature of his

earlier works was evidence neither of a preparatory exercise nor of political blindness, but a conscious choice. The basis for this choice, at bottom, is that Agamben viewed the politics of his time as beneath contempt and hence unworthy of sustained intellectual attention.

There is naturally not much direct textual evidence of this stance in the works in question, but Agamben's recent memoir, *Autoritratto nello studio* (*Self-Portrait in His Studio*, 2017), provides some clues when he discusses his earliest encounters with two of his most important political influences: Hannah Arendt and Guy Debord. Early on, Agamben reports that he began reading Arendt's work shortly before the second seminar with Heidegger at Le Thor in 1968 (ARS 26). This ultimately leads him to relate the story of how he came to write her a letter of appreciation, enclosing a short article that she would later cite in *On Revolution* (28). Yet he also recalls that his enthusiasm for her work was not widely shared, as her characterisation of the Nazi and Stalinist regimes as equally totalitarian led many on the left to view her as a reactionary. This was unfortunate in his view, because it meant that a thinker who 'could have oriented the movements more felicitously instead remained excluded from them' (27).

A few pages later, he reflects on his relationship with Debord, whose *Society of the Spectacle* he reports reading at around the time of its publication in 1967. More important, however, was the friendship he developed with Debord in the late 1980s, which he describes as a moment of political awakening: 'For the first time I found myself speaking of politics without having to bump up against the encumbrance of useless and distracting ideas and authors', among whom he numbers the famous French Marxist theorist Louis Althusser (36). He reports that he agreed with Debord that 'the principal obstacle that impeded access to a new politics was precisely what remained of the Marxist tradition (not of Marx!) and of the workers movement, which were unconsciously complicit with the enemy they believed they were combating' (36–7). And here he draws attention to Debord's contention throughout *Society of the Spectacle* that the Stalinist and capitalist regimes were both equally defined by the spectacle.

In both cases, then, we are dealing with figures who are crucial for Agamben's political thought, with whose work he was familiar from the very beginning of his career, and who do not play a major role in his published writings until around the time of shift of attention toward the political. I would suggest, however, that they did influence his work indirectly insofar as they both pointed toward the conclusion that Communism did not represent a genuine political alternative. This position may also be one that he held on independent grounds as well – namely, through his experience of interacting with actual Communist Party activists. Elsewhere he equates their rigidity and insularity to that of the Roman Catholic Church, as both hold to the principle of *extra ecclesiam non salus*: outside their institutional framework, there can be no salvation (57–8). By contrast, he holds that '*extra* is the place of thought' (58). Later, he even suggests that Italo Calvino's time as a Communist had held back the famous novelist's formidable mind (153).

Agamben's political sympathies have clearly always been with the left, but for much of his early career, the left position was essentially monopolised by an institutional force that he regarded as a destructive fraud. Indeed, in one of his first explicit political interventions, the 1990 essay 'Marginal Notes on *Commentaries on the Society of the Spectacle*', he dismisses the notion that *glasnost* and *perestroika* have changed anything fundamental. More than that, he contributes his own variation on Arendt and Debord's theme of the fundamental sameness of the capitalist and communist spheres, claiming that both are becoming total surveillance states: 'For the first time in the history of our century, the two most important world powers are headed by two direct emanations of the secret services: Bush (former CIA head) and Gorbachev (Andropov's man)' (MWE 86), referring to the former KGB chief who served briefly as General Secretary in the early 1980s. This cynicism about Gorbachev – so out of step with the optimism of mainstream Western commentators about his reform efforts – vividly illustrates Agamben's unwavering conviction that no genuine political alternative could arise from within the confines of Real Socialism.

And as it turned out, he was right – at least about Gorbachev. His reform efforts did not in fact manage to salvage the Soviet system and generate a sustainable model. Just the opposite: by the next year, the Soviet Union had been dissolved out from under Gorbachev. While we could debate whether this outcome was inevitable, it seems fair to say that none of the machinations of Western Communist Party activists, much less any of the intellectual handwringing over the proper stance to take toward the USSR and its party line, contributed materially to the outcome either way. In fact, from our contemporary perspective, the thinkers who were most embedded in that political milieu now seem irrevocably dated, even those who were most unavoidable in their own day – few today regard Jean-Paul Sartre, for example, as one of the great twentieth-century philosophers.

Hence I would suggest that if Communism appeared to be the one live option on the left at that time, and if being a self-conscious intellectual of the left would mean being forced constantly to take a position on it, then Agamben was probably justified in directing his energies elsewhere. We cannot understand what is at stake in these early writings, however, if we insist on viewing them as somehow 'already' political. We have to take seriously the fact that Agamben *really did* direct his energies elsewhere, and that he did so emphatically. Simply on the level of content, he did in fact leave politics aside, as the early works display no sustained engagement with the questions of law, state power, or violence that would be so central to his later work – and this despite the fact that, perhaps uniquely among major twentieth-century philosophers, his primary formal academic training was in law. This is more than merely an absence or lacuna waiting to be filled in, however, as though he found politics to be merely uninteresting at this point and then later changed his mind. Instead, his earliest thought continually enacts his rejection of the narrow constraints of what he understood as politics in his historical moment.

If we read the early works on their own terms, rather than as a prelude to his later political works, it is clear that the unifying thread of this astonishingly diverse body of work – consisting of five books and well over a dozen essays on an intimidating range of topics – is precisely the vindication of individual experience.

Again and again, we see a similar gesture: against those who think in terms of impersonal necessity (whether they be Stalinists or structuralists), Agamben asserts the irreducibility of the individual. This priority shapes his distinctive views on the two most important emphases at this stage in his work: language and the task of criticism. As we will see in the following chapter, by the mid-1980s, the development of his thinking on these two issues was bringing him to a point where he had to at least begin dealing with something like politics, though at that stage he more often preferred to speak of 'community'. Still at that stage, however, it was far from clear how he would take up his meditations on the human relationship to language and the paradoxes of cultural transmission and bend them in a more overtly political direction – above all to Agamben himself, who would require a decade of experimentation and improvisation to retool his intellectual project from a political viewpoint.

Those experiments will be the topic of our next chapter, and we will see then that many (though far from all!) of the key concepts he developed in these works proved fruitful when he did take up political reflection as an explicit intellectual task. My emphasis in this chapter, however, will be on discontinuity and change, in keeping with my goal of presenting Agamben as an exemplar of living, truly historical thought. Starting with his early works on the concept of criticism and poetics, I will chart the emergence and gradual abandonment of his interest in a 'general science of the human', his short-lived attempt to articulate a philosophy centred on the concept of 'voice', and the subsequent investigations of the structure of language that, in retrospect, turned out to lay the foundations for his political work in ways no one ever could have predicted.

Criticism after the end of art

Any serious study of the development of Agamben's thought must start with his first two books, *The Man Without Content* (1970) and *Stanzas* (1977). The two texts are strikingly different from his later works – and, indeed, from each other. The first is a study of the history of the concepts of the artwork and of aesthetic taste in the

Western tradition. The second is a much more varied investigation that mostly centres on medieval theories about the role of
mental images in cognition and specifically in the experiences of
melancholy and love, as they are reflected and reworked in the
poetry of Dante and his troubadour predecessors (the poets of the
Dolce Stil Novo or 'new sweet style'). Whether intentionally or
not, the two works closely parallel Walter Benjamin's two disser-
tations, the first of which focuses on the history of the concept of
criticism and the second of which investigates a formative episode
in his own national literary tradition (the German mourning play,
or *Trauerspiel*). At the same time, we can see a profound Heideggerian influence in Agamben's approach to the history of thought
and, especially in the latter work, in the revelatory importance
he attaches to melancholy, parallel to the role anxiety plays in
Heidegger's *Being and Time*. In both cases, what he takes from his
two great masters is what fits best with the concern with individual experience and intellectual freedom that is so characteristic
of his early period.

The years separating the two volumes (the longest gap
between book-length publications in Agamben's entire career)
were marked by intensive research and intellectual development.
The Man Without Content, published in the wake of Heidegger's
second seminar at Le Thor in 1968, vividly displays the profound
impact of that formative experience. It is the most thoroughly
Heideggerian work in Agamben's corpus, both in approach and
in prose style, to the point where it can sometimes feel like the
work of a different author. *Stanzas*, in turn, is the fruit of a trans-
formative fellowship at the Warburg Institute in London, as well
as his growing identification with Benjamin, whom he once
famously described as 'the antidote that allowed me to survive
Heidegger'.[1] Though *Stanzas* carries a dedication to Heidegger,
who died while Agamben was finalising the text, it also marks
a kind of declaration of independence from his former teacher.
In his memoir, he relates that what stands out to him when he
reflects on the years immediately following the Le Thor seminars
is '[his] immaturity then and [his] inability to remain faithful to
the encounter that had happened'. It was only 'in May of 1976,
at the precise moment when news of Heidegger's death reached

me', that he felt he could truly begin speaking in his own voice (ARS 26). It was then that he decided to dedicate the book to Heidegger, whose name otherwise hardly appears in the text.

Hence by his own account, the works bookend a formative stage in his thinking, in which he was still grappling with his major influences and starting to define his own distinctive approach and concerns. Even the scholars most concerned to attribute unity and consistency to Agamben's body of work have recognised the provisional and experimental nature of these texts, particularly *Stanzas*. In fact, the latter gets very little scholarly attention: Salzani devotes only a few pages to it, and other scholars tend to refer to it only in passing. One exception is Durantaye, who spends a whole chapter on *Stanzas*, but concludes that it represents something of a dead-end in Agamben's intellectual trajectory.[2] By contrast, both Salzani and Durantaye view *Man Without Content* as anticipating the most important aspects of his mature works. And on a superficial level, the book does seem like 'classic Agamben': we get a historical narrative, relying heavily on Aristotle and Heidegger, punctuated by vivid and memorable examples (above all the *Wunderkammer*), and a sudden appearance by Benjamin at the end of the book (what Durantaye has amusingly called the '*Benjamin ex machina*').[3]

Both scholars concede that there are some discontinuities with the later work in *Man Without Content*, but they characterise them as relatively minor. Durantaye even goes so far as to bring this volume forward as indirect evidence of his thesis that the concept of potentiality is the key to Agamben's thought:

> It is perfectly obvious that Agamben's first book is about art, but it is less immediately clear that it is also a book about *potentiality*. Agamben indeed discusses the passage from Aristotle that will remain at the center of his thought for four decades, but he does not use the term *potentiality* extensively, choosing instead an ontological vocabulary largely borrowed from Heidegger.[4]

This understates the case, because he does in fact use the Greek term *dynamis*, which is often translated as *potentiality* – but in a way that completely contradicts his later usage. We will be going into more detail on his mature view of potentiality in the next chapter, but for now suffice it to say that Agamben highly valorises the concept as the mark of what is most distinctively human and what is most promising in an authentic artwork. Here he equates it to the inert 'availability' of 'the industrial product' (MWC 65), in sharp contrast to the work of art.

Other Aristotelian terminology familiar to readers of Agamben's later reflections on art appears in a similarly scrambled form, particularly *poiēsis* and *praxis*. In essentially all of his later works (among which *Creation and Anarchy* provides the most accessible presentation), he follows Hannah Arendt in arguing that Aristotle prioritised *praxis* over *poiēsis*, associating the former with human freedom and the latter with biological necessity and slavery. Here, however, though he does cite Arendt, he reverses the valuation, claiming that Aristotle 'tended to assign a higher position to *poiēsis* than to *praxis*', and associating *poiēsis* with the unveiling of truth and *praxis* with 'the very condition of man as an *animal*, a living being' (69).[5] More than that, he breaks with Arendt's exposition in *The Human Condition* by introducing 'work' as a third category that was supposedly left unthought by the Greeks. His goal here is apparently to maintain some distinction between artistic labour and utilitarian labour in Greek society – a distinction that he will later reject in recognition that the Greeks used the same term, *technē*, for both.

To the extent, then, that Agamben takes up in *Man Without Content* the concepts and passages from Aristotle that will prove so decisive for his later work, he takes them up in a completely unrecognisable way. And he does so, I would claim, not (or at least not primarily) due to an error or mistake that he will later correct, but because in this early text he is concerned to construct a different kind of historical narrative from those found in his mature reflections on art, with a very different goal. Whereas his later works situate the shift from Greek to modern Western concepts of art within a broader genealogy of political and economic structures, his goal in his first book is to establish that the collapse of traditional concepts of art has opened up a new space of freedom for both critics and artists.

This project is not only implicitly but intentionally apolitical, as we can see from his reading of Benjamin, which is both different from Agamben's later approach and very counterintuitive on its own terms. On the one hand, it is not clear that Benjamin has 'the answer' in the way we would expect from the later works. Agamben does credit Benjamin with being 'the first European intellectual to recognize the fundamental change that had taken place in the transmissibility of culture and in the new relation to the past that constituted the inevitable consequence of this change' (104). He also points to Benjamin's theory of citation, which presupposes that 'the authority invoked by the quotation is founded precisely on the destruction of the authority that is attributed to a certain text by its situation in the history of culture' (104), and his account of the collector, who 'is in some way related to that of the revolutionary, for whom the new can appear only through the destruction of the old' (105), as appropriate responses to the breakdown in cultural transmission that Benjamin witnessed. Yet he seems to attribute a kind of impotence and inadequacy to both, associating them with a meaningless 'accumulation of culture' (107) that 'hangs over man like a threat in which he can in no way recognize himself' (108). Thus, as Watkin points out, 'It remains hard to tell if Agamben is glossing Benjamin here or totally dismissing' his theory of citation.[6] Odder still, he reads the 'Theses on the Philosophy of History' in a completely depoliticised way. For instance, he claims that the oft-quoted passage on Klee's 'Angelus Novus' represents 'a particularly felicitous image to describe this situation of the man who has lost his link with his past and is no longer able to find himself in history' (108–9) – a strange interpretation of a text that is obviously about the accumulated weight of historical injustice and oppression.

In the end, it is Kafka who points the way, insofar as he asks 'whether art could become the transmission of the act of transmission: whether, that is, it could take as its content the task of transmission itself, independently of the thing to be transmitted' (114). If it is difficult to understand what he means here, I would suggest that this is in part because Agamben himself does not yet know. Still, his concluding line expresses an intuition, at least, that can help guide our interpretation of the rest of the text: 'According to the principle by which it is only in the burning house that the fundamental architectural problem becomes visible for the first time, art, at the furthest point of its destiny, makes visible its original project' (115). From a certain perspective, yes, the rupture of tradition is a negative thing, but looked at another way, that very negativity represents an opportunity – a new kind of freedom, compared to which the certainties of traditional culture appear as stultifying constraints.

This perspective casts new light on the most memorable example from his first book: the medieval *Wunderkammer* or cabinet of wonders, 'which contained, promiscuously, rocks of an unusual shape, coins, stuffed animals, manuscript volumes, ostrich eggs, and unicorn horns' along with what we would regard as works of art (29), and in which the medieval viewer would perceive not chaos but 'a sort of microcosm that reproduced, in its harmonious confusion, the animal, vegetable, and mineral macrocosm' (30). Agamben is as susceptible as his readers to its charms and initially compares it favourably to the conventional art gallery (31). Yet by the end of the text, this very harmony comes to seem like a trap, the mark of a pre-modern traditional society in which there is 'no discontinuity between past and present, between old and new, because every object transmits at every moment, without residue, the system of beliefs and notions that has found expression in it' and 'an absolute identity exists between the act of transmission and the thing transmitted, in the sense that there is no other ethical, religious, or aesthetic value outside the act itself of transmission' (107). Even if the task of sifting through the rubble of the accumulation of culture is intimidating, it at least opens up the possibility of something new – unlike the *Wunderkammer*, in which superficial variety always points back toward a deadening sameness.

If, at the end of *Man Without Content*, Agamben relies on the artist, as represented by Kafka, to take up anew the task of cultural transmission, in the years that follow he grows increasingly confident in the creative powers of the critic. This shift largely tracks with his ever greater identification with the figure of Benjamin. This adulation reaches a fever pitch in the introduction to *Stanzas*, where he declares, 'there is strictly speaking perhaps only a single book that deserves to be called critical: the *Ursprung des deutschen Trauerspiel* of Walter Benjamin' (S xv). Clearly Agamben hopes that *Stanzas* will count as a second entry in that august category, but here again he takes up Benjamin's influence in a depoliticised way. Where Benjamin's *Trauerspiel* concerned the death of kings and drew him into a debate – well-known from Agamben's later work – with Carl Schmitt on the concept of sovereignty, Agamben's investigation of the Italian literary tradition remains focused on resolutely apolitical topics like the structure of subjective experience and the emergence of notions of romantic love. That this is a conscious choice is clear from the central place of Dante, whose political thought will play a decisive role in *The Use of Bodies* but is here completely absent.[7]

As we will see, *Stanzas* is not as much of an outlier as it may seem. Agamben will continue to engage with medieval love poetry, as well as modern Italian poetry, throughout his career, though most often in the form of individual essays rather than full monographs. At the same time, he pursues that interest almost as a side project, never fully integrating it into his political work. In fact, it is only after the completion of the *Homo Sacer* project that he engages the troubadours in a sustained way in *The Adventure* (2015), where they provide the basis for a meditation on the dynamics of personal integrity and self-discovery – a return, albeit in a different key, to the realm of individual experience in which he began his career.

The general science of the human

Alongside his project on the concept of criticism, Agamben maintained from the very beginning a keen interest in the theory of language. In the works of the late 1970s, that concern becomes ever more central to his thought, even if it is not always evident how his work on linguistics fits with his other concerns. That explanatory gap is most evident in the brief concluding section of *Stanzas*. Entitled 'The Barrier and the Fold', it feels almost like a non sequitur, shifting from medieval poetry to the late writings of Saussure. There he launches a harsh critique of Derrida's views on language, claiming, in Kevin Attell's words, 'that Derrida thinks his way to the outer limit of Saussurian semiology, but remains enclosed within a semiological understanding of language'.[8] This is not the place to adjudicate the complex, and frankly often passive-aggressive, debate between Agamben and Derrida, which Attell has already covered so exhaustively. More relevant to the present is understanding why the question of language is so important to Agamben, and we can find a clue in one of his earliest essays: 'The Tree of Language', published in 1968, two years prior to *Man Without Content.*

The essay, which originally appeared in a special issue of the Italian journal *Ulisse* on 'Language and Languages', is a forceful intervention into the debate surrounding structuralism. As he observes, 'Linguistics, today, has begun to occupy a privileged place amongst the disciplines; seeming to promise a methodological model for every kind of inquiry, from ethnology to literary criticism', and yet – aping Heidegger's approach – he believes that a preliminary question has been skipped over: 'What *is* linguistics?' (TL 12).[9] The simplest answer is that it is a science of language, yet this pursuit is paradoxical in multiple ways. First, even in the natural sciences, quantum physicists have discovered that every measurement is irreducibly affected by the involvement of the observer, to the point where the Uncertainty Principle states that the simultaneous knowledge of a quantum particle's location and velocity is impossible. If this is the case for a realm so distant from our experience, it seems clear that we must equally take into account the human element in the science of language – which is, after all, pursued by human beings who are constrained to use the object of their study, namely language, at every turn. Yet structuralist linguistics has chosen, instead, to ignore the human entanglement in language:

> Linguistics could be cast as a science . . . only by defining its object as a system of signs – a coherent whole made up of entities, each characterized by the indivisible union of two elements, the *signifier* and the *signified* (*signans* and *signatum*). In other words, the birth of linguistics as a science coincides with the definitive entry of language into a semiological

sphere, without remainder. The 'distortion' [on the model of the Uncertainty Principle] that is produced by the inter-action between the scholar and the object-phenomenon in question is, in this case, the reduction of language to a sys-tem of signs. (13)

Hence to create a science of language, linguists had to ignore the fact that human beings actually speak. But even granting that one-sided view of the object of their study, Agamben argues that a further paradox opens up. Every science is based on the principle of sufficient reason, but if we go back to its Greek roots, reason is *logos*, which is to say, word or language. All of this means that – in a very Heideggerian conclusion to a very Heideggerian argument – 'to enquire after the nature of linguistic science leads us to call into question the very possibility of linguistics itself, insofar as it is a science that seeks the reason of language and hopes to oblige language to justify itself rationally' (14).

Agamben then turns to the history of linguistics and uncov-ers the fact that eighteenth-century linguists were determined to uncover the original language spoken by Adam in the Garden of Eden, whose power 'must have been truly remarkable if, accord-ing to Genesis, God had to confound it in order to prevent humans from erecting the tower at Babel that reached "to the heavens"' (15). Though they found it impossible to reconstruct that original language through historical study, they did believe it was 'none-theless possible to construct an artificial language that possesses the same characteristics' (15), which would allow them 'to construct a true and proper tree of Reason' (16). He traces the development of this idealised language to contemporary linguists like Chomsky (17) and points out that Leibniz's efforts toward a fully rationalised language were part of a broader quest for a universal calculation of all things, which 'laid the logical foundations for what we know today as artificial neural networks and cybernetic machines' (18) – a theme of startling contemporary relevance from our present-day perspective, though he has unfortunately not chosen to follow up on it in his more recent works. And against this nightmare vision of a fully rationalised, mathematised, impersonal world, Agamben proposes that we should abandon 'the definition of language as a system of signs, understood as indissoluble unities of signifier and signified' that stands at the basis of linguistic science (19) and turn instead toward a reflection on humanity's relationship to language, since 'it is in language that humankind – that animal endowed with language – draws closer to the problem of its being in the world and recovers, time and again, its fundamental place in relation to Being' (20).

Much has changed by the time we get to the final chapter of *Stanzas*. For one, while the early essay accepts the structuralist claim to be following in Saussure's footsteps (TL 13), here he cites some of Saussure's final unpublished writings to show that he had serious misgivings about the *Course on General Linguistics* and did not wish to see it published. According to Agamben, what Saussure saw toward the end of his life was that, 'far from simplifying the linguistic act, the inclusion of language in the semiological perspective makes it something impossible' (S 155). The implicit question here is: if language were truly a self-enclosed, purely self-referential system of signs, then how could a concrete human being ever actually *speak* it? From this perspective, Derrida's critique of structuralist linguistics, which privileges the signifier over the signified and writing over the voice, evades the fundamental problem, which is the articulation between the two realms. Agamben's argument ends with a call to action that, much like the conclusion to *Man Without Content*, is as ambitious as it is vague: 'Only when we have arrived in the proximity of this "invisible articulation" will we be able to say we have entered into an area from which the step-backward-beyond of metaphysics, which governs the interpretation of the sign in Western thought, becomes really possible' (157).[10]

Though both arguments are different in detail, the overall thrust is the same: structuralist linguistics errs by removing the human element from language. And the conclusion of *Stanzas* expressed an intuition that the question of language was crucial to his overall project, even if – as all young scholars have experienced at one time or another – he was not sure how to integrate it convincingly into the argument of that book. It was not until his next major publication, 1978's *Infancy and History*, that he places language at the very heart of his investigation, centring the whole book on the insight that language is something that *happens* to every individual human being. The title essay begins with the somewhat startling claim that modern man's 'incapacity to have and communicate experiences is perhaps one of the few self-certainties to which he can lay claim' (IH 15).

He cites Benjamin's argument that the roots of this loss of experience lie in the destruction and chaos of the First World War, but argues that the problem is by now more universal: 'we know that the destruction of experience no longer necessitates a catastrophe, and that humdrum daily life in any city will suffice' (15). Where traditional societies enjoyed a bedrock of stable routines and meanings in their everyday lives, contemporary human beings are completely unmoored, to the point of actively rejecting the experiences that are available to them. We can see this above all in the phenomenon of tourism: 'Standing face to face with one of the great wonders of the world . . ., the overwhelming majority of people have no wish to experience it, preferring instead that the camera should' (17).

As in *Man Without Content*, however, this crisis will turn out to be an opportunity. In the chapters that follow, Agamben lays out the history of the concept of experience from Bacon to Husserl. Just as his first book aimed to show us that our access to the artwork had become deeply questionable, so in *Infancy and History* does he argue that all guarantees of our access to our own lived experience have broken down as well. Here, however, the solution is clearer: we must recognise that all experience is mediated by language and that there is nothing automatic or guaranteed about our relationship to language. Every human individual lives through a period of infancy, which etymologically refers to a lack of speech. Yet here we must not be misled. Even if physiological infancy is a stage we outgrow, infancy in the sense of lacking speech 'is not a paradise which, at a certain moment, we leave for ever in order to speak; rather, it coexists in its origins with language – indeed, is itself constituted through the appropriation of it by language in each instance to produce the individual as subject' (55). Recognition of the fact that language comes to all of us from the outside and must be won ever-anew in the act of speech not only helps to account for 'the origin of language in its double reality of *langue* and *parole*' (55) – meaning the existence of language as both an impersonal system and as concrete acts of speech – but also for our very experience of history.

This means that the structuralists were onto something when they put forward linguistics as the foundation of a universal science – their mistake was simply their impersonal and inhuman view of language. If we acknowledge the concrete human experience of language, which is what the somewhat unwieldy term 'infancy' is meant to indicate, then we might be in a better position to attain a holistic view of human phenomena. This is what the next several essays in the volume begin to sketch out. 'In Playland', which surely counts as one of Agamben's most charming writings, develops a theory of culture based on a study of children's toys, in which the tension between diachrony and synchrony in our experience of historical time is traced to the more fundamental tension between free play and its ossification into deadening ritual. 'Time and History' argues against both the cyclical time of the ancients and the 'secularization of rectilinear, irreversible Christian time' in modernity (105) and in favour of a richer concept of time, grounded in the insights of Benjamin and Heidegger, that has room for discontinuity and interruption. The final major essay, 'The Prince and the Frog', stages a defence of Benjamin's critical method against Adorno, who here seems to serve as a stand-in for the conventional Marxism that Agamben has always been at such great pains to escape – an unusually clear illustration of the early Agamben's determination to assert his intellectual independence over against Marxist political conformism.

After a brief reflection on the nativity crib, Agamben concludes *Infancy and History* with a bold methodological statement.[11] Entitled 'Project for a Review', it represents, as Agamben later reveals in the preface to *End of the Poem*, the (unfulfilled) plan he developed for a literary journal with Italo Calvino and Claudio Rugafiori while they were all living in Paris in the early 1970s (EP xi).[12] Here he returns to the reflections on cultural transmission from *Man Without Content*, claiming that 'perhaps no other epoch has been so obsessed with its own past and so unable to create a vital relationship to it' as his contemporary era (IH 160). The goal of the proposed journal is to restore our access to tradition, deploying 'philology, beyond the limits of any narrow academic

conception . . . as the tool of its "destruction of destruction"' (162) –
in other words, to transcend the 'destruction of experience'
with which *Infancy and History* began. By actively and creatively
reconstructing the past, philology can serve as a kind of 'critical mythology', holding out the hope for a new conception of
'poetry as philology and philology as poetry' (163), which would
'restore to criticism its status and its violence' (164). Crucial here
is the possibility of overcoming the distinction between the act
of transmission and the transmitted context, insofar as philology
always critically reconstructs the text under investigation, most
often generating a new version that is not attested in its entirety
in any existing manuscript.

Here we have a programme to go beyond *Man Without
Content*'s reliance on the creative artist (Kafka) to resolve a situation that the critic (Benjamin) can only diagnose, allowing for
a new and more robust form of truly creative and poetic criticism that is, perhaps, represented by *Stanzas*. More than that, a
review carried out along these lines would lay the foundation
of 'an "interdisciplinary discipline" in which all the human sciences converge, together with poetry, whose goal would be that
"general science of the human" which is severally heralded as the
cultural task of the coming generation' (164). This is a cultural
task, it seems safe to conclude, that both *Stanzas* and *Infancy and
History* contribute to in some modest way, given that the 'Project'
was sketched out years before either work. In short, this conception of a 'general science of the human' founded on philology
appears not only to encapsulate the project of the early writings,
but indeed to lay the groundwork for Agamben's later works,
which took an increasingly philological approach over the decades that followed.

Strangely, though, outside of the memoir, the phrase 'general
science of the human' appears only a handful of times in Agamben's writings. The most important is in a postilla added in 1983
to his 1975 essay on Aby Warburg, which presents Warburg's
method of humanistic inquiry in a way that broadly anticipates
Agamben's own approach in *Stanzas*. In the added section, he
reveals that he intended that study to be the first in a series of
essays on exemplary figures who would point the way toward 'a

general science of the human freed from the vagueness of inter-disciplinarity' (P 101). The second study would have focused on the linguist Émile Benveniste,[13] an omnipresent point of reference in Agamben's subsequent work, who is here presented as anticipating the insights of *Infancy and History*. On the one hand, Benveniste's '*Indo-European Language and Society* brought comparative grammar to a limit point at which the very epistemological categories of the historical disciplines seemed to waver', while on the other hand, his 'theory of enunciation', which emphasises the concrete human speaker over against the impersonal system of language, 'carried the science of language into the traditional territory of philosophy' (101). Here again, everything seems to fit together so well – yet Agamben abruptly announces that he never finished the Benveniste essay and abandoned the idea of a series altogether, because he had come to believe that the 'general science of the human' could never actually be achieved.

Voice and its vicissitudes

What went wrong? Agamben does not say, in either the Warburg essay or the memoir. The next reference to the 'general science of the human', found in the 1990 essay 'Philosophy and Linguistics', provides only indirect evidence. There he claims, 'The project of a "general science of the human," which reached its apex at the end of the 1960s, dissolved with the political project of the same years' (P 64) – which would mean that, in retrospect, Agamben's interest in the concept was already anachronistic when he took it up in the 1970s. In my conversation with Agamben in Venice, he cited several factors to account for the shift away from the 'general science of the human': an inability to get the journal envisioned in 'Project for a Review' off the ground (due in large part to logistical obstacles), his sense that academia as a whole was turning away from the structuralist project that lay at the basis of the general science of the human, and his growing conviction that philosophy already represented the desired unification of the human sciences. Thus if Benveniste was, in Agamben's account, moving beyond the sphere of the human sciences into philosophy, Agamben was determined to follow him – something that would require a major retooling of his approach.

If we look to the published works, we find evidence that things were changing rapidly at the end of the '70s. Most notably, infancy quickly falls aside as a key term. In the year after *Infancy and History* appeared, he contributed an entry on 'taste' to an Italian philosophical reference volume (which was ultimately published as the short book *Taste* in 2015), in which he calls for a 'form of cognition, as distinct from sensation as from science and located between pleasure and knowledge'.[14] This energetic essay shares many of the same points of reference as *Man Without Content* and *Stanzas*, perhaps indicating that the hoped-for third form of cognition is a fresh attempt to provide some kind of unity to his emerging interdisciplinary project, but this new conception plays no explicit role in other works of those years.

In the publications of the early 1980s, a new central term begins to emerge: 'voice'. The attempt to unify his project around 'voice' culminates in Agamben's densest and most rigorously philosophical work of the early period: *Language and Death* (1982). This work is a *locus classicus* for the scholarship that is determined to see an unbroken unity in Agamben's thought, as it is the first text in which the figure of the *homo sacer* is mentioned. Yet there is good reason to view it as a turning point – or, perhaps, even as a temporary dead end – in the trajectory of his thought. As we have already seen, in the year after the book appeared, Agamben republished the Warburg essay with the addendum declaring the 'general science of the human' to be unattainable. And after a flurry of activity on the concept of 'voice' (four major essays and a book within a few short years), the term quickly slips into the background of his thought – never fully rejected or repudiated, but never again granted the central role it enjoys in *Language and Death*.

Before diving into the argument of *Language and Death*, it may be helpful to take stock of the intuitions that Agamben is trying to bring together at this stage of his intellectual project. The first is the essential role of individual experience in humanistic inquiry. We can see this in his initial choice of aesthetics as a topic of study as well as in his critique of the one-sidedly impersonal approach of structuralist linguistics. At the same time, the conclusion of *Stanzas* and the core argument of *Infancy and History* show that he agrees with the structuralists on the centrality of language to the human sciences – the problem is to rethink language in a way that takes account of the individual experience of language. Finally, there is a repeated recourse to destruction or negativity – the collapse of the aesthetic tradition, for instance, or the paradoxical foundation of the human experience of language on the human's originary *lack* of language – that reflects what I have characterised as his deep temperamental commitment to freedom and individuality, understood at this stage as a lack of external constraint or conformism.

Language and Death attempts to bring together these priorities by elaborating on a passing remark of Heidegger's as to the 'essential relation' between the two title concepts, which 'remains still unthought' (LD xi). Emboldened by Heidegger's declaration during the seminars at Le Thor about the limit of his own thought – 'You can see it, I cannot' – Agamben proposes in the introduction to flesh out Heidegger's intuition through a 'clarification of the problem of the negative' (xii), which, he claims, leads us back to the problem of Voice. The first step that he proposes toward getting to the bottom of all this is through synthesising Hegel and Heidegger, who represent a kind of culmination of the Western metaphysical tradition. The end goal, however, is a passage beyond the confines of ontology into the realm of ethics.

This agenda is admittedly intimidating, but thankfully Agamben focuses on some of the best-known passages from his two guiding authorities: Heidegger's analysis of Dasein's 'being-toward-death' from *Being and Time* and Hegel's dialectic of sense certainty from *The Phenomenology of Spirit*. From Heidegger, he draws the notion that the foundation of human existence or Dasein is the negativity or nothingness represented by death – the one thing we human beings can be absolutely sure of is that we will one day die, even if we cannot be sure when. In a (very abstract) sense, though, we can be sure *where*, because for Heidegger, Dasein is not so much a substance or essence so much as the place, the 'there', where human existence takes place. And this 'there' is defined by a voice-related phenomena – the 'call (*Ruf*) of conscience', which silently testifies to the fundamental negativity of human existence (2).

Here we seem to have all the major themes promised in the introduction, yet Agamben chooses to pick up a perhaps unexpected thread: the word 'there', or *Da*, which is 'morphologically and semantically connected with . . . the demonstrative pronoun *diese* (this)' (5). 'This' provides the link to Hegel's text, which famously argues that the attempt to designate the concrete object before us in an unmediated way must have recourse to the abstract and empty word 'this', which can equally refer to anything. Hence when we mean to designate the most concrete thing, language thwarts our intentions and expresses something universal, namely 'Being in general'. The most common reading of this passage is that the material thing cannot be said as such in language, but Agamben claims that the really important thing is the meaning that language expresses contrary to our intentions. This means that demonstrative pronouns like 'there' and 'this' have 'the power to introduce . . . humanity into negativity' (15), in the sense of separating our speech from our conscious intentions.

The discussion then shifts into linguistic territory, focused on 'the sphere of the pronoun', which is 'a grammatical category whose definition is always a point of controversy for theorists of language' (19). Tracing the history of the concept of the pronoun from ancient Greek grammarians through medieval and modern linguistics, Agamben repeatedly emphasises that Hegel is far from the first to connect the realm of 'Being in general' to pronouns. Already in Plato and Aristotle, 'grammatical and logical categories and grammatical and logical reflections are originally implicated one in the other, and thus they are inseparable' (20). Insofar as the pronoun served only as a designation with no determinate content, it played a privileged role in reflections on the meaning of Being (and later, as he discusses in Excursus 2, in Christian theological conceptions of divine transcendence).

For modern linguists like Benveniste and Jakobson, by contrast, pronouns serve an apparently humbler role as 'a reference to the instance of discourse that contains them' (23). They thus 'enact 'the conversion of language into discourse' and permit the passage from *langue* [language as a self-enclosed system] to *parole* [a concrete utterance]' (24). Echoing his mildly counterintuitive reading of Hegel's dialectic of sense-certainty, Agamben extrapolates from this to claim that the pronouns' function of 'indication – with which their peculiar character has been identified, from antiquity on – does not simply demonstrate an unnamed object, but above all the very instance of discourse, its taking place . . . Indication is the category within which language refers to its own taking place' (25). And this means that the ontological role that ancient and medieval philosophy assigned to the pronoun is entirely appropriate, because 'metaphysics is that experience of language that, in every speech act, grasps the disclosure of that dimension, and in all speech, experiences above all the "marvel" that language exists' (25).

The next step in Agamben's argument is to look toward the concrete reality that allows this self-indication of language to take place. The answer, obviously, is the voice of the human being who is speaking in that particular case. Yet this seemingly simple observation carries within it unexpected paradoxes. On the one hand, Agamben claims, 'A voice as mere sound (an *animal* voice) could certainly be the index of the individual who emits it, but in no way can it refer to the instance of discourse as such, nor open the sphere of utterance' (35). The voice must be articulated into sounds, syllables, and words, but once that happens, we no longer 'hear' the voice as such – we hear what is being said. Hence the animal voice 'is indeed presupposed by the shifters [or pronouns], but as that which must necessarily be removed in order for meaningful discourse to take place . . . It is *ground*, but in the sense that it goes *to ground* and disappears in order for being and language to take place' (35). This logic of presupposition, wherein a foundational element is at once taken for granted and forgotten, will prove crucial for the *Homo Sacer* project – though as we will see, it will take significant conceptual work to give it the political valence it takes on in that context.

In its more immediate context, this argument is a step beyond the dynamic Agamben had previously designated as infancy, insofar as we are not dealing simply with an initial lack of language, but with a negativity (the submersion of the animal voice through the articulation of meaning) that is foundational to every occurrence of language as such. This shift carries with it a greater specification of his earlier argument that infancy is the foundation of historical experience. He is no longer thinking merely of the empirical fact that language impinges on every individual human being at some moment in time, but is trying to capture a dynamic internal to language itself: 'Inasmuch as it takes place in Voice (that is, in the nonplace of the voice, in its having-been), language takes place in time. In demonstrating the instance of discourse, the Voice discloses both being and time. It is chronothetic' (35), or time-positing. In both cases, Agamben shifts from a simple contrast between language and its outside to a more complex conception of the structure of language itself.

The greater rigour and elegance of the argument, however, comes at a cost, because Voice-with-a-capital-V comes to stand for the foundational *absence* of the animal voice (in the sense of the raw sounds that come out of your mouth) – a confusing and distracting terminological choice, to say the least. Even worse, Agamben chooses to pick a fight with Derrida on this basis, making the tendentious claim that, contrary to Derrida's argument that the metaphysical tradition privileges live vocal speech as the locus of presence over against the absence and negativity, Voice (in his idiosyncratic and counterintuitive sense) is actually the negative foundation of metaphysics (39–40). Even granting that Agamben's sense of Voice can be drawn in some way from the tradition, this seems like an attempt at disproof through the arbitrary redefinition of a term.

Be that as it may, the next several chapters return to Hegel and Heidegger, grounding their accounts of negativity and death in the dynamics of Voice. Having laid out the basic parameters of the problem, Agamben chooses to forego the expected *Benjamin ex machina* – indeed, Benjamin's name is strangely absent from this book – and instead looks to the poetics of the troubadours for a resolution to the deadlocks of the Voice. Through a detailed reading of an exemplary medieval poem by Aimeric de Paguilhan as well as a work by the nineteenth-century Italian poet Giacomo Leopardi, Agamben argues that poetry allows the absent Voice to sing by means of metrical features that, because they do not bear semantic meaning, call attention to the materiality of language. This means that while philosophy is always necessarily cut off from the foundational reality of Voice, which remains forever unattainable for it, the 'musical element' of 'poetic language commemorates its own inaccessible originary place and . . . says the unspeakability of the event of language (*it attains*, that is, *the unattainable*)' (78; emphasis in original).

Poetry thus fulfils the introduction's enigmatic promise of a passage from ontology to ethics, insofar as it points toward humanity's dwelling in or inhabitation of language – a conception that is rooted in the notion of 'having', which is the etymological root of the Greek term *ethos*. The argument that follows weaves its way through Greek tragedy before abruptly turning to the relationship between Hegel's view of the Absolute and the later Heidegger's concept of *Ereignis*. And at the end of this increasingly compressed and at times strained argumentation, we meet for the first time in Agamben's corpus with the unfortunate *homo sacer*, who 'is excluded from the community, exiled, and abandoned to himself, so that killing him would not be a crime' (105).

Scholars have made much of this brief reference to what will become Agamben's central category. For our purposes here, two representative examples will suffice to show the basic range of positions. Prozorov is characteristically exaggerated in his claims of continuity, proclaiming, 'If one is looking for a concise summary of *Homo Sacer*, one need not look any further.'[15] I would beg to differ, as key aspects of the later book are completely absent (most notably the relation with the logic of sovereignty, the role of the state, the connection with Foucault's biopolitics, and the exemplary role of the Shoah). And coming from the other direction, the grounding of violence in the experience of the negativity of Voice is of course completely foreign to the later work. Salzani is more measured, claiming that this passage 'introduces a problem and a terminology that, even if it remains at the level of intuition, will come to constitute the nucleus of the later project of *Homo Sacer*'.[16] This assessment is more realistic, but it overstates the continuity, because the concept does not reappear until nearly a decade later, in *The Coming Community* – and there only in passing (CC 87). If this passage is the seed of his later project, it lies completely dormant for nearly a decade.

To understand why this is so, it is worth reflecting on the place of this brief excursus in *Language and Death*, which is that of an almost total non sequitur. Indeed, it is the last and least convincing conceptual leap in a thread of argumentation that has become increasingly scattered and tenuous. Already, the shift into the ethical realm felt forced, founded as it was upon the connection of a

Greek etymology to a nineteenth-century poet, and what follows becomes ever more difficult to follow. I suggest that this is not simply a sign of laziness or imprecision on Agamben's part, as the opening chapters unfold in a rigorously systematic way. The scattered character of the later portions of *Language and Death* is instead a symptom of the fact that Agamben has not yet laid any foundations for speaking about ethics – much less politics. The problem is the individualism characteristic of his early work. The dynamics of Voice, as was the case with infancy before it, are presented in a way that highlights each person's experience of acquiring language from the outside rather than as an inborn instinct. The poetic experience that Agamben recommends as a solution to the deadlocks of the philosophical approach is also deeply individual, amounting to the poet's (or reader's) contemplation and enjoyment of the sheer fact of language. Far from grounding an ethical position, this aesthetic experience does not yet even bring us to the point of an encounter with another concrete human being. Indeed, he consistently insists that the love poets of the *Dolce Stil Novo*, who best represent the poetic resolution to the philosophical deadlock of Voice, are not even talking about an actual beloved woman at all in their work. In 'The Dream of Language', an essay published in the same year as *Language and Death* (1982), he argues that 'behind the Provençal and Dolce Stil Novo theory of love stands a radical reflection on poetic language' (EP 57). Hence, for instance, Dante's beloved Beatrice was not a real woman he really fell in love with, but rather 'Beatrice is the name of the amorous experience of the event of language at play in the poetic text itself . . . It is because of its absolute originarity that speech is the supreme cause and object of love and, at the same time, necessarily transient and perishable' (58). How do we get from the poet's love for language in the abstract to a reflection on violence and sacrifice?

The exile of thought

Hence if the final pages of *Language and Death* indicate that Agamben was beginning to intuit some political 'implications' of his project, they also indirectly demonstrate that he was not yet in a position to integrate them convincingly. He remedied this, not by throwing himself into the question of the political, but by taking a step back into the familiar territory of the philosophy of language in order to enrich and deepen his understanding. The publications of these years thus have a paradoxical character. On the one hand, they are if anything even less overtly political than his publications of the late 1970s and early '80s, so that the reader who was following Agamben's career contemporaneously would have assumed that the brief note on violence and the sacred in *Language and Death* would turn out a random outlier in the trajectory of his thought. On the other hand, we know in retrospect that they are laying what will turn out to be the conceptual groundwork for his shift toward the political around 1990 – a shift that was in large part precipitated by geopolitical events that neither he nor anyone else was in a position to predict.

What was it about this stage of his thought that proved more suitable to political extrapolation than the work leading up to *Language and Death*? I would suggest the counterintuitive thesis that they lay the groundwork for a shift to the political precisely to the extent that they are more abstract – or, better, more impersonal. Though his earlier writings are often very abstract in their own way, they are nonetheless all grounded in the irreducibility of personal experience, in keeping with his commitment to asserting individual freedom over against the constraints of tradition and conformism. This approach provided him with a unique perspective from which to critique the dominant intellectual forces of his time, from institutional Marxism to structuralism. Yet it also arguably led him to take the conventional account of his object too much for granted, as a stable foil which he played off against his more experiential supplement.

In the years that immediately follow the publication of *Language and Death*, Agamben begins to correct this tendency. In a sequence of important essays – 'Language and History' (1983), 'The Idea of Language' (1984), and 'The Thing Itself' (1984) – he begins to develop his own account of language as such, one that does not centre on the structuralist dichotomy of *langue* and *parole*, even as a foil to be overturned. Instead, he draws on the Stoic theory of language, which 'clearly distinguishes two planes in language: the level of names . . . and the level of discourse' (P 49). Where the structuralist dichotomy juxtaposes the speaker and the impersonal system of language, the Stoic conception displaces the focus to a distinction between two functions internal to language: alongside its discursive function, language also *names* things.

Drawing on Walter Benjamin, Agamben argues that naming represents the fundamentally historical element of language. On one level, this position seems like pure common sense, insofar as we cannot know the names of things other than through the historical transmission of particular historical languages. There is no way to logically deduce that the device on which I am typing this document is called a 'laptop' in English rather than some other name. So far, so structuralist – but Benjamin goes beyond the arbitrariness of the signifier to the arbitrariness (or historical contingency) of every historical language as such. And if the words of our historical languages mean particular things, he asks, somewhat strangely, what does each language *as a whole* mean? Benjamin's answer is pure language, which is symbolically represented in Adam's naming of the animals in the Garden of Eden and in the vision of a universal human language in the messianic era (52–3).

This pure language neither means nor expresses some extraneous content. It is 'speech that does not communicate anything other than itself' (52). This means that it cannot be something like Esperanto, which aims to overcome the historical division among languages while still remaining one historical language among others (55), nor a kind of meta-language based in hermeneutical reflection (56), nor even a supersession of language in the mystical contemplation of God (57–8). Instead, Agamben tells us, Benjamin 'holds that the universal language at issue here can only be the Idea of language, that is, not an *Ideal* (in the neo-Kantian sense) but the very *Platonic Idea* that saves and in itself fulfills all languages' (59). This distinction is not immediately clear, since the conventional interpretation of the Platonic theory of ideas would hold that the Ideas are every bit as unattainable (at least in this life) as the Kantian regulative ideals. Yet Agamben asserts that something else is at stake. Rather than being a transcendent goal that all historical languages endlessly aspire to, 'the Idea of language is language that no longer presupposes any other language;

it is the language that, having eliminated all of its presuppositions and names and no longer having anything to say, now simply speaks' (60).

The next essay in the sequence, entitled 'The Idea of Language', builds on these claims by highlighting the role of presupposition in most accounts of language. Agamben begins with the concept of revelation in the biblical traditions, which all agree that revelation has a linguistic character. Christianity in particular insists that God reveals himself in Christ precisely as Word. Translating this into secular terms, Agamben argues that 'the content of revelation is not a truth that can be expressed in the form of linguistic propositions about a being (even about a supreme being) but is, instead, a truth that concerns language itself, the very fact that language (and therefore knowledge) exists' (P 40). Yet that very fact can never be expressed directly, but only presupposed as the inexpressible foundation of all linguistic utterance. Agamben detects this dynamic in the infamous 'ontological proof' of the existence of God, in which the medieval theologian Anselm of Canterbury argues that no one can make use of the name of God without being constrained to admit that God in fact exists. Agamben agrees with a millennium's worth of critics that this argument does not seem to hold, but he argues that 'there is a being whose nomination implies its existence, and that being is language. The fact that I speak and that someone listens implies the existence of nothing – other than language. *Language is what must necessarily presuppose itself*' (41).

Over the next few pages, Agamben ties this dynamic of presupposition to the concept of voice, using much the same argumentation and even wording as in his discussion of theology in *Language and Death*. Yet he is taking up this theme only to leave it aside. On the one hand, in keeping with his turn to poetry in *Language and Death*, he says, 'Philosophy can only lead thought to the limit of the voice; it cannot say the voice (or, at least, so it seems)' (43). At the same time, he claims that 'the paradox of pure philosophical intention is precisely that of a discourse that must speak of language, exposing its limits without making use of a metalanguage' that would itself presuppose some other language as object of reflection (43). Hence philosophy must somehow overcome the structure of presupposition, and it is (at least apparently) impossible for it to do so from the direction of voice.

Agamben claims that conditions for finding this non-presuppositional form of philosophical language are favourable, insofar as we live in a world in which the impossibility of any metalanguage has become absolutely undeniable:

There is no name for the name, and there is no metalanguage, not even in the form of an insignificant voice. If God was the name of language, 'God is dead' can only mean that there is no more name for language . . . Thus we finally find ourselves alone with our words; for the first time we are truly alone with language, abandoned without any final foundation. (45)

In Agamben's view, most contemporary thought takes this recognition as the furthest horizon of philosophical inquiry. Yet just as with the collapse of the artistic tradition in *Man Without Content* or the evacuation of experience in *Infancy and History*, Agamben believes that this apparent negativity or lack opens up new possibilities for thought. Here, though, instead of calling for an unheard-of future philosophy to take up this task of thought, he once again points toward Plato's theory of Ideas – not only as a way to escape the logic of presupposition, but as a means of establishing authentic community. In the final paragraph of this short essay, he boldly declares:

There can be no true human community on the basis of a presupposition – be it a nation, a language, or even the a priori of communication of which hermeneutics speaks. What unites human beings themselves is not a nature, a voice, or a common imprisonment in signifying language; it is the vision of language itself and, therefore, the experience of language's limits, its *end*. A true community can only be a community that is not presupposed. (47)

The political reference is perhaps unexpected, but it is not the same kind of non sequitur as the passage on *homo sacer* in *Language and Death*. In fact, here he seems to implicitly diagnose what made that latter passage so questionable. As he himself admits in the quoted passage, the experience of voice, even granting that it befalls all speaking beings, is nonetheless an individual experience. It is common in the sense that we all experience it, but it is not experienced *as* common. By contrast, language as a supra-personal system is an irreducibly common reality, is always necessarily experienced as *shared*.

In the essay that concludes this decisive sequence, 'The Thing Itself', Agamben leaves these communal implications of his emerging theory of language aside, in favour of a deeply philological investigation of Plato's theory of Ideas. He chooses to centre his investigation in a text that scholars long regarded as spurious but, at least by Agamben's report, they were beginning to recognise as authentic – namely, the Seventh Letter, whose neglect by the philosophical tradition makes it a text that can 'be considered with a freshness that is probably unattainable in regard to any other Platonic text' (P 27). What follows is a fine-grained reading of the so-called 'philosophical digression' that previous scholars have cited in support of 'the existence of Plato's unwritten doctrines' but which Agamben believes to provide unexpected insight into what Plato means by the phrase 'the thing itself' (29).

Here I will forego a detailed exposition of this dense and erudite essay. In some ways, this is a shame, as Agamben clearly regards it as one of his greatest achievements and an important part of his intellectual legacy. In both the original English edition of *Potentialities* as well as the expanded and somewhat rearranged Italian edition, it is presented as the first entry in the collection, and shortly after the conclusion of the *Homo Sacer* series, he revises and expands upon the argument in *What is Philosophy?* (2016). More important than the intricate details of the argument itself is a recognition of why Agamben would view it in this way. First and most obviously, it embodies his emergent philological method, reconstructing an ancient text (including on the very technical level of emending the existing critical edition; P 32) in a way that allows us to read the entire philosophical tradition differently. To that extent it is undeniably a tour de force. More subtly, yet more importantly for our purposes, it marks a decisive turning point in his conception of language, at once clarifying the logic of presupposition and pointing toward a way to overcome it.

The key here is in the peculiar grammar of the phrase 'the thing itself' (in Greek, *to pragma auto*). As is well known, Plato uses similar phrasing when referring to the Ideas (sometimes also called Forms). Again and again in the dialogues, Socrates rejects his interlocutors' examples of particular things that are just or good or beautiful and insists that he is after justice *itself*, goodness *itself*, beauty *itself*. The various mythological accounts of the soul and its fate in the dialogues give the impression that Socrates believes that these Ideas are discrete entities, albeit ones that exist in a realm beyond our experience, much as the Kantian thing-in-itself is the real object existing apart from our perception of it. If this were the case, then Plato would be putting forth the thing itself as 'an object presupposed by language and the epistemological process', but Agamben argues that Plato is using the phrase 'the thing itself', *to pragma auto*, to mean 'that *by which* the object is known, *its own knowability and truth*' (32). And since we can only know the thing by means of language, this means that the thing itself 'is the very sayability, the very openness at issue in language, which, in language, we always presuppose and forget' (35). While recognising that our normal use of language could not proceed without this act of presupposition, Agamben declares that the task of philosophy is to bring us back into contact with language in its pure sayability, apart from any concrete referent or discourse.

It is difficult to understand what such a philosophical approach would look like, and the work that followed, 1985's *Idea of Prose*, provides at best indirect guidance. On the one hand, the link with the trio of essays culminating in 'The Thing Itself' seems clear enough: the title stems from a phrase of Benjamin's quoted in 'Language and History', which he uses to designate the pure language that exists beyond all meaning or expression, and the work itself is divided into a series of short meditations on the 'Idea' of a particular concept or experience. Yet it lacks the programmatic character of either *Language and Death* or the follow-up essays. Although some of the chapters contain what we might characterise as philosophical arguments, the purpose of each appears to be to evoke a certain mood or attitude rather than to make a definitive philosophical statement. In a sense, it may be Agamben's attempt to fulfil the demand for a work of criticism that would simultaneously be a work of poetry.

The book opens with the story of Damascius, the last head of the Academy in Athens, who went into exile in Persia after the Emperor Justinian shut the school down and who 'determined to devote the last years of his life of writing a work to be entitled: *Aporias and Solutions Concerning First Principles*' (IP 31). In practice, the task proved nearly impossible, as every approach to the problem seemed inadequate and self-refuting – until he turns his attention, after a fit of unexpected inspiration, to the 'writing tablet on which he had been jotting down his thoughts'. This leads to a profound realisation:

> Suddenly he remembered the passage in the book on the soul in which the philosopher compared the potentiality of the intellect to a tablet on which nothing is written. Why had he not thought of it before? It was this that he had been so futilely trying to grasp day after day . . . The uttermost limit thought can reach is not a being, not a place or thing, no matter how free of any quality, but rather, its own absolute potentiality, the pure potentiality of representation itself: the writing tablet! . . . And the entire, lengthy volume the hand of the scribe had crammed with characters was nothing other than the attempt to represent the perfectly bare writing tablet on which nothing had been written. (34)

To the extent that this vignette builds on 'The Thing Itself', it seems to redouble the abstraction of Agamben's call for a confrontation with the sayability of language by putting forward the task of thinking pure potentiality. Again, what could this possibly mean?

As we will see, there is a sense this reflection seems to lay out a programme for Agamben's future philosophical project, which will be increasingly defined by the concept of potentiality. But the status of *Idea of Prose* is just as paradoxical as that of the essays that proceeded it. Although we can recognise in retrospect that these works of the early 1980s provided the staging ground for his political reflections, they culminated in a book that is resolutely apolitical and even quietistic, reflecting a growing disillusionment with the intellectual milieu in which he was forced to work. In the memoir, Agamben describes *Idea of Prose* as 'the work in which I recognize myself more than in all the others, perhaps because in it I succeeded in forgetting myself' (ARS 69) – yet there is an undeniable element of self-reference in the figure of Damascius, who carries on his solitary philosophical labour in a world dominated by anti-intellectual barbarians. As he will declare in the same 1990 essay in which he consigns the 'general science of history' to the same oblivion as the political hopes of the '60s, 'The severe prose of the world of the 1980s tolerates only positive sciences and, alongside them, a philosophy that is more and more oblivious of its destination' (P 64–5).

The story of Damascius ends ambivalently. After the revelation of pure potentiality, he realises that 'now he could break the tablet, stop writing. Or rather, now he could truly begin . . . That which can never be first let him glimpse, in its fading, the glimmer of a beginning' (IP 34). We know, of course, that Agamben's greatest works were still ahead of him. But that optimistic reading was not the only possible one for a reader in the late '80s. Notwithstanding the burst of creativity represented by *Idea of Prose*, one would have been justified in assuming that Agamben had reached something of a stopping point by the mid-'80s. After nearly a decade of relentless production – starting with the one-two punch of *Stanzas* in 1977 and *Infancy and History* in 1978, continuing through the series of programmatic essays in the late '70s and early '80s, punctuated by *Language and Death* in 1982, and culminating in the bold experimentation of *Idea of Prose* in 1985 – Agamben enters a period of relative intellectual hibernation.

Had he really stopped pursuing philosophy at that point, Agamben's body of work would have seemed remarkably cohesive even in its diversity – but surely no one, likely including Agamben himself, would have regarded it as a potential starting point for a pathbreaking reassessment of Western political institutions. Even if that political potential was in some sense 'already there', it took external events to activate it. And as we will see in the next chapter, the path from his early works to the *Homo Sacer* project, like every path from potentiality to actuality, was neither smooth nor straight.

Notes

1. Quoted in Durantaye, *Giorgio Agamben*, 53.
2. See Durantaye, *Giorgio Agamben*, ch. 2, particularly 77–8.
3. Durantaye, *Giorgio Agamben*, 331.
4. Durantaye, *Giorgio Agamben*, 51.
5. Salzani reports the priority of *poiēsis* in *Man Without Content*, but without calling attention to the contradiction with his later position (*Introduzione*, 15).
6. Watkin, *Literary Agamben*, 93.
7. An essay on Dante from around the same time, 1978's 'Comedy' (which was later republished in *End of the Poem*), reinforces this impression, as it provides a much more comprehensive overview of Dante's poetics and theology, yet also leaves aside his political thought.
8. Attell, *Giorgio Agamben*, 2.
9. In quotations from Agamben, all emphasis is in the original unless otherwise noted.
10. The concluding semi-oblique reference to a poetic fragment of Heidegger's on Cézanne appears to be a personal tribute, as Agamben reveals in *The Use of Bodies* that between sessions of one of the Le Thor seminars, he and Heidegger once bonded while contemplating Mt. Ste.-Victoire, of which Cézanne painted countless canvases (UB 188).
11. I leave the later 'Notes on Gesture' aside for reasons described in Chapter 1, note 20.
12. In my conversation with him in Venice, he confirmed that he was the sole author of this text, which he produced in order to spur discussion of the journal project with Calvino and Rugafiori.
13. In our conversation in Venice, he pointed to his preface to the new English translation of Benveniste's masterwork as the fulfilment of his ambition to write this essay on his favourite linguist. See 'The *Vocabulary* and the Voice', in Benveniste, *Dictionary*.
14. Agamben, *Taste*, 24, translation altered.
15. Prozorov, *Agamben and Politics*, 68.
16. Salzani, *Introduzione*, 42.

2
Taking on the Political

This chapter will chart the gradual emergence of the political in Agamben's thought. Broadly speaking, it was a two-step process. The first step was one that was already beginning to take shape in the works covered at the end of the previous chapter: a consideration of social or political phenomena *in general*. The works in this vein, among which *The Coming Community* is the most sustained example, tend to proceed in a way that is at once deeply speculative and strongly normative. Even if we are not sure what Agamben is actually proposing in any given reflection, there is a clear ethical demand at work, supported by a rhetorical pathos that renders even his most obscure proclamations challenging and seductive. The second step was the development of the *Homo Sacer* project, which the preface to *Means Without End* characterises as 'a rethinking of all the categories of our political tradition in light of the relation between sovereign power and bare life' (MWE x).[1] The latter will introduce a new systematic discipline into Agamben's work at the same time that it spurs him to radically expand the range – and, perhaps even more importantly, the concreteness – of his thought.

There is no single cause or event that prompts him to devote increasing attention to the political. Even the fall of the Soviet Union, important as it was for someone with such a strong aversion to institutional Communism, served more as confirmation than as revelation. Indeed, many of his early political proclamations continue to use Communism as a foil, in a way that clearly presupposes its indefinite future existence. For instance, in a 1986 lecture transcript published under the title 'On Potentiality', which represents his first sustained engagement with the title theme, one of his key examples of the 'experience of potentiality' and its ethical demand is the Soviet dissident poet Anna Akhmatova (P 177). In the opening of the previous chapter, we briefly discussed his equation of Bush Sr. and Gorbachev as products of the security services in the 1990 essay 'Marginal Notes on *Commentaries on the Society of the Spectacle*' (MWE 86). The section in which that remark is found reappears that same year in slightly altered form in *The Coming Community*, where Agamben makes the first explicit reference to the figure of the *homo sacer*, who 'could be killed without committing homicide' (CC 87), since its unexpected role in the conclusion of 1982's *Language and Death*. Though the reference to the Shoah is present, the term is introduced primarily to characterise the victims of the Tiananmen Square massacre – once again, the exemplary political subject is resisting a Communist regime.

On the intellectual level, a major precipitating factor was doubtless the famous debate between Maurice Blanchot and Jean-Luc Nancy on the concept of community. Nancy's original essay, 'The Inoperative Community', and Blanchot's book-length response, *The Disavowed Community*, both appeared originally in 1983 – and in 1984, the term 'community' emerged as a crucial point of reference in the conclusions to Agamben's 'The Idea of Language' and 'The Thing Itself'. We know this is no coincidence, not only because of Agamben's close ties with the French intellectual scene, but more importantly because of his close friendship with Nancy, of whom he later says, 'For years, I have felt . . . so close to his thought that it appeared at times that our voices would become confused' (ARS 93). In the memoir, Agamben highlights their convergence on the theme of the voice, but in this context, the determinative factor appears to be their shared distaste for institutional Communism. In the opening pages of 'The Inoperative Community', Nancy affirms that

> the word 'communism' stands as an emblem of the desire to discover or rediscover a place of community at once beyond social divisions and beyond subordination to technopolitical dominion, and thereby beyond such wasting

away of liberty, of speech, or of simple happiness as comes
about whenever these become subjugated to the exclusive
order of privation; and finally, more simply and even more
decisively, a place from which to surmount the unraveling
that occurs with the death of each one of us . . .[2]

Nevertheless, he notes that the word has lost its aspirational
charge, in part 'because the States that acclaimed it have appeared,
for some time now, as the agents of its betrayal',[3] and he proceeds to use the term 'community' as a way of designating the
desires that 'communism' no longer effectively evokes. What is at
stake, though, is not the development of another policy agenda
or party platform, but the task of grasping the communal nature
of humanity as such, which is to say, the ontological ground that
makes particular human communities possible and thinkable.

Nancy's text, then, provides Agamben with the means to
think the political in a distinctively philosophical register. At the
same time, the political events of the 1980s provided a kind of
negative motivation to reconsider the political. This is because the
very squalor and intellectual bankruptcy of the political world of
the 1980s and '90s – which was so profound and thoroughgoing
as to render itself almost invisible – provides a unique window
into the nature of the political. As he says in the preface to *Means
Without End*,

> If politics today seems to be going through a protracted
> eclipse and appears in a subaltern position with respect to
> religion, economics, and even the law, that is so because, to
> the extent to which it has been losing sight of its own onto-
> logical status, it has failed to confront the transformations
> that gradually have emptied out its categories and concepts.
> (MWE ix)

Here we can see another instance of the principle laid out in
Man Without Content that 'it is only in the burning house that the
fundamental architectural problem becomes visible for the first
time' (MWC 115) – only as the political order collapses into utter
meaninglessness and nihilism are we in a position to really think

the political as such. At the risk of belabouring the metaphor, though, we can say there are two possible responses to a burning house: to build a new house or to investigate what caused the old one to burn down. One way to understand the trajectory that will lead to the formulation of the *Homo Sacer* project is that Agamben begins with the constructive task, but becomes increasingly convinced of the necessity of the diagnostic task. In other words, he starts formulating solutions before he has fully grasped the problem they are responding to – leading necessarily to false starts and dead ends.

Commentators have tended to view *The Coming Community* and *Means Without End* as the 'positive' counterpoint to the critical work in the *Homo Sacer* books, but Agamben himself is more ambivalent, saying that the essays in the latter volume 'at times . . . anticipate the original nuclei of those investigations [i.e., the *Homo Sacer* project] and at others . . . present fragments and shards' (MWE x). One such fragment can be found in the above-quoted reflection on Tiananmen, where he goes on to hypothesise that the convergence of both East and West on the politics of nihilistic security betokens 'the worst tyranny that ever materialized in the history of humanity . . . and all the more so in that it is increasingly clear that such an organization will have the task of managing *the survival of humanity in an uninhabitable world*' (87). Neither the reference to climate change – the only one I am aware of in any of his published works – nor his vision of a world ruled by spies will wind up playing any significant role in his later political thought, even though both themes strike me as plausible frameworks for understanding the politics of the last few decades. The same could be said of his 1991 essay 'Sovereign Police', which argues, based on the US's assertion that the first Gulf War was an international police action, that the model of criminality is dominating international relations. Here, as in the revised version of the Tiananmen reflection in *The Coming Community*, we have the reference to bare life (including the privileged instance of the Shoah) and the concept of sovereignty (which is here taken up thematically for the first time in his published writings). Yet things are not yet coming together in a way that is legible as his 'official' position from the *Homo Sacer* project.

The real breakthrough to the *Homo Sacer* schema comes in an essay with the unassuming title 'Notes on Politics'. Published in 1992, it declares:

> The fall of the Soviet Communist Party and the unconcealed rule of the capitalist-democratic state on a planetary scale have cleared the field of the two main ideological obstacles hindering the resumption of a political philosophy worthy of our time: Stalinism on one side, and progressivism and the constitutional state on the other. Thought thus finds itself, for the first time, facing its own task without any illusion and without any possible alibi. (MWE 109)

In the wake of this 'great transformation', we must now recognise that the house is well and truly burning down, and that means that 'terms such as *sovereignty, right, nation, people, democracy,* and *general will* by now refer to a reality that no longer has anything to do with what these concepts used to designate – and those who continue to use these concepts uncritically literally do not know what they are talking about' (110).

Here we find the first formulation of Agamben's basic political position in the *Homo Sacer* period: 'Sacred life – the life that is presupposed and abandoned by the law in the state of exception – is the mute carrier of sovereignty, the real *sovereign subject*' (113). In 1993, he publishes 'Beyond Human Rights', where he puts forward the stateless refugee as the privileged figure of bare life. In 1994, 'What is a Camp?' sees the first statement of his thesis that the Nazi concentration camp represents 'the hidden matrix and *nomos* of the political space in which we still live' (37). And 1995 sees the publication of the first volume of *Homo Sacer*. This choice of the concentration camp, rather than surveillance, or police, or climate change, as the most urgent issue of the post-Soviet world may seem counterintuitive from an American perspective, but we have to remember that the Yugoslav wars, which marked a return to explicit ethnic cleansing on European soil, began almost immediately after the collapse of the USSR – and took place uncomfortably close to Agamben's home in Italy.

Hence we can hypothesise that the fall of the Soviet Union and the genocidal civil war that followed in its wake cleared the space for the development of the distinctive political position he takes in *Homo Sacer*, even if they did not necessarily 'cause' it in any reductive sense. Only in an unprecedented political situation – not just the end of the Cold War order but the re-emergence of concentration camps across the Adriatic Sea – could he truly get to work on the task of radically rethinking the political. At the same time as this task was a response to unpredictable historical events, however, it was also an outgrowth of his own intellectual project, which he had been slowly and haltingly rethinking from a political perspective throughout the 1980s.

We are dealing, therefore, with a period in which the tension between continuity and responsiveness is most immediately evident – and most productive, transforming Agamben from a hermetic aesthetic thinker to one of the foremost political minds of our era. This transformation did not take the form of simply shedding one persona in order to take on another, however. Agamben remained in many ways the aesthetic thinker that he had always been. In 1991, the same year in which he begins formulating his theory of sovereignty, he also published a tribute to a recently deceased friend, the Italian poet Giorgio Caproni, which drew on his much earlier studies of the *Dolce Stil Novo* poets and Romantic aesthetic theory. That essay later appeared in *The End of the Poem*, published in 1996 (the same year as *Means Without End*), which gathered together pieces ranging from the late 1970s all the way to the mid-'90s, including an extremely erudite and philological study of the Provençal poet Arnaut Daniel that appeared in the same year as the volume as a whole (in other words, the year after *Homo Sacer* was published). The preface to this volume refers to the 'Program for a Review' from *Infancy and History*, lamenting that the project never took off and declaring that 'this book merely offers a torso of the idea of which we once tried to catch sight' (EP xiii). Hence the collection appears to be a backward-looking tribute to a project abandoned long ago, an impression reinforced by its publication in the same year as the more forward-looking *Means Without End* – except that roughly a third of *The End of the Poem* stems from only the year or two before its publication.

Thus we must resist the temptation to offer a simplistic narrative of progress. Agamben's earlier work on poetry and aesthetics did not simply 'lay the foundation' for his political project, as though it were a conceptual presupposition that can ultimately be left aside. Poetry and art represented an area of ongoing reflection even as his political project was getting underway – not as a nostalgic indulgence, but, as we will see in this chapter and those to come, as a real laboratory of thought. Even so, the dominant note of this period is political, and so this chapter will pick up where the previous one left off. After tracing the development of Agamben's concept of potentiality in the works of the mid-1980s, it will take up in turn the two main stages of his political evolution – the first, speculative stage centred on the conceptual triad of language, potentiality, and messianism, and the second, more critical stage, which takes up an rearticulates the first triad in terms of a second, consisting of law, life, and sovereignty. As we will see, even as he assembles what will turn out to be his 'official' position for the rest of his career, his experimental process leads to dead ends and regressions.

Language, potentiality, and messianism

In the last chapter, I suggested that Agamben's work of the mid-'80s laid the basis for his political work in a counterintuitive way – namely, by abstracting away from the concrete individual experience of language and reflecting on the structure of language as such. Where *Language and Death*, focused as it was on the problematic of the Voice, could not find a convincing path from the poet's aesthetic contemplation of language to the questions of violence and political community its final pages gestured toward, the essays that followed took up language insofar as it is always necessarily *shared*. Here again, he proceeded by way of abstraction, arguing that all the concrete historical languages of particular human groups ultimately point toward a more fundamental experience of language in itself. And based on his reading of Plato's theory of Ideas in 'The Thing Itself' (1984), he characterised this experience of pure language or language in itself as an experience of its sheer sayability – or, in yet another level of abstraction, as *potentiality* in general.

If the shared experience of language is what allows Agamben to speak convincingly about community, it is his reflections on the paradoxes and aporias of the concept of potentiality that allow him to begin speaking about *power*. This is clearer in the Italian text, where he often draws a terminological contrast between two terms that could equally be translated as 'power': *potenza* (normally translated as 'potential' or 'potentiality') and *potere* (often rendered simply as 'power'). In his political writings, the former term designates the dynamism and openness that makes things possible, while the latter refers to some already existing form of institutional power. Though the translation convention is necessary for maintaining the terminological distinction, it has the unfortunate side-effect of partly obscuring the fact that the Italian reader would see an immediate relationship with 'power' in both terms.

Hence Agamben is now at the point where he has a theory of language as a communal, supra-individual experience and has begun to speak, if only very abstractly, about power. At a basic level, he now has the groundwork for addressing social and political problems much more convincingly than he had been able to do up to this point. More than that, he now has the ability to make normative claims in both areas, insofar as he declares repeatedly that the abstractions he is dealing with carry with them an ethical element. We can see this in his account of Benjamin's theory of language, where pure language is linked with both the Garden of Eden and the messianic kingdom – which is to say, with both the origin and goal of humanity. In the years covered by this chapter, Agamben will increasingly place his emphasis on the latter, messianic element, laying the basis for a distinctly philosophical conception of messianism that is not tied to any particular historical revelation or tradition but to the human experiences of language and potentiality as such.

The concept of potentiality that will ultimately emerge as Agamben's 'official' position in the mature work is one that starts from Aristotle's distinction between act (*energeia*) and potential (*dynamis*). Where Aristotle privileges the act, however, Agamben will privilege potential (and sometimes claim that, contrary to appearances, Aristotle does so as well). And against a common-sense position that would see potential as being somehow 'used up' once it is fully actualised, Agamben will claim that potential continues to infuse human actions, or at least the most authentic and revelatory types of human action (such as philosophical thought or poetic creation). As with his reading of Plato in 'The Thing Itself', he will make a philological correction to the received text of Aristotle, arguing that Aristotle sees every potential as simultaneously an impotential, every ability as an inability. Hence dwelling in our own potentiality, as Agamben calls us to do, necessarily means dwelling in our own impotentiality or impotence, a condition that he connects to the messianic. And ultimately, Agamben will call for a more radical thought of potentiality freed of any relation to actuality.

Overall, this position on potentiality is homologous with his view of pure language as the condition of possibility for all concrete languages, in that both potentiality and pure language are abstracted from any concrete meaning and both carry a messianic valence. Both positions are also derived from creative philological rereadings of foundational texts – a move he will go on to repeat for messianism, with his creative philological reading of the messianic texts of the Apostle Paul in *The Time That Remains*.

From the perspective of Agamben's later work, the main contribution of *Idea of Prose* and the handful of works that follow in the late 1980s is to develop his concept of potentiality. In *Idea of Prose* itself, we already saw how central it was to the story of the exiled scholar Damascius, whose political alienation and struggle with ontological concepts both seem to resonate with Agamben's own position at this point in his career. The concept comes up again in two key sections: 'The Idea of Study' and 'The Idea of Power', which connect potentiality to the idea of the messianic and to the structure of political institutions, respectively, albeit not yet in the way we would expect in his more mature reflections.

In 'The Idea of Study', after recounting the history of the Jewish people in the wake of the destruction of the Temple in Jerusalem, Agamben notes that 'the Jews entrusted the preservation of their identity to study rather than to worship', so that 'study, the Talmud, has become the real temple of Israel' (IP 63). This means that in Judaism, the scholar has 'a messianic significance unknown to the pagan world' (63). This identification of study as an eschatological discipline might initially seem paradoxical, insofar as study 'is per se interminable' – as anyone who has undertaken a serious research project knows very well. Yet there is also something appropriate about the equation of study with redemption, because 'not only can study have no rightful end, but it does not even desire one' (64). In other words, study is an end in itself, a pursuit that can, in principle, provide an eternal satisfaction.

Study is not simply an interminable progress toward an impossible goal, however. It also includes moments of discontinuity and sudden shocks, where the new and unexpected stops the scholar cold, at once stupefying and astonishing him. Hence, 'if on the one hand he is astonished and absorbed, if study is thus essentially a suffering and an undergoing, the messianic legacy it contains drives him, on the other hand, incessantly toward closure. This *festina lente* [making haste slowly], this shuttling between bewilderment and lucidity, discovery and loss, between agent and patient, is the rhythm of study' (64). And this rhythm, he claims, is the best possible illustration of 'the condition which Aristotle, contrasting it with the act, defines as "potentiality"' (64).[4] He then adds that this concept provides the means to understand what Plato was getting at in his Seventh Letter, the text that forms the basis for the essay 'The Thing in Itself', which represented the culmination of Agamben's crucial sequence of essays on the theory of language.

All three elements of Agamben's emergent political thought – messianism, potentiality, and the theory of language – are present here, but the explicitly social or political charge is absent. The focus is not on community, even the scholarly community, but on the experience of the individual student and 'the self-nourishment of the soul' (65). Much the same could be said for 'The Idea of Power', where he aligns pleasure with pure actuality and potentiality with pain. This parallel, he claims, can 'throw light on the hidden links between power and potentiality':

> The pain of potentiality disappears, in fact, the instant in which it passes into act. But there are forces everywhere – even within ourselves – which constrain potentiality to hang fire within itself. Power grounds itself on these forces: power is the isolation of potentiality from its act, the organization

of potentiality. Power bases its authority on this upgathering
of pain, it literally leaves the pleasure of man unfulfilled. (71)

In this situation of endless deferral, potentiality – which here
seems to be synonymous with the human subject itself – is fooled
into regarding the power structure as an ideal, which is tantamount to 'mistak[ing] the height of pain – omnipotence – for the
greatest perfection' (71). Instead, Agamben proposes, potentiality
should seek the 'human and innocent' pleasure of 'enjoy[ing its]
own impotence' (72).

Here we obviously have a more direct reference to the political, but it is in the purely negative terms familiar from Agamben's recurring opposition of individual freedom and political
constraint. As in 'The Idea of Study', the ultimate goal appears
to be individual beatitude, an impression that is reinforced by the
reflection that follows 'The Idea of Power': namely, 'The Idea of
Communism', which is, strangely enough, actually a discussion of
pornography. For Agamben, pornography at once points toward
'the utopia of a classless society' (73) and embodies the dull conformism of bourgeois culture. Hence he praises pornography for
demonstrating 'that the potential for happiness is present in every
least moment of daily life wherever there is human society' (74),
insofar as any chance encounter could lead to the sex act, and
yet he points out that it is constrained to show 'the unremedi-
ably episodic character of every pleasure – the inner aimlessness
of every universal' (74). As he indicates by referring to the para-
phernalia of pornography as 'the emblems of a community that
we can still barely glimpse' (73) – an echo of Nancy's repeated
characterisation of the word 'communism' as an 'emblem' in the
opening pages of *The Inoperative Community*[5] – this odd section
is less a reflection on institutional Communism than on Nancy's
broader notion of community. And it is a profoundly ambivalent
one. While he acknowledges that community is on some level
what we want, he also seems to doubt that it could ever be fully
satisfying: after all, 'nothing is more boring than a man who has
fulfilled his own dreams' (75).

From the perspective of the later work, this connection
between potentiality and pleasure is unexpected, and indeed it

falls aside already in the 1986 lecture 'On Potentiality'. There we begin to see the key elements of Agamben's 'official' position on potentiality come together. After pointing out the importance of Aristotle's distinction between *dynamis* (potential) and *energeia* (act) for Western thought, he turns abruptly to the above-mentioned reference to the poet Anna Akhmatova, in which she is asked if she can bear to write of the atrocities of the Stalinist regime and responds simply, 'I can' (P 177). In this enigmatic response, Agamben does not see the pride of a great poet who knew her gifts were equal to even the most difficult subject matter. Nor – though Agamben does not explicitly note this possibility – are we in the presence of a brave dissident who is willing to take a risk in the hopes that her poetry might lead to political reform. Instead, he claims that Akhmatova was expressing her willingness to undergo 'the hardest and bitterest experience possible: the experience of potentiality' (178).

Rather than elaborate on the ethical or political implications of 'the experience of potentiality', however, Agamben returns to the path of abstraction, elaborating Aristotle's concept of potentiality and its ramifications in a series of short reflections that are at times difficult to follow. He begins with a passage from Aristotle's *On the Soul* on the paradox that the senses themselves cannot be sensed. Whatever it is that gives us the ability to sense things, then, it is not simply one object among others (even when we look in the mirror at our eye, we are not seeing *sight*, our *ability* to see). What's more, we seem to have this capacity even when we are not actually sensing anything. This means that 'potentiality is not simply non-Being, simple privation', as though we were blind every time we were not in fact looking at something, 'but rather *the existence of non-Being*, the presence of an absence' (179). And this fundamental negativity or lack, he suggests, is both 'the origin (and the abyss) of human power, which is so violent and limitless with respect to living beings' (182) and the reason 'why freedom is freedom for both good and evil' (183). In other words, the human experience of potentiality is at the root of both politics and ethics – a claim that will prove foundational for his later political work. Yet his only concrete example of this experience is an anecdote from the life of a dissident Soviet poet, a particularly literal variation on his favoured anti-Communist motif of the brave individual defying impersonal conformism.

Nevertheless, at this stage of his thought, Agamben is consciously aware of the inadequacies of his focus on individual experience and the need to escape its gravitational pull. We can see this perhaps most clearly in a short piece that has become a *locus classicus* for commentators who stress Agamben's continuity: 'Experimentum Linguae', a preface originally added to the French edition of *Infancy and History* in 1989 – meaning that it was written just as he first began formulating his more overtly political works. Given how rare Agamben's explicit reflections on the trajectory of his work are, and how crucial a moment this one represents, it is understandable that scholars have given it such a prominent place. And on the surface, Agamben does make a strong claim of retrospective continuity, declaring that throughout his career, 'I have stubbornly pursued only one train of thought: what is the meaning of "there is language"; what is the meaning of "I speak"?' (IH 6). Yet at the same time, there is an admission of discontinuity, insofar as he admits that for many years he had been planning a book on the concept of voice that 'remains stubbornly unwritten' (3).

Without repudiating this hypothetical ambition,[6] he reiterates his claim from 'The Idea of Language' that voice cannot form the basis of a community and then strengthens it, saying, 'Only because man finds himself cast into language without the vehicle of a voice . . . do an *ethos* and a community of any kind become possible' (10). The problem is that voice is necessarily an absent presupposition of our usual experience of language, but 'the community that is born of the *experimentum linguae*' – the experience or experiment of language to which the essay's Latin title refers – 'cannot take the form of a presupposition', because 'the only content of the *experimentum* is that *there is language*' (10). And at this point, within the space of a few short sentences, he lurches from his most concrete political claim to date to some of the grandest abstractions to be found anywhere in his work:

we cannot represent this [experience of *there is language*], by the dominant model in our culture, as *a* language, as a state or a patrimony of names and rules which each people transmit from generation to generation. It is, rather, the unpresupposable non-latency in which men have always dwelt, and in which, speaking, they move and breathe. For all the forty millennia of *Homo sapiens*, man has not yet ventured to assume this non-latency, to have the experience of his speaking being. (10)

The contrast with the dominant model of languages as defining a particular state or cultural inheritance is clear enough, even if it is not immediately obvious what the alternative is. Yet what follows, declaring that the experience of language which he is invoking is at once universal and yet radically unprecedented, points to an unanswered question in what I characterised as the first stage of Agamben's political work. If potentiality and pure language are truly foundational for human experience, why are they almost universally unexperienced? His references to 'forces everywhere – even within ourselves – which constrain potentiality to hang fire within itself' (IP 71) or to the necessity of 'freedom for both good and evil' (P 183) show an awareness of the problem, yet as explanations they are patently inadequate, even banal. As we will see, Agamben will ultimately need to turn to the task of critique, not simply as a way of 'applying' his political prescriptions, but in order to give them legible content. In these crucial years of political upheaval, however, he will stick to his more speculative, 'solution-first' approach to political philosophy, which reaches what is arguably its most rigorous and seductive form in *The Coming Community*.

Ontology as politics

While *The Coming Community* represents the first major opening toward the political in Agamben's work, there are many ways in which it looks backward. On a certain level, it could be read almost as a synthesis of his previous two books, taking the philosophical rigour of *Language and Death* and combining it with the fragmentary, poetic style of *Idea of Prose*. Indeed, reading *Idea of Prose* and *The Coming Community* in rapid succession during

my chronological study – only two major essays appeared in the
five years that separate them – I viewed *The Coming Community*
almost as an attempt to rewrite *Idea of Prose* in a more political
key, including some passages that were repeated nearly word-for-
word (such as the discussion of Limbo; see IP 77–8 and CC 5–7).
The Coming Community also repeats passages from other writings that appeared in the same year, including significant chunks
of 'Marginal Notes on *Commentaries on the Society of the Spectacle*'
and 'Pardes: The Writing of Potentiality'. Passages from the
latter essay will subsequently recur in 1993's 'Bartleby, or On
Contingency'. Many readers of Agamben have expressed to me
their view that this kind of repetition is pervasive in his body
of work, and it is certainly the case that he frequently restates
similar insights in different contexts. Literal word-for-word tran-
scription of lengthy passages across different publications does
occur at times, but (with the possible exception of his writings
after the publication of *The Use of Bodies*) it reaches its greatest
apex at this point in his career. While it is possible that purely
contingent personal circumstances could account for this phenomenon – perhaps he was simply more pressed for time in these
years, for example – I think we can also view this kind of repetition, perhaps paradoxically, as symptomatic of the rapid changes
his thought is undergoing at this stage. Only when he is scrambling to retool his philosophical project to incorporate an explicit
political element does he need to cling to satisfactory formula-
tions whenever he finds them – almost as a way of locking down
thoughts that would otherwise remain in flux. In periods where
his basic outlook is more firmly established, by contrast, he is
more comfortable finding fresh ways to express similar ideas in
different pieces of writing.

At the same time, from the perspective of his later political
work, what strikes the reader of *The Coming Community* is how
much will *not* be repeated later. This is evident from the first
page, where he introduces the guiding concept for the entire
book: 'whatever being'. This term refers to the sheer existence of
a singular entity, in abstraction from any particular properties or
identities. Yet this abstraction is not a form of indifference, as the
English word 'whatever' most often suggests (for instance, when

uttered by a scornful teenager). Drawing on a Scholastic formulation of the transcendentals, *quodlibet ens est unum, verum, bonum seu perfectum* ('whatever being is one, true, good, or perfect'), he argues that the Latin equivalent for 'whatever being', *quodlibet ens*, 'is not "being, it does not matter which," but rather, "being such that it always matters"'. This is because the Latin term itself refers 'to the will (*libet*)' and hence 'whatever being has an original relation to desire' (CC 1). The best way to understand whatever being is therefore by thinking of the experience of love:

> Love is never directed toward this or that property of the loved one (being blond, being small, being tender, being lame), but neither does it neglect the properties in favor of an insipid generality (universal love): The lover wants the loved one *with all of its predicates*, its being such as it is. The lover desires the *as* only insofar as it is *such* – this is the lover's particular fetishism. Thus, whatever singularity (the Lovable) is never the intelligence of some thing, of this or that quality or essence, but only the intelligence of an intelligibility. The movement Plato describes as erotic anamnesis is the movement that transports the object not toward another thing or another place, but toward its own taking-place – toward the Idea. (2)

There are two aspects of this passage that I would like to highlight. The first is the importance of the theme of love. This had been a major part of Agamben's work ever since his study of the poetry of courtly love in *Stanzas* (where he had in fact connected it to the concept of fetishism), and as recently as 1988, he had published an important essay relating Heidegger's concept of facticity to the experience of love. The second thing to note is the reference to the Platonic Idea, which has been so important to his thought throughout the 1980s. His reflections on his own idiosyncratic reading of Plato's theory of Ideas have tended, up to this point, to be quite abstract and difficult to grasp, and I at least find the notion that experiencing the pure sayability of language is akin to the attitude of love to be a helpful clarification. Later, he will link the concept of whatever being to both potentiality and the messianic, meaning that all three key themes of the speculative phase of his political thought are being explicitly woven together and granted a greater concreteness. The passage on potentiality and whatever being is particularly important. Here Agamben takes up the connection between potentiality and negativity in a new and more rigorous way than he did in 'On Potentiality'. Rejecting the easy reference to potentiality as a source of both good and evil, he states that 'The symmetry between the potentiality to be and the potentiality to not-be is, in fact, only apparent' (CC 35). Where potentiality to be can only come to fruition in some particular act, potentiality to not-be is 'a potentiality that has as its object potentiality itself' (36). And the ultimate instance of this potentiality is thought, which as 'the potentiality to not think' (36) is able to 'turn back to itself (to its pure potentiality) and be, at its apex, the thought of thought' (37). This may appear to be a turn away from anything political into the most self-absorbed individual experience of all, but there is a political seed here in the form of the 'possible or material intellect' (36), which Arabic commentators (above all ibd Rushd, known to the West as Averroës) regarded as a supra-personal reality which individual acts of thought participate in rather than somehow possessing or enclosing and which played a crucial role in Dante's political thought. As when he laid the groundwork for his political thought with his speculations on language, then, here Agamben's account of purely self-referential thought is, despite appearances, actually breaking away from the individualist bent of his previous writings on potentiality.

In his discussions of messianism in *The Coming Community*, Agamben tends not to use the language of whatever being, though he often uses related phraseology such as 'being such' or 'being thus'. In every case, he proposes a paradoxical form of salvation from the very idea of salvation, redemption from the desire to be redeemed. This comes through most clearly in his reflection on Limbo, which is a kind of holding tank for 'unbaptized children who die with no other fault than original sin' and hence were thought to deserve 'only a punishment of privation that consists in the perpetual lack of the vision of God' (5). In Thomas Aquinas's articulation of this doctrine, there is a further twist: they cannot *know* that they lack the vision of God, because otherwise they would feel pain at that lack, which would amount to an active punishment that is inappropriate for souls that have never done anything positively blameworthy. Hence they live in blissful ignorance of God, and in Aquinas's account they will even enjoy the same perfect and impassible bodies as the blessed in heaven: 'The greatest punishment – the lack of the vision of God – thus turns into a natural joy: Irremediably lost, they persist without pain in divine abandon' (5).

Later, drawing Aquinas into dialogue with the short-story writer Robert Walser, Agamben will claim that after the Last Judgment, 'all will be just as it is, irreparably, but precisely this will be its novelty' (39). This means that after the Last Judgment,

> both necessity and contingency, those two crosses of Western thought, have disappeared . . . The world is now and forever necessarily contingent or contingently neces-sary. Between the *not being able to not-be* that sanctions the decree of necessity and the *being able to not-be* that defines fluctuating contingency, the finite world suggests a con-tingency to the second power that does not found any freedom: It is *capable of not not-being* . . . (40)

Elsewhere, drawing on Walter Benjamin, he characterises the messianic world as 'just a little different' from our world – all the content will be the same, yet the world will be affected by a 'tiny displacement' that somehow changes everything (53). 'The tiny displacement', he clarifies, 'does not refer to the state of things, but to their sense and their limits. It does not take place in things, but at their periphery, in the space of ease between every thing and itself' (54). And that 'ease', as he had established in an earlier passage, is 'not so much the place of love, but rather love as the experience of taking-place in a whatever singularity' (25).

Thus the concept of whatever being as love is not only being connected to the themes of language, potentiality, and messianism, but is drawing them more tightly together. Most often, this hap-pens through a logic of association, where certain key terms form relays connecting different passages within the text – meaning that this apparently fragmentary work is actually one of the most intricately structured in Agamben's oeuvre. In my chronological study, I have found that nearly all of Agamben's work rewards rereading, but this is especially the case for *The Coming Community*.

As I noted above, however, this poetic format is paired with a philosophical intention: Agamben is concerned above all with questions of first philosophy, or ontology – and his goal is always to question received binary oppositions. The very term 'whatever being' comes from Scholastic ontology, and within the first page he argues that the concept allows us to escape 'from the false dilemma that obliges knowledge to choose between the ineffability of the individual and the intelligibility of the universal' (1). We have already seen the ways that his messianism challenges another important dichotomy in Western thought, that between contingency and necessity. And in his discussion of thought as the ultimate potentiality, he will claim that 'the potentiality that thinks itself' causes a collapse in the distinction between 'action and passion' (37). Some of his most intricate arguments centre on his reinterpretation of Plato's theory of Ideas. In the long concluding section, he brings the Idea to bear on the distinction between existence and essence, and in an earlier passage he enters into territory normally associated with analytic philosophy, claiming that the Platonic Idea is the solution to Russell's paradox of the 'class of all the classes that are not members of themselves' (71).

All of this may seem very far afield from the political, but Agamben's wager in this book is that the fundamental ontological concepts that structure our understanding of the world have direct political bearing. Hence I agree with Mathew Abbott's characterisation of Agamben's project as one of political ontology.[7] The phrasing of Russell's paradox is a case in point – in English it is most often referred to as the 'set of all the sets that are not members of themselves', but the use of the word 'class' brings it into contact with political questions relating to class and the classless society. Similarly, whatever being, which produces singularities that are not exhausted by categories of identity, holds out the possibility of a form of being that 'would be absolutely irrelevant to the State', which 'in the final instance . . . can recognize any claim for identity', but 'cannot tolerate in any way . . . that the singularities form a community without affirming an identity, that humans co-belong without any representable condition of belonging (even in the form of a simple presupposition)' (86). Agamben sees such a group of whatever singularities in the Tiananmen Square protestors, who made only the most minimal demands but were nonetheless crushed ruthlessly by State authorities. Without justifying the Chinese government's actions in any way, Agamben suggests that the violence did respond to a genuine threat insofar as the protestors demonstrated a form of existence that does not rely on the State's mediation:

> Whatever singularity, which wants to appropriate belonging itself, its own being-in-language, and thus rejects all identity and every condition of belonging, is the principal enemy of the State. Wherever these singularities peacefully demonstrate their being in common there will be a Tiananmen, and, sooner or later, the tanks will appear. (87)

Finally, then, we have some concrete referent for his political prescriptions – one that is not simply the expression of individual conscience (even if the image of the single man standing down a tank is of course the most unforgettable event in those protests), but necessarily collective.

As I mentioned above, this passage on Tiananmen is also the first time that the figure of the *homo sacer*, who is excluded from the protection of the law and can be killed with impunity but not be formally sacrificed or executed, appears – and, crucially, the first time that this figure will be associated with the Shoah. In this, as in many of the basic ontological claims Agamben makes here, *The Coming Community* seems to point forward to the later political work in a very straightforward way. Yet there is a yawning gap between this text and the phase of his career that would begin with the publication of *Homo Sacer*. On the one hand, in the years to come, the concept of love would fall by the wayside – though not to the same degree as 'whatever being', which is never explicitly mentioned again until 2015's *Pulcinella*, or even 'community', which seems no longer to function as a key technical term after this book. On the other hand, many key points of reference are essentially absent in *The Coming Community*, most notably law, life, and sovereignty. He has broken out of his more individualistic approach with his gesture toward the community of whatever singularities that gathered in Tiananmen Square, but insofar as he views the State purely negatively, he is still operating within the terms of his habitual opposition of individual freedom to political conformism. In the years to come, without sacrificing the hard-won insights of this first stage of his political thought, he will spend less time imagining the shape of the coming community than investigating the ways that the existing power structure continually impedes and resists its arrival.

Law, life, and sovereignty

As Agamben develops his critique of Western political institutions, the three themes of what I have called the first, most speculative stage of his political thought remain central: namely, language, potentiality, and messianism. As he moves into his second, more critical phase, he begins to engage with a second triad, consisting of law, life, and sovereignty. This second triad has occupied by far the most critical attention in the reception of Agamben's work, and much of the later scholarship has pushed back on this tendency by pointing out, rightly, that those more overtly political themes cannot be understood apart from his ontological and linguistic concerns. Where I differ from those critics is in their tendency to treat the works of the first stage (or, in many cases, also the earlier works that lead up to that stage) as somehow foundational for the works of the stage that begins with *Homo Sacer*. Without denying that the earlier works help to contextualise *Homo Sacer*, I want to emphasise that his attempt to bring on board the second triad of law, life, and sovereignty pushes him to continue to develop his ontological and linguistic thought. In other words, it is not so much a question of building a political theory on established ontological and linguistic foundations, as of integrating the two areas of thought in such a way that they mutually influence each other.

The first step in framing my reading is to emphasise the extent to which the themes of the second triad are genuinely new. In the case of sovereignty and law, it seems to me that it is simply impossible to deny that they emerge as thematic concerns only in the early 1990s. As always happens when he is attempting to chart new conceptual territory, Agamben initially leans on Benjamin. The 1992 lecture 'The Messiah and the Sovereign: The Problem of Law in Walter Benjamin' is the first time that problem of the sovereign exception is explicitly named as such, on the authority of Benjamin's Eighth Thesis proclaiming that the state of exception has become the rule (P 160). And he takes this concept as his guiding thread in an investigation that he characterises as

> a contribution to the history of the difficult relationship between philosophy and law . . . Here is it not a matter of a problem of political philosophy in the strict sense but of a crucial issue that involves the very existence of philosophy in its relationship to the entire codified text of tradition, whether it be Islamic *shari'a*, Jewish Halakhah, or Christian dogma. *Philosophy is always already constitutively related to the law, and every philosophical work is always, quite literally, a deci-*sion *on this relationship.* (161)

That final sentence, with its two layers of italics, is as emphatic as it is utterly unprecedented. We are accustomed to think of Agamben as a philosopher of law above all, yet prior to this lecture, he has never explicitly addressed the relationship of philosophy and law – much less claimed that this relationship is constitutive of philosophy as such.

Given the roots of his investigation in Benjamin, Agamben's engagement with law and sovereignty necessarily has implications for his theory of messianism. And after many years of deploying messianic themes in a way that is clearly meant to be normative and yet is not explicitly grounded philosophically, this lecture represents the first time that he makes clear the relationship between messianism and philosophy. He lays the foundation for this by asserting that the sovereign state of exception is somehow 'already' messianic: 'Messianic time has the form of a state of exception (*Ausnahmezustand*) and summary judgment (*Standrecht*), that is judg-ment pronounced in the state of exception' (160). Later, observing

that 'in Judaism, as in Christianity and Shiite Islam, the messianic
event above all signifies a crisis and radical transformation of the
entire order of the law' (162–3), he stakes out the following claim:

> The thesis that I would like to advance is that the mes-
> sianic kingdom is not one category among others within
> religious experience but is, rather, its limit concept. *The
> Messiah is, in other words, the figure through which religion con-
> fronts the problem of the Law, decisively reckoning with it.* And
> since philosophy, for its part, is constitutively involved in
> a confrontation with the Law, messianism represents the
> point of greatest proximity between religion and philoso-
> phy. (163)

Never before has Agamben explicitly linked the theme of messianism to law, much less to the crisis of the law. Hence the
rearticulation of his philosophy to address law requires more than
simply 'applying' his pre-existing concept of messianism – he
must rearticulate the latter theme to fit the emerging shape of his
thought. The way he does so does not always match up with his
mature concept of messianism. For instance, he asserts a duality
in the messiah, corresponding to the duality between the actual-
existing state of exception and the 'real state of exception' in
Benjamin (173). Subsequently this distinction will fall aside, as
he will identify the messianic exclusively with the latter pole. In
addition, he makes much of the notion that the Torah in the state
of messianic suspension is a meaningless jumble of letters (165).
Though that image does return in *Homo Sacer* (HS 57), we will
see in the next chapter that he eventually returns to his intuition
on the messianic significance of study from *Idea of Prose*, which
implicitly requires some kind of order or structure in the law.
These observations are not criticisms, however, but rather illustrations of the bold experimentation of this phase of his thought.

The concept of life is a more ambiguous case. The digression
on the figure of *homo sacer* in *Language and Death* does link 'the
sacralization of life' to the abandonment of 'naked natural life'
(LD 106) in a way that looks forward to *Homo Sacer*. When the
concept recurs in the Debord essay and the parallel passage in *The*

Coming Community, the same connection is reaffirmed – but in between, 'life' is every bit as absent as *homo sacer* as an object of explicit reflection, and the references in these writings of 1990 are every bit as brief and fleeting as they were in *Language and Death*.

The first real attempt to grapple with the concept of life as such actually occurs in one of the essays collected in *The End of the Poem*, namely 'Expropriated Manner', the aforementioned tribute to the poet Giorgio Caproni. At the heart of this essay is a rich reflection on the relationship between poetry and life – surely a poignant theme in the context of the eulogy of a friend who had lived for poetry. Asking, 'Why does poetry matter to us?', Agamben isolates two possible positions: 'those who affirm the significance of poetry only on condition of altogether confusing it with life and those for whom the significance of poetry is instead exclusively a function of its isolation from life' (EP 93). Both positions, however, are ultimately inadequate in Agamben's view, and against them he asserts that the real answer can be found in 'the experience of the poet, who affirms that if poetry and life remain infinitely divergent on the level of the biography and psychology of the individual, they nevertheless become absolutely indistinct at the point of their reciprocal desubjectivization' (93).

In other words, and in contrast to some of his earlier writings about the poet's aesthetic contemplation of the sheer fact of language, what is important is not the experience of the individual poet so much as the way that that experience pushes the poet and his work beyond the level of the individual and toward an experience of language that has implications for everyone: 'The poet is he who, in the word, produces life' (93). By this he does not mean that poetry somehow engenders biological life, but rather that it produces a new form of life: 'poetry matters because the individual who experiences this unity in the medium of language undergoes an anthropological change that is, in the context of the individual's natural history, every bit as decisive as was, for the primate, the liberation of the hand in the erect position or, for the reptile, the transformation of limbs that changed it into a bird' (94). This notion of anthropological transformation will become increasingly central to Agamben's work, beginning with 2002's *The Open*, meaning that one of the most important themes of his mature thought finds its origin in a reflection on poetry. In keeping with the pattern of the first stage of his political thought, it is also a 'solution-first' approach to the concept of life, thinking life first of all from the perspective of its greatest promise as it is actualised in the poetic act, which for Agamben will always remain one of the most privileged human activities.

Two important essays from the years that followed 1991's 'Expropriated Manner', namely 'Notes on Politics' (1992) and 'Form-of-Life' (1993), begin to connect his intuitions about possible political alternatives to a basic conceptual scheme recognisable from *Homo Sacer*. In the first essay, which I have already cited above as the first political text to appear after the collapse of the USSR, he lays out the familiar relationship between sacred life and sovereignty, then proposes that we need to start thinking 'the happy life' over against the lies of consumer society (MWE 114), which means investigating the modalities of a 'free use of the common' that breaks down the distinction between what is proper and improper (118). This concept of use will largely remain in the background in the years to come, but it will prove increasingly central as he brings the *Homo Sacer* series to an end in the 2010s.

It is only in the following year, in the essay 'Form-of-Life', that he begins to deploy the familiar distinction – drawn from Hannah Arendt's *The Human Condition* – between *zōē* and *bios*, or between the sheer fact of living and the specific form that a life takes, which is homologous to the relationship between the rights of 'Man' (that is, of a human being in general, without reference to a specific political community) and 'the Citizen'. And here for the first time, the title concept, 'form-of-life', which refers to 'a life that can never be separated from its form' (3), appears as the desideratum of the coming politics. This form-of-life is instantiated above all in the experience of thought, which 'does not mean merely to be affected by this or that thing, by this or that content of enacted thought, but rather at once to be affected by one's own receptiveness and to experience in each and every thing that is thought a pure power of thinking' (9; translation altered). Thought, in this sense, is not a purely personal act of contemplation but 'is always experience of a common power' (9), which is mediated by pure language as pure communicability (10). Drawing on Averroës and

Dante, Agamben claims that thought is always necessarily collective and supra-individual, and this means that 'intellectuality and
thought are not a form of life among others in which life and social
production articulate themselves, but they are rather *the unitary
power that constitutes the multiple forms of life as form-of-life*' (11). It is
this form-of-life as the collective power of thought that the power
structures founded on sovereignty strive to capture and subdue.

In short, in the essays that follow *The Coming Community*
the two triads of language-potentiality-messianism and law-life-
sovereignty are becoming more and more tightly interwoven. I
have spent so much time on these transitional works in order to
emphasise the experimental nature of this process. It is simply not
the case that his political project was somehow 'already there', as
though these essays were gradually revealing it. Instead, the essays
aim to integrate the two triads in ways that are always partial and
often unrecognisable from the perspective of his 'official' position
in *Homo Sacer*. Sometimes those seeming dead ends turn out to be
important for his later work, and sometimes they are never picked
up again – which we should expect in light of Agamben's own
description of the essays of this era as sometimes 'anticipat[ing] the
original nuclei' of the *Homo Sacer* project while at other times they
'present fragments and shards' (MWE x).

The power of presupposition

Only in *Homo Sacer* itself are the two triads fully integrated, but
once again we are not dealing with the simple 'application' of
the first triad to the second or an establishment of pre-existing
parallels. What is so remarkable about *Homo Sacer*, if we read it in
its chronological context, is how much fresh conceptual labour
Agamben is doing in the work that will provide the starting point
for the next twenty years of his output. It is easy to miss the
innovations, however, because so much of his argument seems to
draw on his earlier analyses. Indeed, one of the most striking features of *Homo Sacer*, particularly in the first major division of the
text, 'The Logic of Sovereignty', is how little space the political
concepts actually take up and how often he retreats to the familiar territory of language and ontology. Moreover, the guiding
thread of his analysis is the logic of presupposition, which we have

already encountered repeatedly in *Language and Death* and in the essays that followed. Yet both the familiar concepts and the logic of presupposition take on new forms and implications in their new context.

Following Benjamin's lead, Agamben begins his first main chapter, 'The Paradox of Sovereignty', by taking up Schmitt's theory of sovereignty, which entails that 'the sovereign, having the legal power to suspend the validity of the law, legally places himself outside the law' (HS 15). Schmitt characterises this paradoxically legally sanctioned form of extra-legality as an 'exception', and as Agamben points out, 'the most proper characteristic of the exception is that what is excluded in it is not, on account of being excluded, absolutely without relation to the rule' (17). Instead, 'the rule applies to the exception in no longer applying, in withdrawing from it' (18; emphasis omitted), meaning that 'the exception is truly, according to its etymological root, *taken outside* (*ex-capere*), and not simply excluded' (18). While some theorists of exceptional powers take them to be a departure from the sphere of law into the realm of sheer factual necessity, Agamben counters that 'the situation created in the exception has the peculiar characteristic that it cannot be defined either as a situation of fact or as a situation of right, but instead institutes a paradoxical threshold of indistinction between the two' (18). For this reason, the exception is not a matter of entering a sphere outside the law so much as establishing law's applicability *in general*, that is, of creating a space within which the supposedly 'normal' operation of law (its application to discrete individual cases) can be carried out.

Having established the basic parameters of the sovereign exception in the space of a few pages, Agamben makes his first return to familiar territory, saying that the question of a general applicability of law as a whole reveals an 'essential proximity' between law and language (20). First, the distinction between the applicability of law in general and its concrete application in specific cases is parallel to that between *langue* (the general system of language) and *parole* (a particular act of speech). Second, and more fundamentally,

> just as language presupposes the nonlinguistic as that with which it must retain itself in a virtual relation (in the form of a *langue* or, more precisely, a grammatical game, that is,

in the form of a discourse whose actual denotation is maintained in infinite suspension) so that it may later denote it in
actual speech, so the law presupposes the nonjuridical (for
example, mere violence in the form of the state of nature)
as that with which it maintains itself in a potential relation
in the state of exception. *The sovereign exception (as zone of
indistinction between nature and right) is the presupposition of the
juridical reference in the form of its suspension.* (20–1)

The logic of presupposition thus provides the point of contact
between the linguistic and legal realms, which is the first crucial
step in rigorously integrating the concerns of his second, critical
political work with those of his first, speculative phase.

   This reliance on the logic of presupposition builds on his previous work – indeed, on *Language and Death*, which is where the
logic of presupposition was introduced – but it also highlights
an element of discontinuity, centring on the theme of the voice.
In *Language and Death*, the non-linguistic presupposition of language was the (animal) voice, which can never appear as such
in human language. In the introduction to *Homo Sacer*, Agamben does invoke this theme, citing Aristotle's claim that language
is what distinguishes human beings from other living things and
makes political existence possible:

> Among living beings, only man has language. The voice
> is the sign of pain and pleasure, and this is why it belongs
> to other living beings . . . But language is for manifesting
> the fitting and the unfitting and the just and the unjust. To
> have the sensation of the good and the bad and of the just
> and the unjust is what is proper to men as opposed to other
> living beings, and the community of these things makes
> dwelling and the city. (qtd in HS, 7–8)

Hence in this earlier passage, he states a similar parallel between
language and politics with an emphasis on voice: 'The living
being has *logos* by taking away and conserving its own voice in
it, even as it dwells in the *polis* by letting its own bare life be
excluded, as an exception, within it' (8). Yet he invokes this older

theme to supersede and replace it, saying a little further down, 'There is politics because man is the living being who, in language, separates and opposes himself to his own bare life and, at the same time, maintains himself in relation to that bare life in an inclusive exclusion' (8). His fleeting reference, a few pages later, to the parallel of the relationship 'the link between *zōē* and *bios*, between voice and language' (11), further reinforces the eclipse of the theme of voice that culminates in the designation of the presupposition of language as non-linguistic reality in general (the range of things that language can refer to) rather than voice. Whether intentionally or not, this eclipse of voice in the early pages of *Homo Sacer* seems to recapitulate his transition in the early '80s from the individual experience of voice to the analysis of language as a general structure.

Alongside this apparent departure from his earlier theory of language, there is a new positive development: the notion of the example, which is a kind of inversion of the exception. If exception is 'an *inclusive exclusion* (which thus serves to influence what is excluded), the example instead functions as an *exclusive inclusion*' (21). His example of the example is the grammatical paradigm, in which

> a single utterance in no way distinguished from others of its kind is isolated from them precisely insofar as it belongs to them. If the syntagm 'I love you' is uttered as an example of a performative speech act, then this syntagm both cannot be understood as in a normal context and yet still must be treated as a real utterance in order for it to be taken as an example . . . The example is thus excluded from the normal case not because it does not belong to it but, on the contrary, because it exhibits its own belonging to it. (22)

By contrast, 'the exception is included in the normal case precisely because it does not belong to it' (22). Despite being apparent opposites, however, the very existence of the correlative relationship between them means that they form part of the same system and are 'ultimately indistinguishable' (22). Though he does not clarify what the legal equivalent of the example would be, he does highlight the prevalence of 'exemplary punishment' in the state of exception (23), indicating that it is not enough to favour the example over the exception.

Later, Agamben will use the distinction between constitutive and constituted power, which Benjamin presents as 'the relation between the violence that posits law and the violence that preserves it' (40), to connect the problem of sovereignty with that of potentiality. Here again, the logic of presupposition comes into play, because every constitutional order – which establishes the basic legal order and systems of right for a particular country – necessarily presupposes that the framers of that constitution had a right to found it. In practice, this power is often treated as irrelevant or exhausted, such that the existing constitution is the ultimate foundation of every law and right, but this just redoubles the problem, because it makes it more difficult to distinguish between constitutive and constituted power. Meanwhile, in extreme circumstances, like Nazi Germany or revolutionary Russia, the appeal to constitutive power can render the constituted order a dead letter and create a situation where even the most extreme measures become permissible.

When presented in these terms, the problem seems to have an urgent practical relevance. And in classic Agamben fashion, he proposes to solve this dilemma by turning to the ontological problem of potentiality, claiming: 'in the last analysis, the relation between constituting and constituted power . . . depends on how one thinks the existence and autonomy of potentiality' (44). He begins by observing that for Aristotle, 'potentiality precedes actuality and conditions it, but also seems to remain essentially subordinate to it' (44). In contrast to the Megarians, who claimed that there is no potentiality apart from the act – much like modern constitutionalists who claim there is no constitutive power apart from the existing constitution itself – Aristotle asserts the 'autonomous existence of potentiality' (45), which is the only way for someone to have a skill while not actually using the skill, for instance. This means that potentiality includes a necessary element of negativity or impotentiality, or to quote Agamben's somewhat idiosyncratic rendering of a key moment in Aristotle's *Metaphysics*: 'Every potentiality is impotentiality of the same and with respect to the same' (qtd in HS 45).

So far, this is all familiar from Agamben's previous discussions of potentiality. Yet he introduces a twist by claiming that by 'describing the most authentic nature of potentiality, Aristotle actually bequeathed the paradigm of sovereignty to Western philosophy' (46). Just as the sovereign exception founds the legal order on the possibility of suspending, which is to say *not* actualising, the law, so too is potentiality's autonomy defined by its potentiality not to be realised in action. Hence he claims that 'an act is sovereign when it realizes itself by simply taking away its own potentiality not to be, letting itself be, giving itself to itself' (46). This means that, contrary to traditional readings that clearly privilege actuality, 'it is never clear' whether Aristotle 'in fact gives primacy to actuality or to potentiality'. And this ambiguity stems from the fact that 'potentiality and actuality are simply the two faces of the sovereign self-grounding of Being', so that in the last analysis, 'pure potentiality and pure actuality are indistinguishable, and the sovereign is precisely this zone of indistinction' (47).

If this identification of potentiality, one of his most valorised concepts, with sovereignty, the ultimate object of his critique, were not surprising enough, he goes on to claim that this 'zone of indistinction' corresponds to the figure of 'a thinking that in actuality thinks its own potentiality to think' (47) – which is precisely where Agamben has placed his political hopes in the writings leading up to *Homo Sacer*. Rather than simply contradicting his earlier articulation of potentiality, however, he is radicalising it. It is not enough to privilege potentiality, as he has done up to this point, but rather 'one must think the existence of potentiality without any relation to Being in the form of actuality . . . and think the existence of potentiality itself without any relation to being in the form of the gift of the self and of letting be', a shift in perspective that 'implies nothing less than thinking ontology and politics beyond every figure of relation' (47).

In the final chapter of *Homo Sacer*'s first major division, Agamben turns from this enigmatic demand to the task of reformulating the last leg of his first triad – namely, messianism. He begins by addressing Jacques Derrida and Massimo Cacciari's interpretations of Kafka's parable 'Before the Law', both of which put forward the story of the man from the country before the open door of the law as reflecting the fact that 'law affirms itself with the greatest force precisely at the point in which it no longer prescribes anything' (49). At this point, he turns to Benjamin and Scholem's correspondence on Kafka, in which Scholem affirms essentially the same view as Derrida and Cacciari. Agamben initially seems to reinforce this interpretation with his reference to Kantian ethics, which is all the more demanding insofar as the moral commandment has no determinate content. Yet he ultimately claims that this kind of legal nihilism, in which an empty law remains in force despite being utterly meaningless, does not go far enough. Benjamin provides the model, as ever, when he 'proposes a messianic nihilism that nullifies even the Nothing [of the law's content] and lets no form of law remain in force beyond its own content' (53). From this perspective, Agamben claims, 'all the behavior of the man from the country is nothing other than a complicated and patient strategy to have the door closed in order to interrupt the Law's being in force' (55) – an effort that, contrary to most common-sense readings of the story, Agamben views as successful.

The man from the country thus represents the messiah, who does not defeat or destroy the law so much as stop it in its tracks – and in so doing paradoxically fulfils the law by granting it an existence apart from the logic of exception (57–8). After a discussion of a text by Jean-Luc Nancy in which he puts forward similar views, Agamben once again calls for a thought that would not rely on the logic of relation, and in a long concluding aleph-note that again draws on Nancy's terminology,[8] he introduces the important concept of *désœuvrement* or inoperativity as a way of thinking about the messianic event beyond Heidegger's *Ereignis* (usually translated as 'event of appropriation') and Kojève's end of history.

This refusal of work resonates with one of Agamben's favourite examples of this period, namely Bartleby the Scrivener, who is the focus of an important 1993 essay on potentiality in which he first calls for a new ontology focused on pure potentiality (see especially P 258–9). Agamben ends the chapter by making this connection between inoperativity and potentiality explicit: 'The only coherent way to understand inoperativity is to think of it as a generic mode of potentiality that is not exhausted (like individual action or collective action understood as the sum of individual actions) in a *transitus de potentia ad actum* [passage from potential to act]' (HS 62).[9] That parenthetical, which implicitly invokes Averroistic themes of thought as a collective reality, is important because it shows that the themes of messianism and potentiality are becoming more tightly interwoven in a way that further consolidates Agamben's shift from a more personal or individual perspective to a collective or political one.

Zōē, bios, and bare life

By the end of the first major division of *Homo Sacer*, then, we have an articulation of the two triads, language–potentiality–messianism and law–life–sovereignty, which entails a further development and integration of the former categories, particularly in the cases of potentiality and messianism. In further developing both theories, Agamben moves beyond favouring one side of a dualism and calls, albeit in the enigmatic terms of overcoming 'relation', for a new mode of thinking that will render those dualisms irrelevant.

The exact form this transformation takes differs for each member of the first triad. In the case of potentiality, this results in what we could somewhat reductively call a 'bad' version, which is defined by its relation to actuality and which provides the model for sovereign power, and a 'good' version that pushes the thought of potentiality beyond any relation to actuality. In the case of messianism, where his earlier essay on Benjamin had defined a 'bad' version (the actual-existing state of exception) and a 'good' version (the 'real' state of exception), here he pulls back from defining the actual state of exception as messianic, reserving the term only for the positive conception. The reason for this is presumably that he has come to see the state of exception not as an extreme limit-case so much as the foundation of the entire Western system of power, so that calling the state of exception messianic would be tantamount to calling the entire actual-existing order messianic. By contrast, he does comparatively little explicit work on the 'good' version of language in this context, which likely reflects the fact that he had already so thoroughly developed the theory of the Platonic Idea in his previous writings. Hence the task here is to more fully articulate the 'bad' version of language that is homologous to sovereignty.

Other essays of this period also contribute to this task of overcoming ontological dualisms. I have already mentioned 'Bartleby' (1993) in this connection, and two other important examples are 'Notes on Gesture' (1992), which contemplates a mode of human activity that would be liberated from the dualism of means and end, and 'Absolute Immanence' (1996), which begins developing an alternative notion of causality that 'escapes the logic of presupposition' (P 233). In these essays as in the first part of *Homo Sacer*, we see Agamben repeating the same basic move that led him from his philosophy of voice to the theory of ideas – instead of simply privileging the subordinate or denigrated element in the structure (for instance, voice), he seeks to think the structure in a way that would not subordinate or denigrate any element in the first place. In other words, it is not enough to expose the presuppositional structure of some system, nor even to reverse its terms. The system as such must be brought to a halt, so that it stops producing the presupposed element.

In the case of language – much less potentiality or gesture – this concern could seem very abstract. What grants it urgency is the figure that Agamben declares to be the 'protagonist' of *Homo Sacer*: 'bare life, that is, the life of *homo sacer* (sacred man), who *may be killed and yet not sacrificed*, and whose essential function in modern politics we intend to assert' (HS 8). In contextualising this most famous claim in Agamben's philosophy, it is important to avoid misunderstanding. As is well known, he begins his investigation in *Homo Sacer* from the following observation:

> The Greeks had no single term to express what we mean by the word 'life.' They used two terms that, although traceable to a common etymological root, are semantically and morphologically distinct: *zōē*, which expressed the simple fact of living common to all living beings (animals, men, or gods), and *bios*, which indicated the form or way of living proper to an individual or group. (1)

This distinction, which Agamben ultimately draws from Hannah Arendt, has come in for significant criticism, most often based on the assumption that Agamben's entire argument hangs on a hard-and-fast distinction between the two terms. Yet the important thing – underlined by the reference to a shared etymological root – is that these two terms are part of a single *system* of conceiving life. Hence on the very next page, he draws on Aristotle's *Politics* to reinforce the same basic point with a different vocabulary, claiming that Aristotle begins by 'opposing the simple fact of living (*to zēn*) to politically qualified life (*to eu zēn*)' (2), or more literally, 'the good life'. What is important is not that the Greeks used two distinct terms, always and everywhere, to refer to these two aspects of life. If it were, then Agamben would have undermined his entire argument within a page and a half, since he provides direct counterevidence in Aristotle's usage of different vocabulary. The point, rather, is *that there are two aspects of life*, and politics is concerned with articulating the difference between the two.

In the classical Greek *polis* as conceived by Aristotle, this articulation took the form of consigning *zōē* to the household, which is necessary to the existence of the *polis* without being properly political. In modernity, by contrast, political power tends to legitimate itself as a way of serving and vindicating the biological life of its subjects. In either case, the system presupposes the existence of natural life (what Agamben designates as *zōē*) as the foundation of properly political life (what he calls *bios*). Hence for the Greeks, the household is a supposedly natural form whose head is able to enter into the political space, while for moderns, Man (the naturally occurring human individual) is the bearer of the rights of the Citizen (the member of a particular political community). Perhaps understandably, political analysts tend to focus their attention on the second, more properly political member of this dyad, but Agamben believes the more fundamental question is 'why Western politics first constitutes itself through an exclusion (which is simultaneously an inclusion) of bare life' (7).

And here we come up against a second common understanding. In the argumentation of the introduction, which sometimes seems to move much too quickly, it could seem as though 'bare life' were simply synonymous to *zōē* in the sense of natural life. Yet in political terms, we do not have access to the sheer fact of natural life – we only have life *as* it is taken up in the political system. And in the last analysis, the way that politics asserts its claim over life is by exposing it to violence and death. Under normal circumstances, this violence is mediated through the legal structure, but the most extreme and paradoxical form of asserting this power of life and death is to *exclude* someone from the realm of legality (with all its protections), precisely as a legal punishment. This dynamic of an exclusion that results in an infinitely intensified inclusion is what the Roman legal figure of the *homo sacer* exemplifies, and to that extent he exists as part of a correlative system with the figure of the sovereign who can legally arrogate the right to exercise extra-legal violence: 'the sovereign is the one with respect to whom all men are potentially *homines sacri*, and *homo sacer* is the one with respect to whom all men act as sovereigns' (84). Indeed, in one of the most dense and difficult chapters of the book, 'Sovereign Body and Sacred Body', he suggests that in the extreme case of the sovereign's death, he too seems to assume a status akin to that of the *homo sacer*.[10] Just as fact and law, exception and example, potentiality and actuality all enter into a zone of indistinction in the sovereign exception, so too, in the last analysis can the ultimate political subject and the ultimate figure of bare life.

The relationship between sovereignty and bare life is thus the ultimate proof of the insufficiency of privileging the presupposed, and therefore abjected, element in a system. On the one hand, declaring someone to be *homo sacer* in a certain sense 'privileges' the presupposed natural life or *zōē*, but in doing so it only subjects that person to the system of power all the more intensely. On the other hand, there would be something perverse and even obscene in claiming that reduction to bare life is beneficial or liberatory – particularly given that the most important modern figure of bare life for Agamben is the most degraded victim of the concentration camps, known in camp jargon as the *Muselmann*.

To return to my admittedly simplistic terminology above, the figure of the *homo sacer* or *Muselmann* clearly represent the 'bad version' of overcoming the division between *zōē* and *bios*, between natural and political life. The 'good version', which at this stage still remains largely unarticulated, is 'form-of-life', in which the distinction between *zōē* and *bios*, between life and its concrete form, becomes simply irrelevant insofar as the two coincide and are completely exhausted in one another – eliminating, rather than privileging or separating out, the presupposed excess of natural life underlying its concrete political form.

This form-of-life, Agamben suggests, could allow 'the emergence of a field of research beyond the terrain defined by the intersection of politics and philosophy, medico-biological sciences and jurisprudence' (188), which may well represent the successor to his earlier hopes for a general science of the human. But rather than dive straight into the articulation of that new field of research – in other words, rather than revert to the 'solution-first' approach of his first political stage – he concludes *Homo Sacer* with a recognition of the preparatory critical work that needs to be done: 'First, however, it will be necessary to examine how it was possible for something like a bare life to be conceived within these disciplines, and how the historical development of these very disciplines has brought them to a limit beyond which they cannot venture without risking an unprecedented biopolitical catastrophe' (188).

The third part of *Homo Sacer* had modelled that critical approach to a certain extent, with its study of the disturbing correspondences between Nazi legal and biological thought and certain trends in liberal democracy (above all related to terminally ill patients surviving through life support alone and to questions surrounding euthanasia). Twenty years later, the third major division of *The Use of Bodies*, which concludes the *Homo Sacer* series, will answer the call for the corresponding positive research agenda with a fresh investigation of the concept of form-of-life initially grounded, again, in medical texts (this time from the Hellenistic period).[11] In the meantime, Agamben's next step in the *Homo Sacer* project will be an investigation of his most extreme modern figure of bare life – namely, the *Muselmann* – from a legal and ethical perspective.

The book that resulted, *Remnants of Auschwitz: The Witness and the Archive*, is arguably his most controversial. Many readers have felt uncomfortable with, or even offended by, this text, which at times seems to appropriate the experience of the Shoah to serve Agamben's own philosophical agenda. Though I take the critiques seriously and in some cases share them, addressing them in detail would take me too far afield from the argument at hand. Durantaye is characteristically even-handed in his authoritative account. In Agamben's defence, he argues that 'the criticism leveled against *Remnants of Auschwitz* has focused more on the fact *that* Agamben dares to use such figures and events as Auschwitz and the *Muselmann* as paradigms than on *how* he does so and what his use of them reveals'.[12] Yet he also admits that Agamben did not do himself any favours in producing a work 'where steps in reasoning seem to have been silenced or skipped', making it, in Durantaye's view, 'the only one [of his works] that shows signs of haste'.[13]

I agree with the impression of haste, but given the book's designation as volume 3 of the *Homo Sacer* series, that haste has implications for the project as a whole. I am referring not so much to the out-of-order publication – which, as we will see, is actually a pervasive feature of the entire series – as of a lack of clarity on the stakes and, above all, the method of the project as a whole. Though he claims early on that the most important task when confronting the horrors of Auschwitz is to understand the legal structure that made them possible (namely, the state of exception, which reduced the Jews and other victims to bare life), his emphasis throughout is on the attempt to somehow capture the subjective experience of the camp's victims, and above all the *Muselmann*. This task initially appears impossible, given the *Muselmann*'s radical unresponsiveness and total disconnection from anything recognisable as a normal human existence. Agamben's ultimate goal, however, is to show that the experience of the *Muselmann* – including the seemingly insuperable obstacles to testifying to it – sheds new light on universal features of human experience. Hence in the chapter entitled 'Shame, or On the Subject', Agamben uses the shame experienced by many camp survivors as the starting point for an investigation of the process of subjectivation in general. Similarly, the concluding chapter 'The Archive and Testimony' uses the impossible position of the witness to the camps as a lens to investigate some of his perennial concerns about language.

In the context of Agamben's philosophical trajectory as a whole, this final chapter points both forward and backward. On the one hand, he draws on his older analyses of language, so that, for example, even the concept of 'infancy' puts in an appearance for the first time in over twenty years (RA 146). Yet this reference occurs in the context of a passage that is concerned to relate his theory of language more closely to his new conception of potentiality, leading to a reworking of the categories of modality in light of the figure of the *Muselmann* that in some ways anticipates *The Use of Bodies* (RA 146–8). Perhaps more importantly, he spends much of the first half of the chapter integrating Benveniste's theory of enunciation – a continual point of reference – with Foucault's notion of philosophical archaeology (137–9). As we will see, this latter concept will be central to Agamben's emergent methodological reflections, although here his perspective on archaeology is more ethical than political (141).

Each time I reread this chapter, however, I am struck by how seldom the *Muselmann* explicitly appears in the argumentation. This relative absence is especially unfortunate given Agamben's decision to conclude with a series of transcribed testimonies from former *Muselmänner* recounting their experiences, a clear contradiction of his repeated claims that being a *Muselmann* was a terminal state that no one ever recovered from. Perhaps by now we should be aware that something of the tension between the *Muselmann* and the witness exists in every Western subject, most of whom nonetheless manage somehow to speak. Yet it is difficult to deny that the shift to direct testimony feels abrupt, even glib – an impression I have confirmed in multiple reading groups. The same ambivalence hovers over the second half of the work, with its ever-expanding scope and ever-expanding distance from the concrete figure of the *Muselmann*. From one perspective, these chapters represent an admirable attempt to rework his philosophy in light of the profound ethical demand represented by Auschwitz. From a less generous perspective, however, the entire exercise comes across as insensitive and even self-indulgent.

However one decides on the appropriateness of Agamben's decision to write a book about Auschwitz at all, the more important question for the present argument is how it fits into his development. My view is that *Remnants of Auschwitz* represents a regression to the more personal or individual perspective of his earlier work, after the breakthrough to a more properly political mode of thought in *Homo Sacer* itself. His goals are so unclear – and hence potentially so easy to misconstrue – because the goals of the project remain poorly defined at this point, and his argumentation is difficult to follow because he has not yet established a reliable method to guide his research. Fully articulating the project's goals and methods will take him a full decade, a process that will prove all the more difficult insofar as he will be forced to undertake it not only as the project itself is unfolding, but as it is radically expanding its purview. In a testament to Agamben's discipline and ambition, however, the result is not chaos and confusion but, in my view, the richest and most challenging period of Agamben's work, to which we now turn.

Notes

1. The English translators provide 'naked life' for *la nuda vita*. For the sake of consistency, here and elsewhere I have substituted 'bare life', not out of any strong preference, but in recognition of the fact that it is the more familiar and standard translation of the phrase in the context of Agamben's work.
2. Nancy, *Inoperative Community*, 1.
3. Nancy, *Inoperative Community*, 2.
4. Translation slightly altered.
5. See Nancy, *Inoperative Community*, 1–2.
6. When I met with Agamben in Venice, he revealed that he had actually returned to this project. He showed me the pile of notes on the subject that he had gathered over the years and claimed to have a full manuscript of the completed work.
7. See Abbott, *The Figure of This World*.
8. Incidentally, the aleph-note format is a staple of the later Agamben, but prior to *Homo Sacer*, it appears only once in its familiar form, in the 1982 essay '*Se*'. The only other place it appears is the 1985 essay 'Tradition of the Immemorial', but there the aleph-note format is used for block quotations rather than the learned digressions familiar from his mature works.
9. In my discussion of this passage, I have substituted 'inoperativity', the standard translation of Agamben's term in later work, for Daniel Heller-Roazen's 'inoperativeness'.

10. This argumentative agenda seems to be what is motivating his one-sided critique of Kantorowicz's *The King's Two Bodies*, in which Agamben tries – implausibly in my view – to exclude any Christian theological influence from the funeral rites that Kantorowicz puts forward as evidence of the notion that the king had a notional second body that contained the sovereign majesty and guaranteed the kingship's continuity beyond the death of its individual bearer. See my further discussion of the importance of this passage below.

11. When we keep in mind the medieval medical treatises covered in *Stanzas*, this means that Agamben has engaged with important medical texts from the ancient, medieval, and modern periods of the Western tradition – a little-recognised interdisciplinary achievement.

12. Durantaye, *Giorgio Agamben*, 249.

13. Durantaye, *Giorgio Agamben*, 297.

3
In Search of a Method

In *The Signature of All Things: On Method*, Agamben begins with an understatement: 'Anyone familiar with research in the human sciences knows that, contrary to common opinion, a reflection on method usually follows practical application, rather than preceding it' (ST 7). In his case, this was undoubtedly true. Published in 2008, his explicit reflection on method comes well over a decade after the beginning of the *Homo Sacer* project (1995), in which he had announced a systematic rethinking of the major categories of Western politics starting from the interplay of sovereign power and bare life. In the meantime, he had published volume 3 of the series (*Remnants of Auschwitz*, in 1999), as well as the first and second parts of volume 2, *State of Exception* (2003) and *The Kingdom and the Glory* (2007), respectively. The latter volume was a surprise in many ways. Not only had there been no previous indication that the second volume of the series would be divided into multiple parts, but the book itself – ostensibly a subsection of a subsection of a larger project – was easily his longest to date, amounting to a longer page-count than all the previous volumes in the series combined. In its subject matter, as well, it seemed like an outlier, largely departing from the study of sovereign power to discuss economic modes of thought, by means of a deep dive into the Christian theological tradition. How did this mammoth volume fit into the architectonic of his project?

This huge addition to the series was only the latest in a growing queue of questions about the stakes and approach of Agamben's investigation. I have already suggested that his use of the *Muselmann*

as a kind of paradigm for the ostensibly universal problem of somehow testifying to the inhuman element within oneself raised serious
problems – not only of sensitivity and propriety, but of methodology.
What are his grounds for making such a universal claim on the basis
of one of the most extreme conditions ever imposed upon a human
being? The same could be said for his other major points of reference,
like the distinction between *zōē* and *bios* or the figure of the *homo
sacer*. Is he claiming that Greek terminology or an obscure Roman
legal provision are somehow 'causing' the dynamics of sovereignty
and bare life? Surely that can't be it, but they do appear to be central
to his argument – and so in what way and on what basis would he
respond to classical scholars who dispute his philological claims?

The *homo sacer* and *Muselmann* are hardly the only figures of
ambiguous significance to appear in *Homo Sacer*. Indeed, the book
ends with a series of figures or examples: a class of Roman priests
known as the *Flamen Diale*; the *homo sacer* and related victims of
legal exclusion; the Führer himself; the *Muselmann*; a biochemist
with a terminal disease who began experimenting on himself; and
an 'overcomatose' patient with no brain activity who is being
kept alive by life support alone. These examples are presented
roughly in chronological order – is this a historical narrative of
some kind? What exactly is the status of this series of figures for
his argument?

We do not get much clarification of these questions in Agamben's indirect indication of his general approach in the opening
pages of *Homo Sacer* itself, where he sets himself the task of synthesising Foucault's work on biopolitics with two elements of
Arendt's thought: her critique of modernity's privileging of biological life over properly political action in *The Human Condition*
and her famous theory of totalitarianism (HS 3–4). Agamben's
engagement with Foucault is another of the clear shifts in his
thought in the 1990s. While a fleeting reference in 'Experimentum Linguae', the preface added to *Infancy and History* in 1989,
indicates that Agamben has developed an interest in Foucault's
work (IH 6), it is only in the important essay 'Form-of-Life'
(1993) that he cites Foucault as a major authority on the centrality
of life in modern politics (MWE 7). Overall, it seems clear that
Agamben has taken Foucault on board relatively rapidly. How

deep can the influence really be at this point? This problem of rapid response will only compound in the coming years, as the publications of Foucault's lecture series at the Collège de France will vastly increase the amount of material Agamben is implicitly holding himself accountable to.

By contrast, Arendt has been with Agamben from the very beginning, and as I have noted, she was already implicitly present on the very first page of *Homo Sacer*, in the form of the dichotomy between *zōē* and *bios*. This contrast is taken directly from *The Human Condition*, where Arendt distinguishes between natural and properly human life in the Greek world in very similar terms to Agamben:

> The word 'life', however, has an altogether different meaning if it is related to the [distinctively human] world . . . The chief characteristic of this specifically human life, whose appearance and disappearance constitute worldly events, is that it is itself always full of events which ultimately can be told as a story, establish a biography; it is of this life, *bios* as distinguished from mere *zōē*, that Aristotle said that it is 'somehow a kind of *praxis*.'[1]

In his presentation of the place of *zōē* in the classical *polis*, he also follows Arendt in locating it in the pre-political realm of the household. Yet in a brief chapter entitled 'Vitae Necisque Potestas' (The Power of Life and Death), he notes that, at least in Roman law, the ultimate instance of sovereign authority was that of the father of the household, who not only could choose to accept and raise a child or expose him to death, but in at least some periods of Roman history actually retained the authority to kill his own child into adulthood. And just as the killing of the *homo sacer* falls outside the legal order of right and punishment, so too is the son simply exposed to the arbitrary violence of his father, with no legal sanction or protection.

Agamben's argumentative point here is to confirm that life 'originally appears in Roman law merely as the counterpart of a power threatening death' (HS 87), yet the reference to the household realm raises some questions from an Arendtian perspective.

On the one hand, this overlap between the household and political realms in Roman society fits with Arendt's historical narrative, insofar as she claims the Romans confused the categories of the household and the *polis* that the ancient Athenians, at least at their best, had kept separate. But on the other hand, Agamben complicates matters when he goes on to claim that this apparent deviation from what Arendt sees as the Greek norm is actually revelatory of a deeper dynamic in Greek society itself:

> Hence the situation of the *patria potestas* at the limit of both the *domus* [household] and the city: if classical [Greek] politics is born through the separation of these two spheres, life that may be killed but not sacrificed is the hinge on which each sphere is articulated and the threshold at which the two spheres are joined in becoming indeterminate. Neither political *bios* nor natural *zōē*, sacred life is the zone of indistinction in which *zōē* and *bios* constitute each other in including and excluding each other. (90)

In other words, bare life does not arise from the confusion of *zōē* and *bios*, household and *polis*, but instead it is the reverse – bare life is the more fundamental reality that gives rise to the apparently stable distinctions that Arendt takes to be normative. What, then, is the concrete relationship between the household and the city from this new perspective, and what are the implications of that relationship for a possible revision of Arendt's historical narrative?

The preface to *Homo Sacer* also raises questions about another long-standing influence: namely, Guy Debord, whose *Society of the Spectacle* (and personal friendship) was so crucial in Agamben's turn toward explicitly political writing. In the opening pages of *Homo Sacer*, Agamben does make two fleeting references to the 'society of the spectacle' (6 and 11), presenting it as a self-evident characterisation of our contemporary political situation. Yet it is far from clear how this deployment of Debord fits in with the promised synthesis between Foucault and Arendt, a difficulty that is reflected in the absence of any subsequent citations from Debord's work in *Homo Sacer* or *Remnants of Auschwitz*. Failure to follow up on the 'society of the spectacle' would be more than a matter of the internal coherence of the *Homo Sacer* project. Abandoning Debord as irrelevant to his career-defining project in political philosophy would therefore mean implicitly abandoning all the previous insights that had made Debord appealing in the first place – and in turn, it would mean throwing overboard the very author who had done the most to convince Agamben that politics was truly worthy of philosophical attention. The difficulty is how to connect Debord's analysis of commodities and images to Agamben's seemingly unrelated concerns of sovereignty and bare life.

All of these questions – about his use of concrete historical examples as paradigms, about the status of his apparent claims of historical causality, about the integration of Foucault into his project, about the relationship between the household and the city, and about the role of the 'society of the spectacle' as an organising concept – come to a head in *The Kingdom and the Glory*. In the wake of that text, he establishes a clear methodological perspective in *The Signature of All Things* that will guide his remaining work in the *Homo Sacer* series. His path from *Remnants of Auschwitz*, which arguably represents the greatest methodological overreach of his career, to his mature method is neither straight nor predictable. As at every previous stage of his thought, Agamben proceeds via experimentation. Indeed, while acknowledging the importance of his work of the 1990s, I view the years covered in this chapter as the greatest blossoming of creativity and ambition – the high-wire act of holding his project together, even as the backlog of accrued questions and apparent contradictions threatened to tear the entire thing apart, spurred him to his greatest achievements.

While these years were crucial for the *Homo Sacer* project, what is so remarkable is how much else he produced over the same period. In addition to the two 'official' volumes of the series (*State of Exception* and *The Kingdom and the Glory*) and the supplemental methodological reflections in *The Signature of All Things*, he held two important seminars that eventually became books. The first, based on courses held in the late '90s and published in 2000 as *The Time That Remains*, is a detailed philological analysis of the Letters of the Apostle Paul and their rich legacy in the Western tradition. The second, which addressed both the tension between household and *polis* in Ancient Athens and the apocalyptic elements in the thought of Thomas Hobbes, was given in 2001 but published belatedly (and retroactively incorporated into the *Homo Sacer* series) in 2015 under the title *Stasis*.[2] He followed these two seminars with his well-known investigation of the relationship between humanity and animality in 2002's *The Open*. While the three books are on very different topics, when read together they form a kind of triptych, with overlapping themes and conceptual moves that reveal them to be part of the same basic thought process. And though only one, *Stasis*, would ultimately become part of the series, all three serve as workshops for ideas that will prove crucial to its concluding volumes.

At the same time, Agamben continued to pursue the more aesthetic side of his work. In 1998, he published an essay collection in French under the title *Image et mémoire* (Image and Memory), which collects texts reflecting the influence of Aby Warburg on his thought. In 2003, he augmented that collection with the essay 'Nymphs', a fresh reflection on Warburg's methodology that he would later publish as a short Italian book in 2007. It was far from his only short publication of the period, as most of the essays collected in 2005's *Profanations* had appeared previously in small chapbooks. The same is true of the essays 'What is an Apparatus?' (2006), 'The Friend' (2007), and 'What is the Contemporary?' (2008), which were collected, somewhat arbitrarily, into a single volume in English translation (WA). In addition to being experiments in format, many of these short pieces are experiments in style, echoing the more poetic approach in *Idea of Prose* but with a more personal tone – something that is especially true of the essays in *Profanations*. Yet that book is more than a mere side project, as the most important essay, 'In Praise of Profanation', begins to work through questions about the shape of an alternative politics in ways that will bear fruit in *The Use of Bodies* and beyond.

As my repeated references to the future shape of the *Homo Sacer* series indicate, my emphasis in this chapter will be more on continuity than discontinuity. The reason for this should be clear: at this stage of his thought, Agamben has explicitly indicated that he is engaging in a more systematic, long-term research project.

Without taking for granted that there was a fully pre-given plan for the project that he is simply executing, I do take him at his word that he is implicitly seeking greater continuity than in previous stages of his work. At the same time, given his past practice of working through similar concepts in differing contexts in publications of the same period, we should expect even writings that are not designated as members of the series to bear some relation to his overarching research agenda. That is certainly the case for the first text we will turn to in this chapter, *The Time That Remains*, in which he works through concepts that will prove crucial for his attempt to trace the outlines of an alternative form-of-life in the concluding volumes of the *Homo Sacer* project – and, together with the second half of *Stasis*, it lays the groundwork for the growing emphasis on theology in the later *Homo Sacer* volumes. Then, deviating somewhat from chronological order, I will skip ahead to *The Open*, whose account of the relation between human and animal will prove decisive for the shape of the *Homo Sacer* series. After treating these important preparatory works, I will discuss *State of Exception* together with the first half of *Stasis*, highlighting the ways that they look forward to *The Kingdom and the Glory*. I will then turn to *The Kingdom and the Glory*, giving equal attention to the ways it builds on the previous *Homo Sacer* volumes and the new problems it poses. I will conclude the chapter with a discussion of his mature methodological position as laid out in *The Signature of All Things*. While I will be addressing his shorter works as the opportunity arises, my main concern will be the *Homo Sacer* project, focusing on the ways that it was threatening to come apart even as it was moving toward its endgame.

A philosophical messianism

I have noted the ways that Agamben, beginning in the early 1980s, enriched his thinking on two elements of what I have called the first triad of his political thought, namely language and potentiality, through a creative rereading of foundational texts of the Western tradition. In the case of language, this took the form of a philological reconstruction of Plato's theory of the Idea, arguing that, far from positing the existence of eternal heavenly archetypes of all concepts or even things, Plato is using the Idea (formulated as 'the thing itself') to indicate the very sayability of the thing, the fact of its being in language. The notion of sayability seems to lead Agamben in the direction of 'ability' more broadly, which gives rise to his rereading of Aristotle's theory of potentiality. Both theories, particularly that of potentiality, are progressively developed throughout the '80s and '90s, which is to say, over the course of the two initial stages in the emergence of his explicit political thought.

By contrast, his theory of messianism has had a more ambiguous grounding up to this point. While he is clearly drawing on Walter Benjamin's messianism, which he views as a necessary counterpoint to the sovereign exception, the basis for his messianic references is less clear. Are they mere metaphors? Surely that can't be the case, even despite his consistent pairing of messianic themes with literary figures (above all Kafka and, in *The Coming Community*, Walser). At the same time, he does not seem to expect some literal messiah figure to show up one day and fix things. We are dealing with something more than evocative imagery, then, but something less than an apocalyptic prediction.

While his messianic thought continues to develop in tandem with the themes of language and potentiality, it is only in *The Time That Remains* that he rigorously articulates it. And as with the previous two themes, he does so through a creative rereading of a foundational text: namely, the Letters of the Apostle Paul, which make up a significant portion of the New Testament and represent, in Agamben's account, 'the fundamental messianic text for the Western tradition' (TTR 1). Just as in the case of his turn toward community, Agamben is responding to an important broader turn in European philosophy, not just toward religious themes in general, but to the Letters of Paul in particular. Both the Jewish scholar Jacob Taubes and the atheist philosopher Alain Badiou had devoted books to this early Christian figure,[3] and Agamben acknowledges both books explicitly, dedicating the seminar to the memory of Taubes (3) and disputing Badiou's account of Pauline universalism (51–3). For the most part, though, Agamben charts his own path by structuring his investigation as a commentary on the opening line of Paul's most important text, the Letter to the Romans, which he claims 'contracts within itself the complete text of the Letter, in a vertiginous recapitulation' (6).

What follows, however, is far from a traditional scholarly commentary. Instead, he uses each of the key words and phrases as a starting point for wide-ranging investigations, not only within Paul's letters, but in the Western tradition as a whole. This book itself could thus be said to recapitulate Agamben's project in miniature, insofar as it proceeds not only, via creative philology, to reconstruct the messianic stakes of Paul's letters, but also to document the ways that the Western tradition has betrayed that messianic heritage – and in some cases, how a faithful remnant has sought to reactivate it over against the majority tradition. Perhaps the best example is the 'Second Day' of the seminar, devoted to the word *klētos* or 'called'. He begins by noting another important passage from Paul's letters in which the term plays a key role (1 Corinthians 7:17–22), and which served as the basis for the Protestant concept of 'calling' famously investigated by Max Weber. The passage reads as follows:

> However that may be, let each of you lead the life that the Lord has assigned, to which God called you. This is my rule in all the communities [*ekkēsías*, another word derived from the same family as *kaleō*]. Was anyone at the time of his call already circumcised? Let him not seek to remove the marks of circumcision. Was anyone at the time of his call with a foreskin? Let him not seek circumcision. Circumcision is nothing, and the foreskin is nothing . . . Let each of you remain in the condition in which you were called. Were you a slave when called? Do not be concerned about it. Even if you can gain your freedom, make use of your present condition now more than ever. For whoever was called in the Lord as a slave is a freed person belonging to the Lord, just as whoever was free when called is a slave of Christ.[4]

In *The Protestant Ethic and the Spirit of Capitalism*, Weber famously argues that Luther's translation of *klēsis* with the German term *Beruf* in this and related passages created a dynamic in which a

divine calling to salvation was paired with an equally divine calling to conformism within the secular world, which lends modern
professions or class positions a quasi-religious status.
Agamben argues that Paul's intention in 1 Corinthians was
very different. Paul is not calling for lockstep conformity to the
expectations of one's social role, but neither is he calling for his
followers to treat those roles with total indifference, as though
they simply do not matter in the larger picture of God's plan of
salvation. Instead, further down in the same passage, he advises
us to take up a more complex stance toward our worldly status:
'But this I say, brethren, time contracted itself, the rest is, that
even those having wives may be as not [*hōs mē*] having, and those
weeping as not weeping, and those rejoicing as not rejoicing, and
those buying as not possessing, and those using the world as not
using it up. For passing away is the figure of this world. But I wish
you to be without care' (1 Corinthians 7:29–32, qtd in TTR 23).[5]
In Agamben's view, this passage defines the messianic life as 'the
revocation of each and every concrete factical vocation' (23). This
revocation is not a simple rejection or dissolution, but instead
a redoubling of the calling that 'revokes the factical condition
and undermines it without altering its form' (24). This revocation
opens up the possibility of a new 'use' (in Greek, *chrēsis*) of one's
condition, a kind of extra-legal use that never amounts to a form
of possession: 'The messianic vocation is not a right, nor does it
furnish an identity; rather, it is a generic potentiality that can be
used without ever being owned' (26).

In short, the Pauline concepts of *hōs mē* (as not) and *chrēsis*
(use) provide a means of tying together his theories of messianism, law (in relation to ownership or right), and potentiality – in
such a way that critique and alternative go together. This messianic stance toward categories of identity takes up and sharpens
some of the intuitions that were encapsulated in the analysis of
'whatever being' from *The Coming Community*, but more importantly it looks ahead to the two books that will come to make up
the fourth and final volume of *Homo Sacer*: *The Highest Poverty*
(volume 4.1) and *The Use of Bodies* (volume 4.2). Indeed, a dense
note on the Franciscan movement's ultimately failed attempt to
develop a positive theory of use to ground their claim to live

without any legal claim to property anticipates the core argument of *The Highest Poverty* – indicating, perhaps, how thoroughly Agamben had sketched out the basic shape of the project at this point. Meanwhile, the importance of the term *chrēsis* (use) anticipates *The Use of Bodies*, where the first major division of the text includes a detailed analysis of the semantics of that term. Yet here we seem to be dealing with a less developed intuition, because very little of the discussion in the later text is concretely anticipated here.

Agamben's primary concern in the present context, however, is an analysis and critique of Marxist approaches to the question of class. This leads to a consideration of the modal category of 'exigency' (which Lorenzo Chiesa and I have also translated as 'demand' in other texts), a category that he draws from Leibniz in order to flesh out an alternative to the standard Western dualism between contingency and necessity by indicating the element of potentiality that dwells in every actuality. This term, too, will come back in *The Use of Bodies* in the midst of a lengthy commentary on Leibniz. Here, however, the exposition is brief and somewhat elliptical, and I think it is fair to say that few would have anticipated at this early date the importance of the concept of exigency or demand for his later thought.

Without the benefit of hindsight, what appears to be Agamben's central concern is the notion of messianic time. This is reflected both in its placement halfway through the text in 'Fourth Day' and in its greater length relative to other analyses. Here Agamben seeks to reconcile his theory of the messianic with his theory of language, including his views on poetic experience. This is not to say that the theory of potentiality is left out, because he draws primarily on the French linguist Gustave Guillaume, who thought of language in terms of 'the Aristotelian distinction between potential and act' in his critique of traditional views of time, especially as they are expressed through grammatical tenses (TTR 65). In the conventional account, 'grammar represents verbal time as an infinite line comprised of two segments, past and future, separated by the cutting of the present' (65). For Guillaume, what is lacking is that this view 'presents time as though it were always already constructed, but does not show time in the act of being constructed in thought' (65). This time that it takes to construct time is what Guillaume calls 'operational time' (66), which he believes accounts for the complexity of actual existing structures of tenses. For Agamben, this 'operational time' amounts to 'something like a time within time – not ulterior but interior – which only measures my disconnection with regard to it, my being out of sync and in noncoincidence with regard to my representation of time, but precisely because of this, allows for the possibility of my achieving and taking hold of it' (67). This, he claims, is identical to the structure of messianic time, which he defines as *the time that time takes to come to an end*, or, more precisely, the time we take to bring to an end, to achieve our representation of time' (67).

While he discusses other messianic themes (like the kingdom of God, the eternal Sabbath, and salvation) in connection to this theory of time, Agamben's argument in this chapter culminates in an analysis of the poetic device of rhyme. What rhyme does, he claims, is to render the poem 'an organism or a temporal machine' that displays a 'kind of eschatology' insofar as a poem is defined by the time that it takes to come to an end (79). Rhyme achieves this by creating a complex network of backward and forward references in the poem, whereby key words (most often the final words of the line) resonate with those before and after. This property of rhyme, he claims, is best embodied in the challenging poetic form known as the sestina, one of which by the Provençal poet Arnaut Daniel he analyses at some length. The first stanza of the sestina establishes a set of rhymed words, which are then systematically re-sorted in subsequent stanzas. The pattern implies that the seventh stanza – corresponding to the seventh day or Sabbath – would repeat the initial sequence of words, but instead the poet breaks the pattern with a compressed final stanza known as a *tornada*, which 'returns to and recapitulates the rhyming end words in a new sequence, simultaneously exposing their singularity along with their secret connectedness' (82).

This venture into the territory of poetics is certainly unexpected in the context of an exegesis of Paul's letters. Agamben justifies this move by claiming that Paul's rhetorical structures actually amount to the origin of rhyme, which he leaves as a

'messianic heritage' to modern poetry (87). This claim is, to say
the least, highly idiosyncratic, and the entire discussion of messianic time starts with one that is even more so. After contrasting
the figure of the prophet (who transmits the word of the Lord)
and the apostle (who speaks on his own behalf), Agamben draws
an even more important contrast: 'The most insidious misunderstanding of the messianic announcement does not consist in mis-
taking it for prophecy, which is turned toward the future, but for
apocalypse, which contemplates the end of time' (62). This assertion that Paul must not be confused with an apocalyptic thinker
becomes a common refrain, returning in his discussions of messianic time in *The Church and the Kingdom* and *The Mystery of Evil*.[6]
As I noted above, I am not in a position to judge his philological
reconstructions of Plato and Aristotle, but I do have the expertise
to assert that Agamben is on very questionable ground here. For
most readers of Paul's letters, myself included, it is obvious that he
is an apocalyptic thinker who expects the Last Judgment to occur
very soon – indeed, within his own lifetime and that of most of
his readers. And far from laying out the structure of the messianic
that is common to our experience of language, Paul is concerned
above all with the claim that a particular historical individual,
namely Jesus of Nazareth, is the messiah promised by God, who
has raised him from the grave in anticipation of the coming general resurrection of all the dead. The philosophical and aesthetic
concerns that Agamben sees in Paul's texts are clearly far afield of
the urgent eschatological mission he believes God has entrusted
him with.

What is going on here? I believe that here Agamben is less
concerned with making historical claims about what a certain
individual named Paul had in mind when he wrote certain letters than with making Paul's texts legible for contemporary
readers. He shows this agenda clearly in the concluding section
of the seminar – labelled a 'Threshold or *Tornada*' – in which he
tries to demonstrate a philological connection between Paul's
letters and Benjamin's 'Theses'. At the end of that discussion,
he distances himself somewhat from his historical assertions
about Benjamin's intentions and points toward a more important principle:

> Whatever the case may be [regarding Benjamin's intention
> to cite Paul in the 'Theses'], there is no reason to doubt
> that these two fundamental messianic texts of our tradition,
> separated by almost two thousand years, both written in a
> situation of radical crisis, form a constellation whose time
> of legibility has finally come today, for reasons that invite
> further reflection. (TTR 145)

This very claim reflects a Benjaminian approach, because in contrast to the common-sense view that any interpretation of a text is indifferently possible at any historical moment, 'Benjamin's principle instead proposes that every work, every text, contains a historical index which indicates both its belonging to a determinate epoch, as well as its only coming forth to full legibility at a determinate historical moment' (145). Whatever other eras may have made of Paul, our era renders legible – perhaps even demands – the constellation between Paul and Benjamin that strips away the mythological detritus to get at the core messianic concepts that allow us to grasp the structure of our experience without reference to either a concrete individual messiah or an arbitrary sequence of supposed future events.

What is it about our era that made it possible for Agamben to develop his philosophical theory of messianism out of the Pauline texts? We can find a clue in his most direct discussion of the themes of the *Homo Sacer* project in *The Time That Remains*, namely the section on the state of exception. This follows on his discussion of the crucial category of 'inoperativity', which we will discuss more fully when it comes up in *The Kingdom and the Glory*. Here the important thing to emphasise is that he asserts that Schmitt's theory of the sovereign exception belongs to 'an explicitly anti-messianic constellation' (TTR 104) – placing it in a theological rather than strictly juridical context. For Schmitt, Agamben claims, the state corresponds to the figure of the *katechōn* or restraining force from the Pauline writing 2 Thessalonians 2:3–9, where it is presented as somehow holding back or preventing the rise of the 'man of lawlessness' and thereby the Last Judgment. Early Christian thinkers tended to identify the *katechōn* with the Roman Empire, which, though evil in itself, had a valuable function of preserving order and thereby staving off the apocalypse. Agamben claims that 'every theory of the State, including Hobbes's – which thinks of it as a power destined to block or delay catastrophe – can be taken as a secularization of this interpretation of 2 Thessalonians 2' (110).

In *Stasis*, he further develops the apocalyptic implications of Hobbes's thought, primarily through a detailed analysis of the various drafts of the famous frontispiece. Though his analysis is often fascinating, the crucial point for our present purposes is his concluding line: 'it is certain that the political philosophy of modernity will not be able to emerge out of its contradictions except by becoming aware of its theological roots' (STA 69). This claim marks a decisive shift in the terms of his analysis. While he had drawn extensively on Schmitt's *Political Theology* in *Homo Sacer*, he never explicitly foregrounded the theological element and instead emphasised the Greek and Roman roots of modern political concepts. In fact, he devotes an entire chapter, 'Sovereign Body and Sacred Body', to arguing against Kantorowicz's claim in *The King's Two Bodies* that the medieval rituals surrounding the transfer of power after the death of a king had Christian theological origins, once again asserting the primacy of the Greek and Roman legacy. Between them, *The Time That Remains* and *Stasis* demonstrate the necessity of a critique of Christian theology for the project that Agamben had set himself – an insight that will radically expand the breadth and richness of the project while also posing serious problems of coherence.

The problem of anthropogenesis

Overall, we can see that *The Time That Remains* does more work in terms of introducing concepts and figures that will prove crucial to the final stages of the *Homo Sacer* series than in clarifying the outstanding methodological questions I have identified – indeed, it actually introduces a new one, namely, how to integrate Christian theology into his project. This pattern will hold for much of his writing 'on the side' as he works on the *Homo Sacer* project. In keeping with the instincts toward a 'solution-first' approach that he displayed in his initial shift toward the political, he will use his publications that fall outside the scope of the official series primarily as an opportunity to experiment with concepts that are more oriented toward the project's conclusion. This means that, all throughout the *Homo Sacer* period, he is effectively developing the constructive and critical sides of his project in tandem. His approach on the constructive side is, understandably, more improvisational and tentative than on the critical side, in keeping with the fact that, so far, it is only the predominantly critical volumes that are being registered as members of the series as such. The one exception to this pattern among the three major works of the early 2000s is *Stasis*, which focuses primarily on working through the main concepts of the critical project and which ultimately found its way into the series proper. Hence, though we have already touched on the second half of *Stasis* in connection with *The Time That Remains*, we will wait to discuss the first half together with a later text that will turn out to 'precede' it within the architectonic of the series: 2003's *State of Exception*.

The text to which we now turn is among Agamben's most popular, *The Open: Man and Animal*. Written just as animal studies was emerging as a major field within the humanities, it displays the uncanny sense of timing that is characteristic of Agamben's works of the 2000s. It is also, arguably even more than *The Time That Remains*, crucial for the development of the final stages of the *Homo Sacer* project – to the point where certain sections of *The Use of Bodies* seem almost like an attempt to take the main concepts from *The Open* and read them onto the official record of the series. Indeed, as we will see, the final essay in that concluding volume of the series will treat *The Open* almost as an honorary member, at the same time as it ignores other actual volumes within the project's actual architectonic.

Leaving aside for now the question of its relation to the series, it is worth noting how it appeared from a contemporaneous perspective – namely, as a huge innovation and advance in his thought, arguably even a step beyond the conceptuality introduced in *Homo Sacer*. The theme of the emergence of humanity from its animal origins – a moment that Agamben here designates as anthropogenesis – seems at once more universal and fundamental than the inscription of bare life in the *polis*, and the memorable

discussions of animal behaviour appear to expand the purview of
Agamben's project beyond their previous focus on human experience.[7] This view of the place of *The Open* in Agamben's trajectory
is exaggerated, however. On the one hand, Agamben's attention
to animality is not completely unprecedented. Already in *Homo
Sacer*, he had discussed the figure of the werewolf – drawing, incidentally, on his expertise in medieval love poetry by centring his
discussion on Marie de France's *lai* 'Bisclavret', which tells the
story of a werewolf whose wife betrays him – as a variation on
the theme of the *homo sacer* (HS 107–8). In this context, he can
characterise the bare life of the *homo sacer* and werewolf as 'a zone
of indistinction and continuous transit between man and beast,
nature and culture' (109), hence preparing at least some ground
for a discussion of animal life within the terms of the project. On
the other hand, far from setting the agenda for his subsequent
research, the animal theme virtually disappears after the publication of *The Open*, only to re-emerge as a subordinate moment
within the larger scheme of *The Use of Bodies*.

We are dealing, in short, with an experiment – one that will
bear important fruit, without necessarily being fully successful
on its own terms. The shape of the text itself bears that out, as
the first half is made up of brief vignettes reminiscent of *Idea of
Prose* or *The Coming Community*, while the second half largely
settles into a lengthy exposition of Heidegger's reflections on
animality before concluding with some final meditations on possible alternative ways to approach to our animal nature. Rather
than attempt to give a full account of these early sections, which
appear to be organised by a logic of free association rather than
any argumentative structure, I will point out some highlights.
The first comes in the midst of Agamben's discussion of the
anthropological implications of Kojève's concept of the end of
history, which 'seems to introduce – between history and its end –
a fringe of ultrahistory that recalls the messianic reign of the
thousand years that, in both the Jewish and Christian traditions,
will be established on Earth between the last messianic event and
the eternal life' (O 12). From the perspective of this 'fringe of
ultrahistory' we can see that humanity is not just one biological species among others, but a constant striving or task that is

achieved by the 'anthropophorous' (or 'man-bearing') animal.
Then, just as suddenly, he suggests that

> the body of the anthropophorous animal (the body of the
> slave) is the unresolved remnant that idealism leaves as an
> inheritance to thought, and the aporias of the philosophy
> of our time coincide with the aporias of this body that
> is irreducibly drawn and divided between animality and
> humanity. (12)

This observation serves as the basis for a transition to a section
about the concept of life in Western culture, which 'never gets
defined as such' but instead 'gets articulated and divided time and
again through a series of caesurae and oppositions that invest it with
a decisive function in domains as apparently distant as philosophy,
theology, politics, and – only later – medicine and biology' (13).
As ever, Aristotle is the key point of reference, as he divides the
soul into three distinct 'faculties or potentialities (nutrition, sensation, thought)' (14). The durable influence of Aristotle's division
of life in Western culture means that to understand humanity, we
must view it not as a substance or species, but as a division over
which a 'decision' must be made as to 'what is human and what is
not' (15). This notion that life is never defined, but only divided
up, will prove central to the final section of *The Use of Bodies*, on
'Form-of-Life', just as the slave will play a key role in the first
major division of that text.

After a brief discussion of the difficulties theologians had
explaining the function of human bodies after the resurrection of
the dead and the Last Judgment, Agamben returns to the concept
of the 'fringe of ultrahistory', arguing that we cannot reach it
'without making recourse to first philosophy' or ontology (O 21).
After this bold statement, he seems to retreat into a more tentative stance:

> It is as if determining the border between human and ani-
> mal were not just one question among many discussed by
> philosophers and theologians, scientists and politicians, but
> rather a fundamental metaphysico-political operation in

which alone something like 'man' can be decided upon
and produced . . . For this reason, the arrival at posthis-
tory necessarily entails the reactualization of the prehistoric
threshold at which that border has been defined. Paradise
calls Eden back into question. (21)

We see here a return to a gesture that is repeated countless times
in his thought and is encapsulated in the principle of the 'burning house' from *Man Without Content* that Jessica Whyte has
rightly highlighted: only once a system or institution comes to
an end can we fully understand what is at stake in it. Here he
takes a step further, claiming explicitly that the 'fringe of ultrahistory' represented by the posthistorical state gives us insight
into the pre-historical or originary moment in which the history
of humanity (as opposed to animality) arose.

A review of modern zoological taxonomies and the ambiguous place of the human in them leads Agamben to posit the existence of an 'anthropological machine which – in its two variants,
ancient and modern – is at work in our culture' (O 37). Where
the modern version of the machine tends to separate out the animal element within the human body (such as the *Muselmann* or,
more radically, the overcomatose patient kept alive by life support alone), the ancient version tends to produce 'figures of an
animal in human form', such as 'the slave, the barbarian, and the
foreigner' (37). In the last analysis, however, both converge in the
production of bare life, meaning that 'it is not so much a matter
of asking which of the two machines (or of the two variants of the
same machine) is better or more effective – or, rather, less lethal
and bloody – as it is of understanding how they work so that we
might, eventually, be able to stop them' (38).

This passage is one of the single greatest contributions of *The
Open* to the terminology and approach of the *Homo Sacer* project.
While the 'anthropological machine' and its two variants will not
return explicitly, 'machine' will take on a terminological significance in Agamben's subsequent work, as a way of referring to the
various ideologies and institutions that – thoughtlessly, heedlessly,
quasi-automatically – produce and reproduce the structures and
categories that define the Western world. The term highlights at

once the artificiality or contingency of the ideology or institution in question and the necessity of stopping it – rather than tinkering with it while it is still in operation, for instance – in order to make the space for an alternative. Finally, it points toward the real stakes of Agamben's critical project. He is not investigating Western ideologies and institutions for the sake of reforming or improving them, but to find a way to stop them in their tracks. And how better to understand how to disassemble a machine than to discern how it was assembled in the first place? In the case of the anthropological machine, that means uncovering the moment of anthropogenesis, another term that will prove increasingly important in the years that follow. This is the task of the long analysis of Heidegger, which at the time represented by far the most sustained and systematic engagement with Heidegger's thought in Agamben's entire body of work thus far. Where he is most often content with passing references of ambiguous import, here he works through all the major writings in which Heidegger discusses animality, starting with the 1929–30 seminar *The Fundamental Concepts of Metaphysics*.

In this important work, Heidegger draws on the zoologist Jakob von Uexküll, whose basic concepts Agamben briefly reviews as a kind of prelude to this section. In essence, Uexküll claims that each species of animal has its own distinctive *Umwelt* or environment, which includes only those objects and phenomena that are relevant to the animal's needs and instincts. Agamben focuses on the memorable example of a tick, whose *Umwelt* is exceptionally narrow, consisting only of the demand to climb on a branch, where it awaits the sensation of a passing animal's body temperature, sucks its blood, and lays its eggs. The tick has no understanding of what it is doing or encountering and can be fooled by similar stimuli, sucking on any liquid the temperature of a mammal's blood, for instance. The relationship to this handful of stimuli is the totality of the tick's existence: 'The tick *is* this relationship; she lives only in it and for it' (47). Agamben concludes his discussion of Uexküll by noting that the zoologist mentions a tick kept in 'a condition of absolute isolation from its environment' for eighteen years, during which time it remained alive (47). Yet what kind of life could this possibly be?

In the ensuing discussion of Heidegger, it becomes clear that this bizarre moment of suspension is actually the key to the distinctively human mode of existence. Taking up Uexküll's concepts, Heidegger argues that the passage from the animal *Umwelt* or environment to the properly human world is not a gradual enrichment, but instead a radical deactivation represented by the mood he defines as profound boredom. In this state, our investment in the reality around us completely falls aside, so that no stimulus can motivate us and all avenues of experience appear to be closed. But it is only this gesture of withdrawal, Heidegger claims, that opens up the human world.

Here Agamben differs from his teacher, claiming instead that boredom is not a form of openness, but a kind of redoubling of the animal's captivation by the narrow range of stimuli within its more limited *Umwelt*. This means that the human being or 'Dasein is simply an animal that has learned to become bored; it has awakened *from* its own captivation *to* its own captivation' (70). And if Heidegger is right that the experience of certain fundamental moods – like profound boredom or, more famously, anxiety – is revelatory of the root of metaphysical concepts, then we have here a case for viewing the bored human being's curious redoubling of animal captivation as the root of first philosophy. This, at least, is what he claims in the climactic section entitled 'Anthropogenesis', where he declares:

> Ontology, or first philosophy, is not an innocuous academic discipline, but in every sense the fundamental operation in which anthropogenesis, the becoming human of the human being, is realized. From the beginning, metaphysics is taken up in this strategy: it concerns precisely the *meta* that completes and preserves the overcoming of animal *physis* in the direction of human history. This overcoming is not an event that has been completed once and for all, but an occurrence that is always under way, that every time and in each individual decides between the human and the animal, between nature and history between life and death. (79)

This implies that it is possible to disrupt or potentially redirect this process, particularly now that we are living in a posthistorical state in which 'the [anthropological] machine is idling' (80). And the concluding reflections – on Benjamin, the Renaissance painter Titian, and the Gnostic theologian Basilides – all in their own way point toward a new use of our animality that might arise once the anthropological machine has been rendered inoperative.

Just as the notion of the machine would prove more important than the specifically anthropological model, so too here does the concept of anthropogenesis turn out to be more important for Agamben's later thought than the specific context of animality in which it arises. Indeed, the notion of somehow returning to and redirecting the contingent moment of anthropogenesis becomes an ever more insistent concern, beginning especially with *The Sacrament of Language* (2008). The connection between first philosophy (which, for whatever reason, he increasingly prefers to call ontology rather than metaphysics in the years to come) will remain important as well, though the emphasis will be more on language – which does appear as a theme in *The Open*, but not one that plays a determinate role in his conclusions – than on any supposedly 'pre-human' animal experience. In other words, anthropogenesis will take a form more akin to the poetic experience of 'anthropological change' described in 1991's 'Expropriated Manner' (EP 94).

This later shift may shed some light on *The Open*'s ambiguous relationship to the *Homo Sacer* project. While it makes significant terminological and methodological contributions, at the end of the day Agamben's analysis here does not quite fit with the critique of the logic of presupposition that structures the rest of the project. To put it simply, in *Homo Sacer* there is no access to the pre-political natural life, to the thing-in-itself outside of language, to the pre-legal fact – all of them are after-effects of the gesture of presupposition itself. By contrast, here Agamben seems to posit the availability of an animal experience that really does exist outside the anthropological machine and serves to found it. Hence, perhaps, *The Open*'s place as a particularly fruitful thought experiment rather than a fully realised contribution to Agamben's career-defining series.

The city and the household

In the following year, Agamben went on to publish a text that proved, if anything, even more popular than *The Open*, solidifying his reputation – particularly among American academics – as a kind of political prophet: *State of Exception*, which is designated as volume 2 of *Homo Sacer*. The book is the product of a brief window when Agamben was very active in the US, giving the seminars that would become *The Time That Remains* and *Stasis* at several prestigious American universities. (That window would eventually close when Agamben refused to travel to the United States in protest of a new requirement for foreign visitors to submit to fingerprinting, which he viewed as an unacceptable biopolitical measure.[8]) The US influence is particularly clear in *State of Exception*, where he cites American academics like Judith Butler and Sam Weber (SE 4 and 55, respectively), whom he had met while offering his seminars at their institutions. More important is his explicit reference to the USA Patriot Act, which granted George W. Bush the authority to effectively reduce any alien suspected of involvement in terrorism to the status of bare life (3–4), and Bush's 'decision to refer to himself constantly as the "Commander in Chief of the Army" after September 11, 2001', which Agamben views as an assertion of Bush's sovereign power (22).

Seldom had Agamben so directly asserted the immediate contemporary relevance of his thought, and in those dark days of the War on Terror, *State of Exception*, arguably even more than *Homo Sacer* itself, was required reading among left-leaning American academics. The appeal of *State of Exception* over its predecessor was not only its 'ripped from the headlines' feel. Where *Homo Sacer* had briefly outlined the structure of the state of exception and concentrated primarily on establishing homologies with the realms of language and ontology, *State of Exception* displays greater focus on the political and legal implications of its title concept, including a lengthy history of emergency powers in most modern European countries (11–22) – culminating, of course, with Bush's War on Terror. Yet this apparent clarity and contemporary relevance was a double-edged sword. While it helped to popularise his ideas, injecting them into that tense political climate led to a simplification and moralisation of his analysis, as though his purpose were simply to denounce the state of exception as illegitimate.

In reality, the ultimate stakes of the text lay not in the state of exception as such, but in the deeper structures of Western politics and law that it points toward – structures that bear directly on the complex relationship between city and household. I believe that we can gain greater clarity on the goals of *State of Exception* if we restore *Stasis* to its original chronological context – namely, as a product of the years immediately preceding the publication of the better-known book. The connection between the two texts is immediately obvious from their very first pages. Where *Stasis* claims that 'a theory of civil war is completely lacking today, yet this absence does not seem to concern jurists and political scientists too much' (STA 1), *State of Exception* asserts that 'there is no theory of the state of exception in public law, and jurists and theorists of public law seem to regard the problem more as a *quaestio facti* [purely factual question] than as a genuine juridical problem' (SE 1). Given that *State of Exception* makes repeated, albeit always passing, references to civil war as a case in which sovereign emergency powers are evoked to fight a threat to the stability of the state, then, we might perhaps conclude that *Stasis* is addressing a subtopic within the broader framework of the state of exception – an impression that its later designation as volume 2.2 of the *Homo Sacer* series reinforces.

Taken in chronological sequence, however, *Stasis* appears less as a preparatory exercise on a subordinate problem than as a pathbreaking investigation of one of the outstanding questions I have flagged for the *Homo Sacer* project as a whole: namely, that of the relationship between the city and the household. Agamben's point of reference for his brief but decisive analysis is a short essay by Nicole Loraux entitled 'War in the Family', where she highlights the ancient Athenians' belief that civil conflict, which they designated by the term *stasis*, was not a question of politics, but rather of the *oikos* or household. In other words, the true source of *stasis*, of lethal conflict within the community, was not political disagreement, but family disputes – a conclusion reflected vividly in the tradition of Greek tragedy.

For much of the short first division of *Stasis*, Agamben mostly limits himself to a summary of the main claims in Loraux's essay (which at the time was not widely available) and her better-known book *The Divided City*, before expanding upon what he calls – using here for the first time a term that will be central to his later methodological reflections – the *Entwicklungsfähigkeit* or 'capacity for development' in her findings (STA 5). In summarising her conclusions, he points out that *stasis* as Loraux understands it 'calls into question the commonplace that conceives Greek politics as the definitive overcoming of the *oikos* in the *polis*' (10). Just the opposite is the case, as the conflict or *stasis* that originates in the *oikos* represents a constant threat to the *polis*. What is more, the *polis* cannot even resolve the problem of *stasis* on its own terms, but must rely on the *oikos* as the site for 'the reconciliation of what it has divided' (11). Relating Loraux's ideas to his analysis of *zōē* and *bios* in *Homo Sacer*, he claims that the relationship between the *oikos* and the *polis* is 'not an overcoming, but a complicated and unresolved attempt to capture an exteriority and to expel an intimacy' (13). To fully capture that dynamic, however, he must go beyond Loraux's identification of *stasis* with the household or *oikos*. Instead, he claims, *stasis* actually 'constitutes a threshold of indifference between the *oikos* and the *polis*, between blood kinship and citizenship' (15) or 'a zone of indifference between the unpolitical space of the family and the political space of the city' (16). This means that *stasis*, far from being a disturbance of the political realm, is actually the means by which Greek society politicised itself – which is shown in the curious fact that Solon's original laws for the Athenians mandated that anyone who failed to participate in a *stasis* by claiming neutrality must be stripped of citizenship once the *stasis* has concluded. Far from being a deviation from the duties of citizenship, as we moderns would see it, *stasis* or civil war was actually a requirement.

Agamben concludes his analysis by claiming that '*stasis* does not originate in the *oikos*; it is not a "war in the family," but forms part of a device that functions in a manner similar to the state of exception' (22). This 'device' – an anticipation of the language of the 'machine' that will emerge in the following year in *The Open* – politicises the *oikos* in the same way that the state of exception

inscribes *zōē* into the legal order. Politics thus becomes not a separate realm from the household or *oikos*, but 'a field of forces whose
extremes are the *oikos* and the *polis*' (22), meaning that 'politics is
a field incessantly traversed by the tensional currents of politiciza-
tion and depoliticization, the family and the city' (23). And after
a brief moment of equilibrium in classical Greece, the West has
tended to alternate between either trying to convert the city into
the household or else fully politicising every aspect of life without
remainder.

   This argument, which concludes the first major division of *Stasis*, is closely connected with the final chapter of *State of Exception*.
There Agamben is concerned with the Roman concepts of *auctoritas* (authority) and *potestas* (power), which map, broadly speaking, onto the distinction between the household and the city. On
the one hand, *auctoritas* is grounded in the father's power over his
household, which is assumed to be immediate and natural, unmediated by law, while on the other hand, *potestas* represents the
exercise of concrete legal offices or powers. Within the classical
Roman political system, the Senate represented *auctoritas*, while the
other formal magistracies exercised *potestas*. The Senate's role was
fundamentally passive and advisory: it 'cannot express itself without being questioned by the magistrates and can only request or
"counsel" . . . without this "counsel" ever being absolutely binding' (SE 77). Its role was similar to that of the legal figure of the
auctor, whose approval was needed 'in order to confer legal validity
on the act of a subject who cannot independently bring a legally
valid act into being', such as a child or slave (76). In both cases,
Agamben observes, it is 'as if for something to exist in law there
must be a relationship between two elements (or two subjects):
one endowed with *auctoritas* and one that takes the initiative in
the strict sense' (76), namely the representative of *potestas*. Hence,
while the two elements 'are clearly distinct', they nonetheless form
'a binary system' of the kind that we should by now find familiar.

   Under normal circumstances, the *auctoritas* of the Senate (as rep-
resentatives of the supposedly natural and unmediated authority of
the fathers) served only to advise and legitimate the concrete acts
of *potestas*. In extreme cases, however, the Senate could declare
a *iustitium* or 'standstill' of the law (41). This declaration did not

amount to any legal authority or office, such as martial law or temporary dictatorship. The *iustitium* does not empower or authorise any person or action, but simply advises all citizens to take whatever action is necessary to solve the emergency. In other words, it represents a complete *absence* or void of legal power. And this, Agamben declares, is what is truly intolerable to modern legal theorists, above all Carl Schmitt – the notion that there could be a sphere of action completely separate from law. To avoid this impossible conclusion, they instead scramble to inscribe every action and situation within *some* relationship to the law, even the limit case of the purely negative one seen in the state of exception.

By contrast, Walter Benjamin, in his critical reformulation of Schmitt's theory of sovereignty, was seeking to think precisely a sphere of action that would be free of all relation to law. He designates this with the puzzling term 'pure violence', and Agamben is quick to clarify that purity here does not indicate some innocent original state of non-contamination, but rather the removal of its 'relation to something external' (SE 61). Law views every action that falls outside its sphere as illegitimate violence, and hence 'pure violence' indicates an attempt to do that gesture one better by refusing even that negative relationship with law. Here Agamben draws a parallel to the theory of language that he had already drawn from Benjamin: 'just as pure language is not another language, just as it does not have a place other than that of the natural communicative language, but reveals itself only in exposing them as such' – in other words, allowing us to think the sheer fact that *there is language* – 'so pure violence is attested to only as the exposure and deposition of the relation between violence and law' (62).

As an example of what this relation to the law might look like, Agamben turns to Kafka's short story 'The New Attorney', in which Bucephalus, the former warhorse of Alexander the Great, decides to become an attorney in his retirement and spends his time, not practising law, but simply studying the law books (SE 63). Building on the association he had established in *The Open* between animality and the messianic, he argues that this story provides an image of a messianic relationship to the law: 'What opens a passage toward justice is not the erasure of law, but its deactivation and inoperativity – that is, another use of the law', which takes the form of 'play' (64):

> One day humanity will play with law just as children play with disused objects, not in order to restore them to their canonical use but to free them from it for good. What is found after the law is not a more proper and original use value that precedes the law, but a new use that is born only after it. And use, which has been contaminated by law, must also be freed from its own value. This liberation is the task of study, or of play. And this studious play is the passage that allows us to arrive at that justice that one of Benjamin's posthumous fragments defines as a state of the world in which the world appears as a good that absolutely cannot be appropriated or made juridical. (64)

In this memorable passage, Agamben takes up some themes from *Infancy and History* and *Idea of Prose*, but transposes them into a newfound political key, and in so doing he points toward some of the central insights of *The Use of Bodies*. It is, in short, a masterful conclusion.

Strangely, however, *State of Exception* does not actually end there. Instead Agamben transitions abruptly to a passage that revisits *Homo Sacer*'s analysis of the funeral of the emperor, which relies upon the key terms from the final chapter on *auctoritas* and *potestas* without fully explaining them. This is only one of many deeply questionable organisational decisions (above all the unexplained alternation between the contemporary and ancient Roman contexts) that conspire to obscure the true stakes of the argument: namely, the description of the bipolar system of *auctoritas* and *potestas*, of which the state of exception (which most readers, in keeping with Agamben's title, view as the main point of the book) represents only one extreme iteration.

As in *Stasis*, Agamben notes here that some form of equilibrium is possible: 'As long as the two elements remain correlated yet conceptually, temporally, and subjectively distinct (as in republican Rome's contrast between the Senate and the people, or in medieval Europe's contrast between spiritual and temporal powers) their dialectic – though founded on a fiction – can nonetheless function in some way' (86). Yet the system is always threatened with collapse and destruction, because when the two poles 'tend to coincide in a single person, when the state of exception, in which they are bound and blurred together, becomes the rule, then the juridico-political system transforms itself into a killing machine' (86). The task of the critic is 'the patient work that, by unmasking this fiction, separates what it had claimed to unite' (88), for example, life and law or *auctoritas* and *potestas* – a claim that begins to contextualise *Homo Sacer*'s repeated calls to move beyond the category of relation. As in *The Open*'s analysis of the 'anthropological machine', the goal here is not to reform the system or return it to a more stable balance – for instance, to stop relying on exceptional emergency powers and return to the 'normal' rule of law – but to fully grasp it in order to understand how to dismantle it.

The mystery of the economy

After *State of Exception*, many observers (myself included) expected that Agamben's next major work would be the fourth and final volume of the *Homo Sacer* series, on 'form-of-life'. On a superficial level, the series seemed complete: the first volume laid out the terms of the project, and the second and third volumes went into greater detail on sovereign power and bare life, respectively. Yet in terms of Agamben's declared ambition of 'a rethinking of all the categories of our political tradition in light of the relation between sovereign power and bare life' (MWE x), the project was far from complete. There are simply too many political concepts and institutions that have been left out of the analysis or, at best, treated only in passing – among them economics, religion, and even the 'normal' functioning of the state – for him to claim to have completely rethought the Western political tradition. More than that, it is not immediately clear how these topics would fit into his analysis as it stands in the first three volumes.

An important essay dramatises Agamben's dilemma here in miniature: 'In Praise of Profanation', a fresh text included in 2005's *Profanations*, which otherwise collected a series of brief

reflective essays that had originally appeared in small chapbooks.
The essay opens by counterposing the act of consecration – which
renders things sacred and thus 'indicated the removal of things
from the sphere of human law' – and the correlative gesture of
profanation, which 'meant, conversely, to return them to the
free use of men' (Pr 73), a free use that is exemplified in children's play (75–6). If the problem with sovereign power is that
it reduces human life to the status of *homo sacer*, here we seem to
have a means to free humanity of that status. Yet much of the
essay is taken up with unexpected obstacles to profanation: the
Christian tradition, which largely betrays the messianic impulses
of its founding moment, and its misbegotten offspring, the capitalist system, which Benjamin claims 'develops parasitically from
Christianity' (80). As the 'religion of modernity' (80), capitalism
represents 'nothing but a gigantic apparatus for capturing pure
means, that is, profanatory behaviors' (87).

   This analysis is surprising on any number of levels. The first
is the very fact that Agamben is directly addressing capitalism
at all. In keeping with his resistance to conventional Marxism,
Agamben has always been reluctant to address capitalism as such –
indeed, even in his 1990 essay on Debord, who certainly was not
shy about critiquing capitalism, Agamben cannot bring himself to
use the term unequivocally, preferring instead to refer to 'capitalism (or whatever other name we might want to give to the process dominating world history today)' (MWE 82). The second is
his reliance on the terminology of religion. In *Homo Sacer* he was
so determined to distinguish his political and legal sense of *sacer*
from the religious sphere that he devoted an entire chapter, 'The
Ambivalence of the Sacred', to discrediting modern theories of
the sacred originating from the discipline of religious studies. And
although we now know that Agamben had already recognised in
Stasis the necessity of interrogating the theological roots of modern political concepts, he nonetheless leaves Christianity aside in
State of Exception and even doubles down on his critique of Kantorowicz for supposedly overemphasising the Christian valence
of royal funerals in *The King's Two Bodies* (SE 83). *The Time That
Remains* does include critiques of various Christian thinkers, yet
the emphasis was on Paul's messianic potential. Even with that

book in mind, then, the focus on a critique of Christianity as such is a new development.

In an important essay published the following year, 'What is an Apparatus?' (2006), Agamben reveals that these concerns have been at the forefront of his thought since the completion of *State of Exception* in 2003: 'Over the past three years, I have found myself increasingly involved in an investigation that is only now beginning to come to its end, one that I can roughly define as a theological genealogy of economy' (WA 8). That investigation would be published in the following year under the title *The Kingdom and the Glory: Toward a Theological Genealogy of Economy and Government.*[9] As the subtitle indicates, it not only takes up the three 'missing' topics I list above, but seeks to weave them together. And in doing so, it reopens one of the outstanding issues that may have seemed settled in *State of Exception*, namely the relation of the household and the city, which Agamben had clarified by uncovering the bipolar system of *auctoritas* and *potestas*. Here, that system

> takes the form of the articulation between Kingdom and Government and, ultimately, interrogates the very relation – which initially was not considered – between *oikonomia* and Glory, between power as government and effective management, and power as ceremonial and liturgical regality, two aspects that have been curiously neglected by both political philosophers and political scientists. (KG xii)

On both fronts, Agamben is radically expanding the scope of his investigation into areas that he more or less admits to be new, and hence he is right to say that 'the inquiry into the genealogy – or, as one used to say, the *nature* – of power in the West, which I began more than ten years ago with *Homo Sacer*, reaches a point that is in every sense decisive' (xi). At the risk of overdramatising, he seems to be presenting this book as a make-or-break moment for the viability of his project.

Yet it would be a mistake to overemphasise the degree of novelty here. Not only does he maintain the framework of *auctoritas* and *potestas* from *State of Exception*, but he also presents his investigation of *oikonomia* – a Greek term that initially denoted the management of the household or *oikos* and eventually became the root of our term 'economy' – as a continuation and internal critique of 'Michel Foucault's investigations into the genealogy of governmentality' (xi), hence maintaining contact with one of the primary authorities for the original *Homo Sacer* and, more specifically, the new lecture courses that were becoming available over those years. And the theme of glory provides a means, at long last, to integrate Debord's concept of the 'society of the spectacle' (which the preface to *Homo Sacer* presented as an obvious point of reference without arguing for its relevance) into the project in a rigorous way.[10] What makes this move possible is a recognition that the spheres of the media and public opinion are the democratic equivalent of the formal ceremonies and acclamations of monarchical and fascist regimes, which means that Debord's insights into the ways that capitalism devolves into an endless accumulation of images can be repositioned as an insight into the deep structures of 'a society in which power in its "glorious" aspect becomes indiscernible from *oikonomia* and government' (xii).

Indeed, the vindication of Debord appears to be one of the ultimate goals of this massive tome, as revealed by his central role in the concluding 'threshold'. Yet that same section reveals that this is not simply a matter of tying up a loose end from the preface to *Homo Sacer*, but also a response to geopolitical events, specifically developments within the European Union. The 2000s saw the introduction of the euro as a shared currency, which intensified the economic restraints the EU imposed on its member nations. At the same time, the EU expanded rapidly to include many former Communist states and even former Soviet Republics. Both the restraints on democratic politics and the lack of a shared political culture raised questions about the legitimacy and viability of the European project, and Habermas and others suggested that the development of a pan-European 'public sphere' may put the EU on firmer footing. In the 'threshold', Agamben rejects the terms of this debate, declaring that Europe is already dominated by the society of the spectacle and that a reorganisation of the public sphere would not fundamentally change that reality.

The expansion of the European Union was only one example of the broader economic triumphalism of the post-Cold War era, and in his analysis of economic modes of thought, Agamben aims to discredit the identification of capitalism with freedom. Here we can detect an echo of one of Agamben's other primary sources for the project, namely Hannah Arendt, who in *The Human Condition* posits, on the basis of Aristotle's description of the ancient Greek *polis*, a qualitative difference between the economic realm (which is associated with mere natural necessity and slavery) and the properly political sphere (characterised by distinctively human pursuits among free people). This inheritance from Arendt likely accounts in part for the fact that he had not previously viewed the economic realm as worthy of serious attention, and as we will see, it will also shape his argumentative approach, which aims ultimately to dispense with the economic and return to the 'properly' political realm of glory.

Achieving such a wide range of goals in tandem, while maintaining substantial continuity with the previous three volumes of the series, obviously requires a complex argumentative strategy. Yet Agamben arguably overcomplicates his approach by framing his investigation around a debate between Carl Schmitt and the little-known German theologian Erik Peterson about the possibility of a Christian political theology, in Schmitt's sense of a homology between earthly and divine modes of sovereignty. Broadly speaking, Peterson argues that Schmitt's theory is illegitimate in two senses. First, God's nature as Trinity of three persons has no parallel in the created world, and hence no homology is possible in principle. Second, Christianity is *already* political insofar as its public liturgy participates in the angelic liturgy in the heavenly Jerusalem, and therefore the connection of Christianity with any merely earthly *polis* would represent apostasy. Agamben's goal is not to mediate the dispute, however, but to highlight a shared omission in both thinkers' accounts: namely, the centrality of *oikonomia* in the theological sources they marshal in support of their arguments.

The chapter that follows traces the etymology and history of the term *oikonomia*. In the original Greek sources, as I note above, it denotes the management of the household or *oikos*, but its usage evolved to encompass any form of flexible management over heterogeneous interests, in settings ranging from managing a crowd through political rhetoric to holding together a multinational empire. In the New Testament, Agamben claims, the term referred primarily to Paul's improvisational and flexible approach to carrying out God's plan of spreading the Gospel to all nations, which he refers to as 'the *oikonomia* of the mystery' (23).

Gradually, however, Christian thinkers begin reversing the term into 'mystery of the *oikonomia*', which opened the door to a specifically theological view of *oikonomia* as a way of denoting God's *own* management of creation rather than his apostle's management of his divine task – and, in the relation among the Trinitarian persons, God's management of his relationship with himself, in the truly divine *oikonomia*. Since God's ultimate goal is redemption, this economy is an economy of salvation.

Over the course of the next three chapters, Agamben traces the development of the divine *oikonomia* of salvation into the doctrine of providence, which is to say, of God's indirect management of the created world. This is not the place to enter into the fine details of the theological and philosophical debates Agamben analyses, but the emphasis throughout is on the emergence of a bipolar 'providential machine' that coordinates between God's will and individual free choices, between universal divine decrees (primary causes) and particular events (secondary causes), between transcendence and immanence (KG 140–1). This theological model informs the liberal-democratic theory of governance, and the concluding appendices provide some tantalising first steps toward a genealogy that would connect Agamben's medieval sources to modern political theory.

Agamben's true quarry is not economy but glory, however, and the next chapter, 'Angelology and Bureaucracy', provides the transition point. As the title suggests, within the theological system, the angels serve as God's 'middle management', helping to coordinate the divine intent with the immanent events of creation, but they also perform another important function: worshipping and glorifying God. After the Last Judgment, the angels will devote themselves entirely to the pursuit of God's glory, since there will be no need for any further divine management – with one exception, namely hell. There, the demons (who are fallen angels who rebelled against God) will continue to 'manage' the population of the damned, carrying out the tortures that God has mandated. He uses this association between *oikonomia* and hell as the pretext for a rare joke: 'this means that, from the perspective of Christian theology, the idea of eternal government (which is the paradigm of modern politics) is truly infernal' (164). In other words, far from saving us and setting us free, the secular *oikonomia* in which we live has consigned us to unending suffering – a claim that seems retrospectively prophetic when we recall that the financial crisis, which served as the pretext for the self-inflicted agony of austerity throughout Europe, occurred one short year after *The Kingdom and the Glory* was published.

Having concluded that there is in fact no redemption to be found in the *oikonomia*, Agamben devotes the rest of the book more or less exclusively to the analysis of glory. After briefly demonstrating that Peterson's apparent belief that liturgy could save us from Schmittian fascism was naive, he devotes the long final chapter – amounting to over 20 per cent of this lengthy text – to 'The Archaeology of Glory'. There he identifies an apparent paradox: while theologians insist that God is inherently glorious to the highest possible degree, they nonetheless insist just as firmly that worship or glorification of God is necessary. Over the course of a long and meandering investigation, which includes some rare attention to the Hebrew Bible as well as an unexpected detour into Indic sources, Agamben gradually builds the argument that human worship is actually what *creates* God. And since the divine glory serves no further purpose or goal, what we are ultimately worshipping when we worship God is our own *inoperativity*, of which glory represents 'the capture and inscription in a separate sphere' (245). This term has come up several times before, but it is only at this point that he explains it in detail:

> Human life is inoperative and without purpose, but precisely this *argia* [lack of work] and this absence of aim make the incomparable operativity of the human species possible. Man has dedicated himself to production and labor because in his essence he is completely devoid of work, because

he is the Sabbatical animal par excellence . . . the govern-
mental apparatus functions because it has captured in its
empty center the inoperativity of the human essence. This
inoperativity is the political substance of the Occident, the
glorious nutrient of all power. (245–6)

By contrast, a truly messianic approach would deactivate this
apparatus and thereby allow us to dwell once more in our inoperativity. We can anticipate this messianic reality in the present
world not by simply destroying or negating the apparatus, but by
deploying 'a special indicator of inoperativity', namely the Pauline
'hōs mē, the "as not"' (248). The Christian tradition forgets this
messianic heritage, however, and 'a doctrine of glorious life that
isolates eternal life and its inoperativity in a separate sphere comes
to substitute that of the messianic life' (249). Even if the language
of separation superficially contradicts Agamben's prescriptions in
The Open and *State of Exception*, his return to his core concepts of
pure potentiality and form-of-life (250–1), just before an abrupt
concluding turn to the discussion of Debord and the EU's 'public
sphere' mentioned above, indicate that this investigation has been
guided by the same messianic intention as the previous volumes.

Paradigm, signature, archaeology

Such, at least, is the basic outline of *The Kingdom and the Glory*,
though this summary leaves out a great deal. The fact that Agamben
was able to generate a book as rich and diverse as *The Kingdom and
the Glory* – which, along the way to achieving all the goals internal
to his own project, also manages to radically rearticulate the history
of the development of Christian doctrine – over the course of only
three years of intensive research is remarkable. At the same time,
I hope that my outline of the general flow of the argument highlights the extent to which he is barely holding together the various
threads. While the organisational problems in *State of Exception* were
most likely a matter of front-loading the material most relevant to
contemporary events, here the unclear organisation and reliance
on somewhat contrived transition points (above all the joke about
the hellishness of contemporary governance) seems to reflect the

intrinsic difficulty of tackling all the tasks he had set himself in the context of a single volume.

The challenge that *The Kingdom and the Glory* presented was not only that of incorporating new themes and concepts into the project of *Homo Sacer*. Achieving that required the second-order work of developing methods for doing so. Much of this methodological work was apparently done 'on the fly', above all in the first chapter. There he declares:

> One of the theses that we shall try to demonstrate is that two . . . political paradigms, antinomical but functionally related to one another, derive from Christian theology: political theology, which founds the transcendence of sovereign power on the single God, and economic theology, which replaces this transcendence with the idea of an *oikonomia*, conceived as an immanent ordering – domestic and not yet political in a strict sense – of both divine and human life. Political philosophy and the modern theory of the sovereignty derive from the first paradigm; modern biopolitics up to the current triumph of economy and government over every other aspect of social life derive from the second paradigm. (KG 1)

This claim raises the question of how the theological 'derivation' actually functions, and he notes an important difference between the two cases. While he initially appears to accept Schmitt's dictum that modern political concepts are secularised theological concepts, he claims that 'theology is itself "economic" and did not simply become so at a later time through secularization' (3). This is the beginning of an attempt to keep the political and the economic rigorously separate, which culminates in his condemnation of the *oikonomia* to hell – and which seems to me to be a regression compared to his subtler articulation of the relationship between the household (*oikos*) and city (*polis*) achieved in *Stasis* and *State of Exception*. Nevertheless, this arguable step backward is accompanied by a decisive step forward. The long aleph-note that follows complicates the notion of secularisation, arguing that Schmitt is not speaking primarily of the historical origin of political concepts, but asserting that 'in modernity, theology continues to be present and active in an eminent way' (4). The important thing is not to assert an absolute identity between the two realms, but to note 'a particular strategic relation that marks political concepts and refers them back to their theological origin' (4).

It is at this point that Agamben introduces a key methodological term, claiming that 'secularization is not a concept but a signature', which he defines, following Foucault and the Italian philosopher Enzo Melandri, as 'something that in a sign or concept marks and exceeds such a sign or concept by referring it back to a determinate interpretation or field, without for this reason leaving the semiotic to constitute a new meaning or a new concept' (4). Signatures thus constitute 'pure historical elements' allowing the researcher to track the connections between 'different times and fields', and in that sense he claims that 'Foucault's archaeology and Nietzsche's genealogy . . . are sciences of signatures, which run parallel to the history of ideas and concepts, and should not be confused with them' (4). Later he will reiterate this methodological point when justifying his use of theological sources to investigate the concept of governance: 'the genealogy of a political concept or institution may be found in a field that is different from the one in which we initially assumed we would find it . . . archaeology is a science of signatures, and we need to be able to follow the signatures that displace the concepts and orient their interpretation toward different fields' (112). He also defines certain key terms – most importantly 'order' and 'glory' – as signatures, though strangely not *oikonomia*.

We can presumably infer that Agamben's own procedure is supposed to exemplify the approach outlined, and so to that extent we can discern what he means by archaeology or genealogy (though not the difference, if there is one, between them). Yet the explicit methodological principles, taken in themselves, do not give us much to go on other than the somewhat tautologous claim that archaeology or genealogy is the study of signatures and that a signature is the kind of thing one should look for when undertaking an archaeology or genealogy. Nor do we learn the relationship between the new term signature and the already established term 'paradigm', which is used at various points in *Homo Sacer* without being explicitly defined. Indeed, though at times it seems to be a technical term, as when he claims that the camp is 'the hidden paradigm of the political space of modernity' (123), at other places he seems to use it more loosely, as when he claims that 'Aristotle actually bequeathed the paradigm of sovereignty to Western philosophy' in his theory of potentiality (46). Sometimes his usage even appears contradictory, as he can refer to the *homo sacer* as a paradigm of bare life (107) and also claim that it is a member of a broader paradigm that includes the sovereign (100).[11] The use of the same term to designate political theology and economic theology in *The Kingdom and the Glory* seems to compound rather than clarify the problem.

In the following year, Agamben finally takes a step back to reflect on these lingering methodological questions in *The Signature of All Things*. Following Walter Benjamin's principle 'that doctrine may legitimately be exposed only in the form of interpretation', Agamben presents his own method in the form of 'investigations on the method of Michel Foucault, a scholar from whom I have learned a great deal in recent years' (ST 7). This book thus gives Agamben the opportunity to clarify the questions I have identified above about the use of exemplary figures and historical causality, together with the integration of Foucault into the *Homo Sacer* project. At the same time, this wide-ranging text serves as an occasion for Agamben to rethink long-standing influences (Benjamin, Warburg, Benveniste) and preoccupations (linguistics and the theory of Ideas) in light of the broader perspective of his emerging thought. Though I do not have the space to fully address all of the latter discussions, the fact that they play such a prominent role in this text highlights the extent to which *The Kingdom and the Glory* prompted Agamben to pause and clarify the main concerns of his thought. All of his reflections in *The Signature of All Things* are ultimately united under the heading of archaeology. While he had discussed this Foucauldian term briefly in *Remnants of Auschwitz* – where it served as a framework for thinking about the ethics of testimony (RA 140–4) – it is only in the context of *The Kingdom and the Glory* that it becomes a guiding point of reference for his investigation.

By this point, it should be clear that Agamben is not going to provide some kind of step-by-step formula that will allow his readers to duplicate his distinctive mode of philosophical investigation.

Instead, the main achievement of *The Signature of All Things* is to distinguish Agamben's approach from certain common-sense ideas about scholarly objectivity. Indeed, it is precisely the unexpected nature of his method that Agamben highlights in the opening lines of his reflection on the concept of a paradigm:

> In the course of my research, I have written on certain figures such as *homo sacer*, the *Muselmann*, the state of exception, and the concentration camp. While these are all actual historical phenomena, I nonetheless treated them as paradigms whose role was to constitute and make intelligible a broader historical-problematic context. Because this approach has generated a few misunderstandings, especially for those who thought, in more or less good faith, that my intention was to offer merely historiographical theses or reconstructions, I must pause here and reflect on the meaning and function of the use of paradigms in philosophy and the human sciences. (ST 9)

Much of his detailed discussion of Foucault and his influences is beyond the scope of the present investigation, but the most crucial point actually bears on one of Foucault's most famous examples, namely the panopticon, which Agamben claims 'functions as a paradigm in the strict sense: it is a singular object that, standing equally for all others of the same class, defines the intelligibility of the group of which it is a part and which, at the same time, it constitutes' (17). When Foucault uses the panopticon as a way of understanding prisons, schools, and, in the last analysis, the modern state as a whole, he is not claiming that Bentham's hypothetical schema somehow 'caused' all of those phenomena. Instead, Agamben clarifies, 'Paradigms establish a broader problematic context that they both constitute and make intelligible' (17).

In keeping with Agamben's concern to break down familiar binaries, he argues that the paradigmatic method breaks with the binary of inductive vs. deductive reasoning: 'while induction proceeds from the particular to the universal and deduction from the universal to the particular, the paradigm is defined by a third and paradoxical type of movement, which goes from the particular to the particular' (19). To help clarify this dynamic, Agamben has recourse to the concept of an example, which is 'deactivated from its normal use, not in order to be moved into another context but, on the contrary, to present the canon – the rule – of that use, which cannot be shown in any other way' (18). And where *Homo Sacer* had presented the example as part of a binary system with the exception, here Agamben argues that the example provides a means to escape the logic of presupposition. Rather than presupposing certain given principles that are then to be applied in some other field, the example or paradigm puts forth a hypothesis, not as an unquestionable principle but as a heuristic device that helps us to see a given group of phenomena in a way we otherwise could not have. To that extent, to treat a singularity as a paradigm is to treat it as a Platonic Idea, which 'is not another being that is presupposed by the sensible or coincides with it: it is the sensible considered as a paradigm – that is, in the medium of its intelligibility' (26). Hence the apparent contradiction I flagged above between viewing *homo sacer* as both a paradigm and a member of a broader paradigm is no contradiction at all, because the whole point of a paradigm is to establish a network of intelligibility among a broader group of paradigmatic phenomena.

Agamben concludes his reflection on the paradigm by connecting it with the archaeological method. Contrary to the misunderstandings of more traditional scholars who saw him as making very questionable historical claims, he explains,

> *Homo sacer* and the concentration camp, the *Muselmann* and the state of exception, and, more recently, the Trinitarian *oikonomia* and acclamations are not hypotheses through which I intended to explain modernity by tracing it back to something like a cause or historical origin. On the contrary, as their very multiplicity might have signaled, each time it was a matter of paradigms whose aim was to make intelligible a series of phenomena whose kinship had eluded or could elude the historian's gaze. (ST 31)

Even if there is a historical element to his investigation, then, it is not a question of linear time or the chain of cause and effect. Rather, the *archē* that Agamben seeks in archaeology involves a 'crossing of diachrony and synchrony' and 'makes the inquirer's present intelligible as much as the past of his or her object' (32). This means that in an archaeological investigation of the type Agamben is practising, 'the capacity to recognize and articulate paradigms defines the rank of the inquirer no less than does his or her ability to examine the documents of an archive' (32).

In other words, Agamben's method is less empirical than intuitive, and he signals his distance from traditional scholarship by opening his chapter on signatures with a practitioner of a dead science: the alchemist Paracelsus, who saw signatures as structuring the natural world as well as the human world. Whether or not Agamben would embrace this ontological claim about non-human realities, Paracelsus represents for him a mode of inquiry that is not defined by 'a causal relation' (35), but necessarily implicates the researcher. The model here is the human relation to language, which Paracelsus defines as the 'originary signature' (35) that marks the world in a way that makes it intelligible to human beings.

From here, Agamben pursues a more paradigmatic method, cycling through a number of related examples of the dynamics of signatures. One that is particularly helpful is the effect of an artist's literal signature on a painting. When an artist – Titian, for example – signs the painting, it has no effect on the actual content of the painting, but 'merely puts the painting in relation to the name of a man' (39). Yet due to the cultural expectations surrounding artists and artworks in Western culture, becoming aware of the artist's signature 'radically modifies how we look at the painting in question' (40). The experience of viewing some anonymous example of the oft-repeated theme of the Annunciation is very different from that of the same representational content that we recognise as 'a Titian'. We can find the same dynamic in popular culture, where the 'clue' in a detective story 'represents the exemplary case of a signature that puts an insignificant or nondescript object in effective relation to an event (in this case, a crime . . .) or to subjects (the victim, the murderer . . .)' (70).

In both cases, what the signature introduces is an element in excess of the content of the thing signed, and this, Agamben claims, is the core of Foucault's archaeological method. Indeed, Foucault argues that 'there is never a pure sign without a signature', and this irreducibility of the excess of the signature entails that we can

never manage 'to separate and move the signature to an originary
position' (79). Hence 'Foucauldian archaeology never seeks the
origin or its absence', which is where his method differs from that
of Nietzsche's genealogy (79). Yet Agamben suggests that there is
a path beyond Foucault's method of 'inquiring into [signatures']
vital relations with signs and events of discourse' – perhaps pointing toward the *Entwicklungsfähigkeit* or 'capacity for development'
that he defines as the goal of all true philosophical reading (8) – a
practice that 'reaches back beyond the split between signature and
sign and between the semiotic and the semantic in order to lead
signatures to their historical fulfillment' (80).

The final essay in the volume is devoted to tracing the outlines
of this new science of signatures, which begins by clarifying the
meaning of the *archē* that archaeology seeks. The term in Greek
means origin or beginning, but in Agamben's view it 'can never
be identified with a chronological datum' (82). Instead, by carefully working backward through the tradition, an archaeological
investigation finds not the origin or moment of arising of the tradition, but the gap that forever separates the tradition from its origin. What that gap allows us to see is that the originary moment
is not back there in the historical past, but present in the here and
now – as what the tradition is forever seeking to efface without
ever quite managing to do so. And in the last analysis, that impossible, inaccessible origin that the entirety of the human tradition
both testifies to and denies is the moment of 'anthropogenesis',
which means that the *archē* sought in a philosophical archaeology 'is not a given or a substance, but a field of bipolar currents stretched between anthropogenesis and history, between the
moment of arising and becoming, between an archi-past and the
present' (110). To the extent that an archaeological investigation
puts the investigator into contact with anthropogenesis, therefore,
'the gesture of the archaeologist constitutes the paradigm of every
true human action' (108).

In the next chapter, I will discuss the ways that this methodology plays out in the final stages of the *Homo Sacer* project, but here
I will briefly highlight its relation to Agamben's earlier work. I have
noted the resonance between the notion of anthropogenesis and
the 'anthropological change' inherent in poetry that Agamben
described in 'Expropriated Manner' (EP 94), and in that context,

we could say that archaeology is the philosophical equivalent
to that poetic experience. Throughout Agamben's work, from
Man Without Content forward, philosophy seems to trail behind
poetry in his thought, requiring hard labour to match the more
intuitive achievements of the poets – and here at last, the philosopher seems to have caught up. The practice of philosophical
archaeology also seems to fulfil the long-standing desire for a truly
trans-disciplinary discipline that had once found expression in his
hopes for a 'general science of the human'. And it does so by, in a
sense, picking up where the mid-century human sciences left off,
before the rise of comparative grammar and cognitive sciences
in the late 1970s and early '80s (ST 108–11). More specifically,
it means picking up the trail of the last great heroic figure of
that era, Benveniste, whose theory of enunciation and articulation of comparative linguistics (in the form of the Indo-European
hypothesis) become if anything more omnipresent in the second
half of the *Homo Sacer* series. Yet this is not a simple return to a
previous preoccupation, because the stakes of his investigation
have changed – it is no longer a question of simply understanding
human phenomena, but of somehow putting ourselves in a position to become human in a new and different way.

Notes

1. Arendt, *Human Condition*, 97.
2. From various sources, I had heard rumours that the delay in publication of *Stasis* stemmed from Agamben's remarks about terrorism as
   a form of global civil war in the concluding note of the text, which
   his publisher supposedly found too controversial or insensitive in the
   wake of the 9/11 attacks. When I met with him in Venice, Agamben
   clarified that nothing of the kind had happened and explained that he
   had simply not been in a position to finalise the text in the early 2000s.
3. See Taubes, *Political Theology of Paul*, and Badiou, *Saint Paul*.
4. This quotation is based on the New Revised Standard Version, which
   is regarded as the primary scholarly translation, and edited in light
   of Agamben's preferred rendering. The text in the existing English
   translation of *The Time That Remains* is based on the antiquated King
   James Version – an unfortunate habit among translators, who would
   surely not accept a four-century-old translation of any other text
   when many modern alternatives exist.

5. This quotation is taken straight from the existing English translation, which here conforms more strictly to Agamben's idiosyncratic rendering.

6. Agamben, *The Church and the Kingdom*, 5, and *The Mystery of Evil*, 13–14.

7. In fact, Prozorov, who is otherwise so determined to find a lockstep continuity in every stage of Agamben's work, argues that *The Open* represents the *sole* discontinuity in his trajectory, in which Agamben supposedly breaks away from his previous anthropocentrism. This makes *The Open*, in Prozorov's account, 'a brief text that is nonetheless one of the most important in Agamben's entire *oeuvre*' (*Agamben and Politics*, 151), which allows him to put forward a periodisation of Agamben's career that grows more idiosyncratic and questionable as it goes along: 'the work on language and community of the late 1970s to early 1980s, on law and the state in the late 1980s to 1990s, on history and messianism in the late 1990s to early 2000s and on humanity/animality during the 2000s' (6). Not only does this periodisation ignore his continued work on law and the state throughout the 2000s, but it treats this slim volume as though it were virtually the only thing he wrote during that entire decade.

8. See Arne De Boever's discussion of this decision, and the article that announced it, in *Plastic Sovereignties*, 43ff.

9. I have slightly altered the subtitle of the existing English translation, which I believe to be both unidiomatic and misleading – clearly the book is more than simply a manifesto arguing in favour of the idea of a theological genealogy of economy and government, and at the same time, despite its gargantuan size, *The Kingdom and the Glory* presents itself as but a first step in that genealogy, whose appendices point toward further work to be done.

10. This return to the theme of the spectacle is perhaps what prompted Agamben to republish the essay *Nymphs*, a study of Warburg's theory of images that had originally appeared in the French collection *Image et mémoire*, as a short book in Italian in the same year, 2007, in which *The Kingdom and the Glory* appeared.

11. All this is to say that Durantaye's reconstruction of Agamben's paradigmatic method on the basis of *Homo Sacer* and fleeting references in earlier works, with its implicit claim that that method was fully developed (and hence Agamben's critics were implicitly responsible for discerning it) at that time, appears to me to be unrealistic; see *Giorgio Agamben*, ch. 6 passim.

4
Abandoning the Project

In the prefatory note to *The Use of Bodies* (2014), Agamben begins by managing his reader's expectations for this final volume of the *Homo Sacer* series. 'Those who have read and understood the preceding parts of this work', he says, 'know that they should not expect a new beginning, much less a conclusion' (UB xiii). Nor, indeed, should they expect a positive manifesto laying out some kind of political agenda. Rather, 'we must decisively call into question the commonplace according to which it is a good rule that an inquiry commence with a *pars destruens* [critical part] and conclude with a *pars construens* [constructive part]', and recognise that 'the latter coincides, at every point and without remainder, with the former' (xiii). The general shape of the book bears that out – far from focusing on prescriptive declarations, it instead consists of a series of intricate archaeological investigations that, much as in the earlier volumes, begin to trace out alternatives only in their final moments.

On a logistical level, too, Agamben warns us not to expect a clean break or shift in perspective relative to the earlier works, insofar as *The Use of Bodies* gathers materials from the full range of the *Homo Sacer* period: 'Some of the texts published here were written at the beginning of the investigation, which is to say, almost twenty years ago; others – the greater part – were written in the course of the last five years' (xiii). In presenting texts from a span of two decades as part of a single volume, *The Use of Bodies* can serve as a model in miniature for the series as a whole, which Agamben would go on to publish in a single-volume omnibus format, presenting the various volumes and part-volumes in their architectonic order, which often conflicts with the order of publication. Yet the gesture of *The Use of Bodies* is more radical, because the single-volume *Homo Sacer* at least preserves the original dates of publication for the various parts, while the concluding volume does nothing to flag the dates of the materials it brings together.

As I discuss later in the chapter, Agamben gave me some general indications of which parts of the work included earlier material, though he did not go into detail. Even without his explicit guidance, however, it is possible to deduce the likely dating of certain key sections. A particularly interesting case is the epilogue, 'Toward a Theory of Destituent Potential', where he begins by asserting the unity of the *Homo Sacer* series. Characterising the project as an 'archaeology of politics' – hence retrospectively applying the methodological terminology he only arrived at halfway through the series to the previous volumes – he claims that the overall goal was 'to call into question the place and the very originary structure of politics, in order to try to bring to light the *arcanum imperii* [secret of power] that in some way constituted its foundation and that had remained at the same time fully exposed and tenaciously hidden in it' (263). From this perspective, 'the identification of bare life as the prime referent and ultimate stakes of politics' was only a necessary first step (263). The real breakthrough was the identification of the logic of presupposition, which turns out to structure every major Western institution. Once we note the existence of this presuppositional logic, we can see that 'the strategy is always the same: something is divided, excluded, and pushed to the bottom, and precisely through this exclusion, it is included as *archē* and foundation' (264).

The ultimate origin of this structure of presupposition, Agamben suggests, is the 'event of language that coincides with anthropogenesis', in which 'language excludes and separates from itself the non-linguistic, and in the same gesture, it includes and captures it as that with which it is always already in relation' (264). He then proceeds to demonstrate how this pattern plays out in *State of Exception* (in the relation between *potestas* and *auctoritas*), *The Kingdom and the Glory* (in the relation between 'rule and governance' and 'inoperativity and glory'; 265), and *The Open* (in the relation between human and animal life). This presentation is odd in many ways. First of all, the description of the dynamic in *The Kingdom and the Glory* seems incomplete, since Agamben had revealed the providential machine to have a bipolar aspect as well. Does the economic realm not function according to a bipolar structure? Less subtly, he includes *The Open*, a book from outside the series, in the list, without mentioning any of the volumes that came after – most notably, *The Use of Bodies* itself, which takes up and develops some key themes from *The Open* in order to incorporate them into the official architectonic of the series.

What can explain this discrepancy? The simplest answer is that he does not refer to the subsequent volumes because they had not been written (or at least published) at the time that he drafted that section of the epilogue. And since the next official volume of the series, namely *The Sacrament of Language*, was published the year after *The Kingdom and the Glory*, I can only assume that the passages on the unity of the *Homo Sacer* project in the logic of presupposition stem from shortly after he completed *The Kingdom and the Glory*. This reinforces the sense that the latter work forced him to grapple more explicitly with the shape of the project as a whole – and that once he had succeeded in asserting the unity of the other existing *Homo Sacer* books after the potential rupture of *The Kingdom and the Glory*, he was apparently satisfied. Hence he was comfortable with the epilogue's review of the project as it stood, as though the unity of the series was obvious once the *Kingdom and the Glory* problem had been solved.

In contrast to this (thankfully averted) threat to the series' continuity, all the volumes between *The Kingdom and the Glory* and *The Use of Bodies* relate to a project that was clearly part of the plan from the very beginning: an investigation of Franciscanism, as an example of a communal form-of-life that sought to live apart from the law by asserting that they not only contingently failed to own anything, but lacked the very capacity for ownership. For instance, though the topic of *The Sacrament of Language* (2008, volume 2.3), namely the oath, was unexpected at the time, in retrospect it is clear that it serves the purposes of the later study of monasticism and particularly the Franciscans, *The Highest Poverty* (2011, volume 4.1), where Agamben is at great pains to distinguish monastic vows from a legally binding oath.

Even here, though, his investigations in *The Kingdom and the Glory* continue to produce complications, above all by highlighting the importance of 'a phenomenon that is absolutely central in the history of the Church and opaque for modern people: the liturgy' (HP xii). The realisation that 'the great temptation of the monks' was not sensuality but 'the will to construct their life as a total and unceasing liturgy or Divine Office' prompted a change in plans. Where he 'proposed initially to define form-of-life by means of the analysis of monasticism', he reports that he 'has had to contend with the unforeseen and, at least in appearance, misleading and extraneous task of an archaeology of office (the results of which are published in a separate volume with the title *Opus Dei: An Archaeology of Office*)' (HP xii).[1] In turn, the preface to *Opus Dei* (2012, volume 2.5) confirms that Agamben views that volume as a necessary supplement to *The Kingdom and the Glory*:

> In *The Kingdom and the Glory* we investigated the liturgical mystery above all in the face it turns toward God, in its objective or glorious aspect. In this volume our archaeological study is oriented toward the aspect that above all concerns the priests, that is, the subject to whom belongs, so to speak, the 'ministry of the mystery.' (OD xi)

In other words, *The Kingdom and the Glory* prompted not only changes to the original plan for *The Highest Poverty* – in which the legal and liturgical elements sometimes seem poorly integrated or even simply juxtaposed, leading me to suspect there may have been an early draft of the text focused solely on the relation of monasticism to law – but also led to the addition of an unforeseen volume into the project. And when finalising the whole series, Agamben would ultimately change the place of *The Kingdom and the Glory* in the architectonic, shifting it from volume 2.2 to volume 2.4 (presumably to pair it more clearly with *Opus Dei*, volume 2.5) and belatedly introducing *Stasis* into the series in its former slot.

Apart from the lingering after-effects of the integration of *The Kingdom and the Glory* into the series, however, the development of Agamben's thought in this period is much more straightforward.

Though there are new influences and some tacit references to current events, in these years Agamben is much more concerned to follow out the internal logic of the task that he has set himself. This task takes two steps, broadly speaking. The first leads us to *The Highest Poverty* (volume 4.1), with the supporting materials found in *The Sacrament of Language* and *Opus Dei*. The second concludes the series with *The Use of Bodies* (volume 4.2). As we would expect, he continues to work on side projects: the two essay collections *Nudities* (2009) and *The Fire and the Tale* (2014), a collaboration with the Italian artist Monica Ferrando in *The Unspeakable Girl* (2010), the lecture series *Creation and Anarchy* (delivered in 2012–13 and published in 2017), and three short pamphlet-style books on theology, namely *The Church and the Kingdom* (2009), *The Mystery of Evil* (2013), and *Pilate and Jesus* (2013). As in the previous stage of his work, these materials often serve as test-beds for concepts and arguments that will take up their most fully developed forms in the *Homo Sacer* volumes.

Overall, this period of Agamben's work presents the greatest obstacles to a chronological approach, because he was clearly juggling multiple projects simultaneously. Hence for ease of presentation, I will take a slightly more thematic approach, organised broadly around the two steps I have identified above. As in the previous chapter, while I will make reference to the more occasional works when appropriate, my focus will remain on the members of the series itself and the ways that they take up and further develop his hard-won archaeological method.

Taking on language

As I have noted, *The Sacrament of Language* functions partly as set-up for the investigation of monasticism that Agamben had long planned to include in the *Homo Sacer* series. Yet it is much more than a preparatory exercise. Published in the same year as *The Signature of All Things*, 2008, it is the first book to make use of the archaeological approach explicitly outlined there. Its archaeology of the oath serves not only as a more concrete example for that method, but as a way of clarifying and deepening its stakes. The text thus duplicates some short passages and examples from *The Signature of All Things*, almost as a way of reading it onto the official record – a move he will later repeat in *The Use of Bodies* for certain key insights from *The Open* and *The Time That Remains*. At the same time, the gesture of moving *The Kingdom and the Glory* to come after *The Sacrament of Language* in the architectonic of the series retrospectively situates the former volume in terms of the more fully articulated archaeological methodology of the latter.

In addition, *The Sacrament of Language* provides Agamben with an opportunity to reconsolidate his project by grounding it in one of his longest-standing concerns: the experience of language. Indeed, in light of the centrality of language in Agamben's thought, it is remarkable that *The Sacrament of Language* is the only volume of the *Homo Sacer* project that deals primarily with that theme. *Homo Sacer* frequently discussed linguistic concepts, and *Remnants of Auschwitz* also delved into linguistics to a degree that was perhaps surprising given its ostensible topic. In both cases, however, the analysis of language serves a larger argumentative approach: respectively, as a means of establishing the homology among the linguistic, ontological, and political fields, and as a framework for reflecting on the problem of testimony. Here language is the main event.

Agamben's study opens with a reflection on the centrality of the oath to the Western political tradition, based upon a study of the oath by the Italian scholar Paolo Prodi. The project Agamben proposes for his book is not so much a critique or expansion of Prodi's investigation, but rather a kind of philosophical supplement that goes beyond the scope of a purely historical study to seek out the origin and nature of the oath. Part of the challenge here is that the oath lies 'at the intersection of religion and politics' (SL 1), which makes it difficult for traditional scholars in either discipline to fully account for it on their own terms. Agamben proposes a solution to this dilemma that at once helps to clarify his stance toward traditional disciplines and the ways his current approach relates to some of the most long-standing goals of his work:

> Since, however, an eclectic compendium of the results of individual disciplines does not seem scientifically reliable and the model of a 'general science of the human' has been

out of favor for some time now, the present study proposes
to undertake not an investigation into the oath's origin but
rather a philosophical archaeology of the oath. (2; translation altered)

This archaeology asks, ultimately, 'What anthropological level – a
decisive one in every sense – is implicated in [the oath], so that
all of man, in life and death, can be called into account in it and
by it?' (2).

Agamben begins his study by reviewing some of the key sources
cited by Prodi and Nicole Loraux. There he finds that, according
to the consensus of modern scholars and ancient authors alike,
'the oath's primary function, in its various forms, is that of guaranteeing the truth and efficacy of language' (4). Yet the Greek
sources in particular confirm that 'the oath appeared, according
to all evidence, from the very beginning to be completely inadequate to the task, and a simple penalty for lying would certainly
have been more effective' (7). This strange impotence of the oath
is expressed in the belief, found in many Greek texts, that the oath
exists primarily to prevent perjury – a paradoxical claim given that
no perjury is possible in the absence of an oath. Yet Agamben
argues that this apparent contradiction points to the possibility
that the oath 'contained the memory of a more archaic stage,
in which it was concerned with the very consistency of human
language and the very nature of humans as "speaking animals"'
(8). The problem here was not so much that human beings have
a tendency to lie, but rather 'a weakness pertaining to language
itself, the capacity of words themselves to refer to things and the
ability of men to make profession of their condition as speaking
beings' (8).

This suggestion serves as a transition to a discussion of the
nature of the *archē* in this archaeological study. Here, picking
up on his reference back to the 'general science of the human',
Agamben draws upon the 'paradigm' of an archaeological study
in the 'linguistics and comparative grammar' of the twentieth
century (8–9). He has in mind here the reconstruction of the
Indo-European language, which made it 'possible to go back,
through etymology and the analysis of meanings, to otherwise

inaccessible stages of the history of social institutions' (9). The question, of course, is whether something like the original Indo-European language, and the society suggested by it, actually exists, and Agamben insists that each of the hypothetical Indo-European linguistic forms, 'if we want to be rigorous, is only an algorithm that expresses a system of correspondence among the existing forms in historical languages' (9), meaning that 'one could never extrapolate from Indo-European any events that are supposed to have happened historically' (10).

Both Émile Benveniste (here as always the last representative of the heroic era of linguistics) and his contemporary Georges Dumézil (the coiner of the phrase 'the fringe of ultrahistory', which Agamben had already used in several places without explicitly naming him) were aware of the epistemological dilemma that their project had run up against, and Agamben believes that his vision of a philosophical archaeology provides the resolution. The *archē* is not an ancient historical origin for which we happen not to have documents, but

> a force working in history, exactly as the Indo-European language expresses first of all a system of connections among historically accessible languages; just as the child in psychoanalysis expresses a force that continues to act in the psychic life of the adult; and just as the 'big bang', which is supposed to have given rise to the universe, is something that never stops transmitting its background radiation to us. Yet unlike the 'big bang', which astrophysicists claim to be able to date, even if only in terms of millions of years, the *archē* is not a given, a substance, or an event but a field of historical currents stretched between anthropogenesis and the present, ultrahistory and history. (11)

Agamben's investigation of the oath 'will mean therefore steering the analysis of the historical data . . . in the direction of an *archē* stretched between anthropogenesis and the present', which will help us to see the ways in which the oath points toward an experience that 'calls into question the very nature of man as a speaking being and a political animal' (11). At the same time, it clarifies the contemporary relevance of such an apparently recondite study: 'Ultrahistory, like anthropogenesis, is not in fact an event that can be considered completed once and for all; it is always under way, because *Homo sapiens* never stops becoming man, has perhaps not yet finished entering language and swearing to his nature as a human being' (11). The implication is clear: gaining access to the moment of anthropogenesis is not a matter of learning our historical origin so much as finding a way to reimagine and redirect the origin we continually find ourselves performing.

At this point, having in some ways reviewed and expanded upon concepts from *The Signature of All Things*, Agamben returns to the chapter on 'The Ambivalence of the Sacred' from *Homo Sacer*. In its original context, that chapter served primarily to debunk existing explanations of the sacred in religious studies in order to clear the field for his own political definition. Here he takes up the same concerns as a way of contrasting the archaeological method with the widespread conception among scholars in the humanities that 'explaining a historical institution necessarily means tracing it back to an origin or context that is sacred or magico-religious' (12). As Agamben argues, however, this hypothetical purely religious phase is never attested in the sources, which instead show us people who are 'religious and also irreligious, faithful to the oath and also more than capable of perjury' (13). Instead of presupposing an archaic world in which every human activity and institution is somehow religious, Agamben proposes that when we find a phenomenon (like the oath) that seems to blend religious categories with those from another realm (like law), we should not project an imagined religious past, but recognise that we have come upon 'an internal limit, the comprehension of which, by calling into question the accepted distinction, can lead to a new definition of the phenomenon' (17).

What follows is a close reading of various texts on the oath from the Greek, Roman, and Christian traditions, the fine-grained details of which are beyond the scope of the present study. For our purposes, the important thing to recognise is the way that the oath serves as a lens for tracing all major human institutions back to an originary experience of language. This analysis comes to a

head in his analysis of performatives, those strange speech acts –
which are very often oaths or at least oath-like – that apparently
conjure into existence the condition that they name. This is the
context in which Agamben ties his argument most explicitly to
the key categories from *Homo Sacer*: 'Just as, in the state of exception, the law suspends its own application only to found, in this
way, its being in force, so in the performative, language suspends
its denotation precisely and solely to found its existential connection with things' (SL 56). To take the example of a marriage
ceremony, saying 'I do' is semantically a description of what one
is doing (namely, taking this person to be one's lawfully wed-
ded spouse), but this semantic meaning is at once suspended and
intensified, insofar as this utterance does not function as a mere
description – it is the very deed itself.

Agamben claims that these performative speech acts point back
to a 'constitutive experience of speech' that, drawing a term from
Foucault, he calls 'veridiction', in which the subject actually 'coincides integrally with the act of speech', an experience he connects
to the Pauline experience of faith (58). Actual existing historical
language, by contrast, reflects a split in this originary experience,
which opens up the possibility of lies and perjury and thereby gives
rise to the apparatuses of law and religion, 'both of which seek to
tie speech to things and to bind, by means of curses and anathemas,
speaking subjects to the veritative power of their speech, to their
"oath" and to their declaration of faith' (58). Far from serving as
the foundations for the experience of the oath, religion and law
grow out of it and represent various attempts at 'the technicaliza-
tion of the oath' that will guarantee its efficacy by binding us to our
word (59). In historical sources, this veridictional aspect of the oath
is most closely connected to promissory oaths, which aim to guarantee future conduct or outcomes. In an important aleph-note, he
connects the assertorial side of the oath, which aims to confirm the
truth of a statement about a past or present state of events, with
logic and science. And between these two paradigms, he places
'philosophy, which, abiding in both truth and error, seeks to safe-
guard the performative experience of speech without renouncing
the possibility of lying and, in every assertorial discourse, experiences the veridiction that takes place in it' (59).

In short, Agamben has rooted every major human institution –
including philosophy as the critique of every major human
institution – in the experience of language to which the oath
attests. In particular, he clarifies that the experience of language
is foundational for the dynamics of the sacred that he traced in
Homo Sacer, which from this perspective appears as a variation on
the curse that accompanies every oath:

> The interpretation of *sacertas* [sacredness] as an originary
> performance of power through the production of killable
> and unsacrificeable bare life must be completed in the sense
> that, even before being a sacrament of power, the oath is a
> consecration of the living human being through the word
> to the word. (66)

This means that it is not enough to break with the sovereign production of bare life – more fundamentally, 'only a politics that has
broken this original connection with the curse will be able one
day to make possible another use of speech and of the law' (66).

At this point, in some of the most powerful pages in his entire
oeuvre, Agamben begins to lay out the implications of his study of
the oath in terms of anthropogenesis. He laments that most scholars in the humanities, represented here by Lévi-Strauss, see language from a primarily epistemological perspective, 'as if, in the
becoming human of man, there were not necessarily and above all
ethical (and, perhaps, also political) implications at issue' (68). Language is not primarily about what we can know, in other words,
but about how we should live. That means that the distinction
between human and animal language 'cannot reside solely in the
peculiarity of the instrument, which later analyses could find –
and, in fact, continually do find – in this or that animal language',
but lies instead in the fact that the human being has '*put his very
nature at stake in language*' (68). Using an important concept from
The Time That Remains for the first time in the *Homo Sacer* series
proper, he claims that the oath is an echo of 'the demand, decisive
in every sense for the speaking animal, to put its nature at stake
in language and to bind together in an ethical and political connection words, things, and action', which is the ultimate root of

what we understand as history (69). This history, in Agamben's view, has run aground, but as always, the fact that the old regime is breaking down represents an opportunity. Here his description of our present circumstances ties together the analyses of *Homo Sacer* and *The Kingdom and the Glory*:

> On the one hand, there is the living being, more and more reduced to a purely biological reality and to bare life. On the other hand, there is the speaking being, artificially divided from the former, through a multiplicity of technico-mediatic apparatuses, in an experience of the word that grows ever more vain, for which it is impossible to be responsible and in which anything like a political experience becomes more and more precarious. (70)

On the final page, he repeats the same fundamental diagnoses, characterising our era as 'a moment when all the European languages seem condemned to swear in vain and when politics can only assume the form of an *oikonomia*, that is, of a governance of empty speech over bare life' (72).

These critiques of the contemporary order help to weave together different segments of the series, but at the same time they double down on the problematic distinction between the political and the economic – and above all, the denigration of the economic and corresponding valorisation of the political that I have elsewhere dubbed 'Arendt's axiom'[2] – that he established in *The Kingdom and the Glory* and that arguably conflicts with his more nuanced analyses of the relation between city and household or *potestas* and *auctoritas* in *Stasis* and *State of Exception*. And with this in mind, we can also recognise that the economy is the one realm that Agamben has not explicitly grounded in the experience of the oath, much as 'Toward a Theory of Destituent Potential' does not specify the place of the economic in terms of the presuppositional logic that unites the series as a whole. Indeed, the fact that his analysis of economy is designated a 'genealogy', in contrast to the 'archaeologies' of the oath, of glory, and of office, may indicate that a proper archaeology of economy, with all the redemptive potential that implies, is simply not possible. In this purely negative status of *oikonomia*, we can perhaps see one last outgrowth of the anti-Communism that shaped both his early avoidance of politics and the specific form his later engagement with politics would take. If there is one unshaking conviction of Agamben's political work, it is that the *oikonomia* will not – indeed, radically, irrevocably *cannot* – save us.

What can save us, then? The answer appears to be the practice of philosophy as 'constitutively a critique of the oath', which opens up a new experience of language (72). In the closing pages, his only concrete advice is to 'call into question the prestige that language has enjoyed and continues to enjoy in our culture, as a tool of incomparable potency, efficacy, and beauty' (71). In earlier passages, he points to the messianic practice of Paul and Jesus as a way of escaping the curse of the law (see 38, 41–2), which I have discussed at great length elsewhere.[3] If none of these suggestions seem particularly clear or concrete, that only highlights the magnitude of the problem Agamben has set himself. Even if anthropogenesis as it has been experienced in the Western world is contingent, it nonetheless continues to resonate through everything we understand as history, law, religion, and even language itself. By unifying his analyses of all the major Western institutions so forcefully in *The Sacrament of Language* – the text of Agamben's that I believe best encapsulates his mature thought – he has also further compounded the difficulty of imagining any real alternative.

The trap of liturgy

Deviating somewhat from chronological order, I will now jump ahead to *Opus Dei* (2011). I have already noted how the preface to *Opus Dei* presents it as a necessary supplement to *The Kingdom and the Glory*, while in *The Highest Poverty*, Agamben reveals that it was an equally necessary supplement to his study of monasticism. Both of these pairings are appropriate and clarifying, and I would claim that we can also pair it with *The Sacrament of Language*, as *Opus Dei* further develops some of Agamben's key insights into the roots of ontological and ethical categories from that volume. Alongside these thematic connections, there is ample textual evidence that the core concepts from *Opus Dei* were on Agamben's mind throughout this period. Indeed, certain passages in *The Unspeakable Girl* (published in 2010, thus the year before *Opus Dei*) anticipate Agamben's analysis of the Christian liturgical mystery, against which he counterposes the model of the Eleusinian mysteries in ancient Athens as a possible alternative – yet another example of Agamben's 'solution-first' approach to political analysis. And the published lecture series *Creation and Anarchy*, first offered in 2012–13, weaves concepts from *Opus Dei* together with analyses from *The Use of Bodies*, which he was finalising at the time.

Overall, then, despite this volume's avowedly supplemental and even unexpected place in the series, the problems Agamben is grappling with in *Opus Dei* permeate much of his work in the years surrounding its publication. Even if he intended it merely as a preparatory exercise for *The Highest Poverty*, the text itself reveals that the implications of the liturgical mystery far exceeded his initial expectations. What is at issue in *Opus Dei* is not simply a historical clarification of the role of liturgy in Christian history, providing necessary background for the study of monasticism in *The Highest Poverty*. The book is ultimately about a profound ontological transformation that took place over centuries of theological reflection about the functioning of the Christian sacraments and the role of their human ministers in the process. The investigation proceeds by way of fine-grained textual analysis, with even more Greek and Latin than usual, but its ultimate stakes are far from a pedantic scholarly dispute. The shifts in vocabulary Agamben is tracing here are 'essentially terminological and political' at once, because 'a terminological transformation, if it expresses a change in ontology, can turn out to be just as effective and revolutionary as a material transformation' (OD 79). This claim – which one could almost pass over, as it seems to be almost a passing remark in the context of a discussion of the theologian Ambrose's appropriation of Cicero's *De Officiis* – implicitly provides the rationale for Agamben's own attempts, in *The Use of Bodies*, to transform the key concepts of Western ontology. After all, if a transformation in ontology can happen once, why could it not happen again?

Despite its importance, however, anecdotal evidence suggests that *Opus Dei* is among the least-read of Agamben's recent books, and it is admittedly off-putting in many ways. For most readers, the title itself evokes nothing so much as a notorious cult-like group of Catholic extremists, and the subtitle, *An Archaeology of Office*, does little to clarify the stakes of the work (a problem I attempted to mitigate in my published translation by rendering it as *An Archaeology of Duty*, a decision I subsequently came to regret). The book does little to clarify its own structure, as it rapidly jumps back and forth in time, sometimes across thousands of years. Hence I will begin my analysis by offering a brief summary of the text that highlights the flow of the argument. As we have increasingly come to expect over the course of the *Homo Sacer* series, Agamben begins with a linguistic analysis, in this case of the Greek term *leitourgia*, the root of our liturgy. In ancient Athens, the term referred to various types of public services incumbent upon the citizens, including but not at all limited to services relating to the gods – hence liturgy had a political character. The bulk of the first chapter traces the history of how Christian writers came to appropriate the term in order to characterise, in a first step, Christ's priestly ministry as the culmination and abolition of Jewish sacrificial rites and, in a second step, the priesthood's role in mediating the benefits of Christ's sacrificial act. This linguistic shift represents a transformation of Christianity from a charismatic community (typified by the letters of Paul) to a more bureaucratic and hierarchical community.

The first chapter concludes by noting that the personal qualities of the priest – his personal morality, even his personal faith – became increasingly divorced from the effectiveness of his sacramental action, and the second chapter documents the ways that theologians came to articulate the gap between the person of the priest and his priestly activity. It begins with a discussion of a twentieth-century theologian, Odo Casel, who represents a particularly extreme notion of the effectiveness of the liturgy, in which he claims that we do not merely receive the benefits of Christ's past salvific act but carry out that act in the present. The shift here is from the notion of an effect, which is separate from and consequent to a pre-existing cause, to the notion of *effectiveness*, in which that distinction seems to break down: 'While in the vocabulary of classical ontology being and substance are considered independently of the effects that they can produce, in effectiveness being is inseparable from its effects; it names being insofar as it is effective, produces certain effects, and at the same time is determined by them' (41). We are dealing, then, not merely with the intricacies of obscure religious practices, but with the opening up of a 'new ontological dimension that is affirmed first in the liturgical sphere and is then to be extended progressively until in modernity it coincides with being as such' (41).

After tracing this ontological transformation – which, as the remainder of the second chapter demonstrates, included a self-conscious reworking of Aristotelian and Neo-Platonist categories on the part of theologians – Agamben then moves backward in time to study the transition between the Greek traditions in which the New Testament was embedded and the Latin Scholastics who did the most work in developing the ontology of effectiveness. The key figure here is Cicero, whose *De Officiis* proposes that the Greek term *leitourgia* be translated into Latin as *officium* or 'office'. Where the Greek term presupposes some sense of political belonging and the corresponding duty, Cicero's favoured Latin term 'has nothing to do with what we are accustomed to classify as morality' but instead focuses 'on what is respectable and appropriate to do according to the circumstances, above all taking account of the agent's social condition' (67). In other words, it is more a work of etiquette than of ethics properly so called, and that is because *officium* as Cicero envisions it 'is neither a juridical or moral obligation nor a pure and simple necessity: it is the behavior that is expected among persons that is socially codified, but the compulsory nature of which is sufficiently vague and indeterminate' that it does not imply any genuine moral constraint (72).

It is this amoral concept that Ambrose will later take up and appropriate for the Christian tradition – more or less plagiarising Cicero's *De Officiis* and simply replacing pagan examples with biblical ones. Despite its apparent lack of creativity, however, Ambrose's *De Officiis* will play a decisive role in the development of Christian thought, by associating the liturgical act, not with the political duty of free citizens, but with what is necessary to do based on one's place in a hierarchical system. Eventually, it comes to seem that it is the social role or office itself that produces the effects, rendering the priest in his capacity as a human person

simply an indifferent instrument. Regardless of what kind of man
a priest is, 'the correct fulfillment of the priestly function necessarily and automatically implies the actualization of the *effectus*'
or liturgical effectiveness, creating a *'circular relation between being
and praxis, by which the priest's being defines his praxis and his praxis,
in turn, defines his being*. In *officium* ontology and praxis become
undecidable: the priest has to be what he is and is what he has to
be' (81).

In the concluding threshold to the third chapter, Agamben
claims that this self-enclosed dynamic is 'the disquieting inheritance that modernity, from the moment it put duty and office at
the center of its ethics and its politics, has more or less consciously
accepted without the benefit of an inventory' (88). The final chapter is dedicated to tracing that process into modernity, culminating
in the empty self-referentiality of Kant's ethics and Kelsen's theory
of pure law. It begins, however, with a return to the Aristotelian
theory of potentiality and act, of which the ontology of effectiveness represents a self-conscious mutation. This mutation is not
entirely a betrayal of Aristotle, however, because his theory already
carried the seeds for something like the ontology of effectiveness.
Key here is Aristotle's theory of habit (Greek, *hexis*, from *echō*, 'I
have'), which serves to clarify the sense in which one can 'have' a
potentiality when it is not actualised. Like potentiality itself, *hexis*
or habit is defined by the 'possibility of not using it' (95), and this
opens up the question of how it could pass into act. Aristotle's
solution to this aporia is the theory of virtues, which are defined as
'something that, in habit, renders it capable of passing into action
and of acting in the best way' (96).

The well-known circularity of Aristotle's virtue ethics – in
which we recognise good people by their good actions, which
they do precisely because they are good people, etc. – anticipates
the paradigm of *officium*, and in fact it is precisely in the theory
of the virtues that Aquinas considers the question of religious duty
(OD 102ff.). From here, Agamben traces a genealogy up to Kant,
for whom the only virtue is effectively the 'respect' by which we
constrain ourselves to obey our own self-posited law (113). From
the point of view of this contentless commandment, this empty
'you must', Kant reworks all the categories of traditional ontology,

which makes him the key representative of one of the two ontologies that Agamben detects in the Western tradition:

> the first, the ontology of the command, proper to the juridical-religious sphere, which is expressed in the imperative and has a performative character; the second, proper to the philosophical-scientific tradition, is expressed in the form of the indicative . . . The ontology of *estō* and of 'be!' refers to a having-to-be; that of *esti* and of 'is' relate to being. Clearly distinct and in many ways opposed, the two ontologies live together, struggle with each other, and nevertheless never cease to intersect, to hybridize, and to prevail over one another by turns in the history of the West. (120)

And indeed, Kant is not only the culmination of the ontology of having-to-be, but 'represents the moment when the ontology of command and having-to-be reaches its most extreme elaboration and, by penetrating into the ontology of substance and being, seeks to transform it from within' (121).

These two ontologies develop *The Sacrament of Language*'s categorisation of human institutions according to either the veridictive and promissory or the assertorial aspect of the oath, a connection that Agamben confirms by referring to the oath and the performative in the lead-up to his exposition of the two ontologies (119). In the earlier volume, however, that categorisation remained almost a passing aside, whereas here it is presented as a structuring principle of the entire Western tradition. From this perspective, then, we can say that in this concluding part of volume 2, we reach the true core of the 'Western machine', the ontological engine that powers its transformations over time. While this two-fold ontology does not play a major role in *The Use of Bodies*, its key implication – namely that if there are already multiple ontologies, a new one may also be possible – structures the argument of the central section of that book.

Agamben will continue to work out the implications of the two ontologies outside the official series, however, beginning in *Creation and Anarchy*, where he proposes an 'archaeology of command' – a task that is paradoxical insofar as 'the Greek term *archē* has two meanings: it means both "origin, principle" and "command, order"' (CA 51). This association is particularly clear in the monotheistic traditions, where the origin of the universe is precisely the divine command. Agamben proposes that 'a good definition of religion would be that which characterizes it as the attempt to construct an entire universe on the basis of a command' (59). It is an ambition that our ostensibly secular modern societies have come closest to actualising through the religion of capitalism (61), to which the final lecture of the series is devoted. Once again, the economic realm is one of nihilism and hopelessness – and thus, by an exceptionally roundabout path dictated by his allergy to institutional Communism, capitalism emerges in these later works as one of the primary objects of Agamben's critique.

Escaping liturgy and law

I have highlighted the ways that *Opus Dei* can be paired with other *Homo Sacer* volumes, but the clearest pairing is with *The Highest Poverty*. Both volumes appeared in rapid succession, and in keeping with a pattern that has marked the *Homo Sacer* series from the beginning, they appeared out of their architectonic order, with *The Highest Poverty* (4.1) coming a few months before *Opus Dei* (2.5). When it came time to prepare the English translations, Agamben insisted that both should be translated by the same person (me, as it turned out) and that the order of publication be duplicated in English. Hence, despite the fact that *Opus Dei*'s analysis of liturgy was, by Agamben's own account, foundational for his account of monasticism in *The Highest Poverty*, this critique followed the articulation of a positive alternative (or at least an attempt at one). Here, perhaps, we have a very literal instantiation of Agamben's rejection of the common-sense 'rule that an inquiry commence with a *pars destruens* [critical part] and conclude with a *pars construens* [constructive part]' (UB xiii).

A similar dynamic is at work in one of Agamben's minor publications from the same period: *The Unspeakable Girl*, a study of the mythical figure of Kore (better known as Persephone) and her role in the Eleusinian mysteries in classical Greece. This short essay was published alongside illustrations by the artist Monica

Ferrando, who also compiled an anthology of ancient sources on Kore, and hence indicates Agamben's continued interest in experimenting with different publication formats. For our purposes, however, the more important point is his sharp contrast of the Eleusinian mysteries with the Christian liturgical mystery outlined by Odo Casel. Though both liturgies imitate divine actions through dramatic theatrical gestures, the Eleusinian mysteries do not put their initiates into contact with a transcendent reality, nor indeed do they teach them anything, in the sense of some esoteric content. While mystery initiates were encouraged to remain silent about what they had experienced, Agamben hypothesises that

> the point of the silence was not to keep the uninitiated ignorant but intended for the benefit of the initiates themselves. In other words, it is possible that those who had been given an experience of the unknowable – or, at least, the *discursively* unknowable – were encouraged to refrain from attempting to put into words what they had seen and felt. (UG 12)

Ultimately, Agamben claims, what the initiates experienced in the vision of Kore was 'the power and potentiality of a joyfully and intransigently *in-fantile* existence' (13). This experience was not a fringe activity – akin, perhaps, to the New Age 'spirituality' of our day – but something that philosophers like Aristotle had to contend with. Indeed, through a philological reconstruction of Aristotle's views on the mysteries, Agamben concludes that the vision of Kore, which amounts to the vision of 'a young girl at play', represented for Aristotle 'the ideal figure for the supreme initiation and the completion of philosophy' (21). It is this experience that grants initiates 'a complete life' (23) – not by adding some other content to it, but simply by displaying it as such. This placed the burden on the initiates to respond to what they had experienced, not through codifying it into a doctrine, but through the comic adventure of life itself. And here we can see the contrast with the apparatus of Christian liturgy, because where the 'efficacy of the Christian mysteries is guaranteed in any event and every possible situation because it is not the work of man [but] the work of God'

(32), 'precariousness is the adventurous and nocturnal dimension in which the pagan initiate moves' (33).

Agamben will continue to follow up on these themes in his later works, particularly after the closure of the *Homo Sacer* series. In opening the fourth and final volume of the series, however, he sets the Eleusinian mysteries aside in favour of an investigation that he had clearly been planning since at least the late 1990s: a study of monasticism as an attempt 'to construct a form-of-life, that is, a life that is linked so closely to its form that it proves to be inseparable from it' (HP xi). While this choice of an example may seem strange from a contemporary perspective, monasticism has much to recommend it. Unlike the Eleusinian mysteries, which must be reconstructed based on indirect evidence in the sources, monasticism is thoroughly documented. Hence, even if scholars might dispute particular claims in Agamben's study, no one doubts that the phenomenon of monasticism actually happened in the real world. And unlike his previous positive example of an alternative community – the Tiananmen protestors – monasticism proved durable over the long term. This was possible because, instead of simply protesting against or resisting an existing structure, the monks created new structures of their own, structures that Agamben believes to be qualitatively different from the law and liturgy of the Western machine.

The study proceeds in three steps, corresponding to the three major divisions of the work. The first studies the monastic rules that the various communities used to order their shared life. Here the goal is to distinguish the rule from law, a task that initially seems difficult insofar as many monastic rules seem to dictate the lives of the monks much more intensively and minutely than any legal code. What is crucial here is the relationship between life and rule, which he contrasts with the relationship between life and law in a passage that attempts to distinguish the monastic vow from a binding legal oath: 'The one who promises does not obligate himself, as happens in the law, to the fulfillment of the individual acts expected in the rule, but puts into question his way of living, which is not identified with a series of actions or exhausted in them' (55). Indeed, the rule is not an imposition on the monk's life, but ideally grows out of the life he is choosing: 'it is not so much the form of life that is to be derived from the rule as the rule from the form of life' (69).

This model of the relation between life and rule is so foreign to that of life and law that, as Agamben demonstrates in the second part of the text, the real temptation of the monks was not to transform their rule into a law, but to transform their entire life into a non-stop liturgy through 'a total liturgicization of life and a vivification of liturgy that is just as entire' (82). This monastic liturgy is different in important ways from the liturgy of the mainstream Church, which 'had extracted a liturgy from life' and inscribed it 'into a separate sphere, whose proprietor was the priest, personifying the priesthood of Christ' (83). From this perspective, the more totalising liturgy of the monks was potentially subversive to the limited and occasional liturgy of the Church, and Agamben even claims in an aleph-note that 'the Protestant Reformation can be seen legitimately as the implacable claim, promoted by Luther (an Augustinian monk), of the monastic liturgy against the Christian liturgy' (84). Yet for Agamben – following Benjamin in following Max Weber – at the end of that road, far from a genuine alternative form-of-life, is the totalising liturgy of capitalism.

The real goal of Agamben's analysis is the third part on the Franciscans. By Agamben's account, they do not seem to have found the liturgy as great a temptation as their forebears, and hence their true innovation is not liturgical but legal. Where previous monastic orders had simply withdrawn from society in order to lead the form-of-life they had chosen, the Franciscans mingled with the broader society and lived a life that embodied a critique of the entire legal order – that is to say, a life without any property or ownership. And though Francis will ultimately give his followers a rule, his initial claim is simply to be living out the Gospel itself. In sum, the Franciscans put themselves on a collision course with both secular and ecclesiastical authorities, and in keeping with the political structures of the time, that conflict will play out as a debate with the various popes over the meaning of their claim to live without property.

Much of the final third of *The Highest Poverty* is given over to a reconstruction of the debate between the popes and the Franciscan thinkers who sought to vindicate their distinctive form of life – a debate that the Franciscans ultimately lost. This appar-ently recondite history is crucial, Agamben claims, because in his view, 'Franciscanism can be defined – and in this consists its novelty, even today unthought, and in the present conditions of society, totally unthinkable – as *the attempt to realize a human life and practice absolutely outside the determinations of the law*' (110). The debate over the meaning and legitimacy of the Franciscan claim to live without property thus supplies a framework for under-standing what such a life might look like and a map of the pitfalls that led to the collapse of the Franciscan project.

Both the promise and the downfall of the Franciscan effort are encapsulated in a single term: *usus* or use. We have already seen the importance of finding a new use for the law and for other human institutions in *The Time That Remains*, *State of Exception*, and *Profanations*, and we also know in retrospect that Agamben devotes the first major division of *The Use of Bodies* to the concept. And even within the timeframe of the current chapter, Agamben added some compelling reflections on finding a new use for the body in particular in 'Nudity' and 'The Glorious Body', the cen-tral essays in *Nudities* (2009). Hence several commentators – most notably Jessica Whyte,[4] who devotes her entire final chapter to the theme of use despite writing well before the publication of *The Highest Poverty*, much less *The Use of Bodies* – have anticipated the central role of use in Agamben's attempt to articulate an alter-native to the Western machine.

Even in *The Highest Poverty*, however, Agamben is not yet developing a 'positive' theory of use, largely because in his view the Franciscans failed to develop 'a definition of use in itself and not only in opposition to law' (139). At every step of their argu-ment, they distinguish between *usus facti* (or de facto use) and *usus iuris* (de jure use). And as the argument with the papacy progresses, the space for *usus facti* gets smaller and smaller. One key move on the part of the pope was to take on the ownership of all the prop-erty that, in normal terms, would have belonged to the Francis-cans, leaving them merely the de facto use. While this seemed like a helpful concession, it was actually a trap, which led to the pope defining de facto use apart from ownership out of existence, even for immediately consumable goods. By attempting to establish their own privileged space within the regime of the law, the Franciscans wound up guaranteeing that they would be incorporated into the legal order. Hence in the closing pages, after pointing out the conceptual resources that Paul's theory of the *hōs mē* or 'as not' could have offered to the Franciscan theorists, Agamben points toward Francis's more radical demand for a 'life which maintains itself in relation, not only to things, but even to itself in the mode of inappropriability and of the refusal of the very idea of a will of one's own' (140). Such a conception could lay the groundwork for a conception of use that 'no longer means the pure and simple renunciation of the law, but that which establishes this renunciation as a form and a way of life' (142). When it comes time to begin developing a genuine 'positive' theory of use, however, Agamben will go a step further than this by starting with a figure who, far from needing to renounce the law, was always already excluded from its rights and privileges: namely, the slave.

Toward a theory of use

Before diving into Agamben's fully articulated account of use, it may be helpful to take a step back and provide an overview of *The Use of Bodies*. The book is roughly as long as *The Kingdom and the Glory*, but where that text presented itself as a continuous, if complex, argument, *The Use of Bodies* brings together three separate studies – the first on the concept of use and particularly on Aristotle's claim that the life of the slave is characterised by 'the use of the body', the second on the archaeology of ontology that ends with the first steps toward a new form of ontology that Agamben designates as 'modal', and the third on (at long last!) the concept of 'form-of-life'. Along with the epilogue that I have already mentioned above, the book also includes extended reflections on three figures who have been crucial for the project: a prologue on Debord and one 'intermezzo' each on Foucault and Heidegger. These latter sections may hearken back to an early plan for the book, because David Kishik reports, 'In 2001, Agamben still believed that this planned book of profiles' – namely, those he mentions in his early essay on Aby Warburg – 'would eventually become the final installment of his *Homo Sacer* project, to be dedicated to the notion of form of life'.[5] In their current form, the reflections on Foucault and Heidegger do serve to bridge the gaps between the sections between which they appear. Nevertheless, it is not difficult to imagine Agamben publishing each of the respective sections (which are all comparable in length to *State of Exception*, for instance) as separate volumes.

Hence from the book's very form, it is obvious that we should not expect a definitive statement. *The Use of Bodies* is less a conclusion than a continuation, and a remarkably open-ended one. While the epilogue does make an attempt to assert the unity and coherence of at least the first half of the *Homo Sacer* series, there is no explicit justification for the unity and coherence of the final volume itself. This inconclusiveness reflects Agamben's view of the nature of his project as such, which 'like every work of poetry and of thought, cannot be concluded but only abandoned (and perhaps continued by others)' (UB xiii). And in fact, as I have noted, the year following the publication of its final volume, the series expanded to include *Stasis* – a book that was itself expanded in the definitive Italian compilation of the series, where Agamben appends a charming essay arguing that war is essentially a game that got out of hand. In that definitive edition, even *The Use of Bodies* was slightly extended, with an enigmatic aleph-note on the 'Nocturnal Council' from Plato's *Laws* (a note that was included in the English edition). Even leaving aside his decision to keep fiddling with the structure and contents of the series up until the very last moment – an understandable impulse for someone trying to conclude a two-decade, career-defining project – his approach remains as experimental and improvisational as ever. There are places where he seems to be retreading material that he developed in various essays and other side projects over the years, but he continues to innovate up to the very end.

This innovation is clearest in the first section, which bears the title of the volume as a whole: 'The Use of Bodies'. Though Aristotle's *Politics* has been a central point of reference since the original *Homo Sacer*, the focus on the figure of the slave is unexpected. The works of the early 2000s included some passing discussions of slavery – most notably Paul's self-designation as a slave (TTR 12–13) and a largely unexplained reference in *The*

Open (O 12) – but the analysis here goes far beyond either in terms of depth and rigour. Indeed, the close reading of Aristotle's theory of slavery, with careful cross-references that even take into account the periodisation of Aristotle's works, is more intricate and daring than anything he has attempted on the text of Aristotle up to this point – a standard that will only be exceeded in the following section on the archaeology of ontology. This is all the more noteworthy given that an analysis of the figure of the slave was not anticipated at any previous point in the project, something that Agamben confirmed to me when I met with him in Venice. There is an irony here: having consigned the realm of *oikonomia* to hell, Agamben opens *The Use of Bodies* with a figure who, at least for Aristotle, defines the form of power that is most characteristic of the *oikos*, namely the despotic power of master over slave. Even in the project's last moments, then, Agamben continues to expand it in ways that threaten its coherence.

In addition to being unexpected, this analysis is risky, insofar as, aside from *Remnants of Auschwitz*, it is arguably the piece of his writing most likely to cause offense. After all, how can one possibly dare to find redemptive potential in Aristotle's apologetics for slavery? Agamben believes that the case is not so clear-cut, noting that 'it has legitimately been asked whether the doctrine of Aristotle, which the moderns have always understood as a justification of slavery, would not have had to appear to his contemporaries as an attack' (UB 8). In any case, he asserts that our modern sensitivities are out of place here and that a genuine scholarly approach must undertake, 'in place of outrage, a preliminary analysis of the problematic context in which the philosopher inscribes the question and the conceptuality through which he seeks to define its nature' (8). What results is a tour de force of reading against the grain. Where most readers are inclined to denounce Aristotle for illegitimately depriving the slave of the characteristics of humanity, Agamben's entire project up to this point has prepared us to see those characteristics as burdens rather than benefits. Hence, instead of assuming that the slave-owner sets the standard for humanity, Agamben proposes to read Aristotle's definition of slavery as pointing toward a new and different experience of humanity, one that our regnant definitions of humanity have denigrated and repressed (cf. 21).

From that perspective, the slave does not lack the necessary requisites of humanity – as Agamben points out, Aristotle never questions whether the slave is actually human (10) – so much as call all those traits into question. Where Aristotle claims that the properly human activity is the working of the soul according to reason, the slave is characterised by only a use of the body. Where human activity is characteristically goal-oriented, the slave's use of the body is 'unproductive' or *argos* (22; cf. KG 246). More than that, the very assumption of individuality is called into question, insofar as the slave's 'use of the body defines a zone of indifference between one's own body and the body of another' (23) – a body that is, furthermore, 'situated in a zone of indifference between the artificial instrument and the living body . . . and, therefore, between *physis* and *nomos*' (23). The result is a practice that is 'neither *poiēsis* nor *praxis*, neither a production nor a praxis, but neither is it assimilable to the labor of moderns' (23). And this paradoxical, barely legible human action, is nonetheless foundational to the political order:

> The slave, who is defined by means of this 'use of the body', is the human being without work who renders possible the realization of the work of the human being, that living being who, though being human, is excluded – and through this exclusion, included – in humanity, so that human beings can have a human life, which it to say a political life. (23)

This foundational role renders the slave similar to bare life, which 'stands at the threshold that separates and joins' *zōē* and *bios* (20), yet there seems to me to be a key difference here. Bare life, above all in the figure of the *Muselmann*, represents an unlivable extreme, a terminal state (at least in Agamben's initial presentation in *Remnants of Auschwitz*) where no shared life is imaginable. The slave, by contrast, 'represents the capture within law of a figure of human *acting* that still remains for us to recognize' (23; emphasis added).

What follows is a detailed analysis of the Greek term *chrēsis* and *chresthai*, the noun and verb forms, respectively, of 'use'. Though modern interpreters are determined to understand the Greek verb on the model of our modern conception of 'utilisation', in which a subject takes up an object for his or her own ends, Agamben insists that 'precisely the subject/object relationship . . . emerges as inadequate to grasp the meaning of the Greek verb' (27). In reality, the verb *chresthai* is in the middle voice, which combines the properties of something like a reflexive and intransitive verb in English. A good example is the Greek verb for 'to sleep', which can have a form that means simply that a person is sleeping (an action where subject, object, and location are difficult to distinguish) and another that indicates putting someone to sleep (hence displacing the action from one's own subjective position). This odd grammatical form, Agamben declares, 'is situated in a zone of indetermination between subject and object (the agent is in some way also object and place of action) and between active and passive (the agent receives an affection from his own action)' (28).

Here Agamben turns to an example that was central to his 1996 essay on Deleuze, 'Absolute Immanence', and that will return in Part II's archaeology of ontology: Spinoza's analysis of the reflexive active verb in his Hebrew grammar. To clarify this unfamiliar verbal form, Spinoza has recourse to his native Ladino (the equivalent of Yiddish for Spanish Jews of Spinoza's time), where the verb 'to walk' is *pasearse*, which can more literally be translated as 'to "walk-oneself,"' a formulation 'in which agent and patient enter into a threshold of absolute indistinction' (29). The implications of this verbal form are not solely grammatical, but also ontological, insofar as 'the sphere of the action of the self on the self corresponds to the ontology of immanence, to the movement of autoconstitution and autopresentation of being, in which not only is it not possible to distinguish between agent and patient but also subject and object, constituent and constituted are indeterminated' (29). In this ontological shift, subject and object as the key categories of action and causality 'are thus deactivated and rendered inoperative, and, in their place, there follows use as a new figure of human praxis' (30).

Much of the rest of this first part of *The Use of Bodies* is taken up with a critique of the general tendency in philosophy to subordinate this experience of use to the goal-directed activity designated as care. While he begins with an analysis of Foucault and Plato, his primary target here is Heidegger. This leads to one of the most extended close readings of Agamben's great teacher anywhere in his oeuvre – including fine-grained analyses of *Being and Time*, where 'readiness-to-hand' (the everyday use of things) is left aside in favour of care. After examining alternative conceptions of use in the Stoics and the Franciscans, Agamben takes up the question of technology, which the Greeks were of course well acquainted with but which only enters the sphere of ontology with the Scholastics' invention of a new, fifth cause alongside Aristotle's famous four causes: the instrumental cause, which Agamben traces back to their theories of sacramental effectiveness and, beyond that, to the slave whose body is available for the use of others. More or less passing over the modern experience of slavery,[6] he argues that both ancient slavery and modern technology bear on 'the ultimate achievement of anthropogenesis, the becoming fully human of the living human being' (78). Far from defining our access to the realm of the authentically human, Agamben argues that ancient slavery and modern technology

> represent in a certain sense the capture and parodic realization within social institutions of this 'use of the body', of which we have sought to delineate the essential characteristics. Every attempt to think use must necessarily engage with them, because perhaps only an archaeology of slavery and, *at the same time*, of technology will be able to free the archaic nucleus that has remained imprisoned in them. (78)

From this perspective, we can see that 'the slave constitutes in the history of anthropogenesis a double threshold, in which animal life crosses over into the human just as the living (the human) crosses over into the inorganic (into the instrument), and vice versa)' (79). Yet neither model has delivered the freedom that it promised.

After so much Heidegger, Agamben once again performs Durantaye's *Benjamin ex machina*, quoting a fragment in which Benjamin defines justice 'not as a virtue, but as a "state of the world"', in which we experience the world 'as absolutely inappropriable' (81). The remainder of this division consists of three examples of phenomena that define us without our ever being able to fully appropriate them: our own body, our language, and landscape. While the example of language, which can never be purely 'ours' but is constitutively shared with others, is relatively intuitive, the other two are perhaps less immediately clear. In the case of the body, Agamben draws on analyses from Levinas of bodily experiences that we cannot escape but we can equally not assume as our own – experiences like nausea, or 'an uncontestable urge to urinate' (85). In those experiences, we cannot help but experience our own body, and Agamben draws parallels with Husserl and Edith Stein's investigations of the experience of the body of the other. Against their claim that our 'own' body is always primary, Agamben argues that there are circumstances – for instance, watching trapeze artists achieving some death-defying feat (83) – where we cannot help but experience the body of the other in the same inappropriable way we experience our own.

The example of landscape is at once more unexpected and more profound. What he means is not simply the landscape 'out there' that we are witnessing, but the experience itself as a point of indetermination between ourselves and the object of our observation. From a certain perspective, there is no 'landscape' (or, for that matter, no city skyline) without an observer, yet that does not imply that landscape is all in our heads – nor indeed that anyone can 'own' a landscape in this sense. Instead, Agamben argues that what is in question in landscape is our 'relationship with the environment and with the world' (88), which 'represents, with respect to the animal environment and the human world, an ulterior stage' (91). To support this view, he cites works on animal behaviour, claiming that many species contemplate the landscape, with no apparent ulterior motive (89) – his first engagement with non-human forms of life since *The Open*. Agamben goes through much the same material in the *Creation and Anarchy* lectures, as though trying out this material before finally incorporating it into the final draft of *The Use of Bodies*, and there he includes a sentence that is omitted in the latter text, which underlines the profound ontological consequences of a right understanding of landscape: 'Landscape is the house of Being' (CA 50). Where Heidegger famously grants that title to language, for Agamben it is the experience of landscape that is ontologically prior, insofar as it grants the living being – human and animal alike – an experience of 'the world as inappropriable' (91).

While there is some older material that Agamben here reads into the official record – most notably the example from Spinoza, but also some material from 1991's 'Expropriated Manner' that we will discuss in the conclusion – Part I of *The Use of Bodies* is less a consolidation than an expansion of his project. The analysis of the slave has provided him with a way to address topics that, in retrospect, were considerable lacunas in his project of rethinking all Western political institutions – not only slavery itself, but labour and technology. Overall, this section embodies Agamben's claim that the constructive and critical moments of a philosophical work cannot be separated.

Ontology and anthropogenesis

Throughout his analysis of slavery and the use of the body it implies, Agamben emphasises its ontological implications. This unique form of human action requires us to rethink very basic categories, including some that have been central to Agamben's work thus far. Hence, for instance, he can claim that 'Aristotle . . . has divided what we are here seeking to think as use and has called *dynamis* and *energeia* [potentiality and act] that which results from the division' (UB 59). The transition to ontology is expected, then, and yet the next major part of *The Use of Bodies*, 'An Archaeology of Ontology', feels less like a continuation or extrapolation than a new beginning. Indeed, far from promising to work out the ontology that corresponds to the slave's use of the body, Agamben begins by opening the question of 'whether access to a first philosophy, that is, to an ontology, is today still – or once again – possible' (111). Drawing implicitly on *Opus Dei*'s claim that Kant's work represents the moment when the ontology of command

began to colonise the ontology of being, Agamben highlight's
Kant's role in rendering ontology increasingly problematic, to the
point where 'it is not thinkable except in the form of an archaeology' (111). Despite the obstacles, however, such an archaeology is
worth carrying out, because ontology is not just a set of abstract
logical distinctions, but

> opens and defines each time the space of human acting and
> knowing, of what the human being can do and of what it
> can know and say. Ontology is laden with the historical
> destiny of the West not because an inexplicable and meta-
> historical magical power belongs to it but just the contrary,
> because ontology is the originary place of the historical
> articulation between language and world, which presents
> in itself the memory of anthropogenesis, of the moment
> when that articulation was produced. To every change in
> ontology there corresponds, therefore, not a change in the
> 'destiny' but in the complex possibilities that the articulation
> between language and world has disclosed as 'history' to the
> living beings of the species *Homo Sapiens*. (111)

And we know that such changes are possible because anthropogenesis is 'the event that never stops happening, a process
still under way in which the human being is always in the act
of becoming human and of remaining (or becoming) inhuman'
(111). In other words, anthropogenesis is not only not in the past,
but could open a new and different future.

Broadly speaking, Agamben's argument proceeds via three
steps, corresponding to the three chapters in this section. First,
he lays out the foundational ontology of Aristotle, which sets the
terms for all later developments. His focus here is on the logic of
presupposition, which has been a key point of reference throughout the project but here attains a new level of rigour and philological grounding. At the same time, he presents Plato's approach
as a path not taken, in a passage that finally reads Agamben's key
findings from 'The Thing Itself' onto the official record of the
Homo Sacer series. Second, he traces the ways that the tensions in
Aristotle's system opened up the possibility for transformations

in ontology, but in ways that intensify rather than ameliorate its most undesirable aspects. Here the key term is *hypostasis*, which marks a shift toward a more operative ontology and, in the context of Trinitarian theology, prepares the way toward modern theories of subjectivity. Finally, he mines the Scholastic and early modern philosophical traditions for materials that could be used in constructing a modal ontology, which would represent a genuine alternative to the logic of presupposition. Agamben had seemingly prepared the ground for this in Part I, where at one point he states that

*being, in its originary form, is not substance (*ousia*), but use-of-oneself, is not realized in a hypostasis but dwells in use.* And 'to use' is, in this sense, the archimodal verb, which defines being before or, in any case, outside its articulation in the ontological difference existence/essence and in the modalities: possibility, impossibility, contingency, necessity. (56)

At the end of Part II, however, use appears only briefly and somewhat inorganically, in a short paragraph that comes at the end of a repetition of his earlier analysis of the mode of immanent causality illustrated by Spinoza's example of the Ladino verb *pasearse* (165). It is difficult to avoid the conclusion that these two brief cross-references were late additions meant to bring together two texts that were composed separately, with different (though broadly compatible) argumentative goals.

As in previous chapters, I do not intend to discuss the philological niceties – in which these chapters are exceptionally dense, even relative to Agamben's usual standards – in great detail. More important for our purposes is how his close readings of Aristotle bear on his project in *The Use of Bodies* and the *Homo Sacer* series more generally. As I have suggested, they serve primarily to deepen his account of the logic of presupposition, and the key contribution here – aside from its greater philological documentation – is the notion that presupposition includes an irreducibly *temporal* element. There is a pastness about the element that is presupposed, which can never appear in the present but always refers back to an imagined moment before the presupposition took place. In the case of linguistic presupposition, we imagine extra-linguistic reality as what exists prior to our attempt to grasp it with language. While we tend to distinguish between logical and temporal priority, Agamben claims they are ultimately the same, and indeed that the logic of presupposition is actually what generates our sense of time and history: 'The ontological apparatus is a temporalizing apparatus' (127). This means that Heidegger's project of rearticulating Being in terms of time is, ultimately, knocking on an open door and is doomed to repeat the pitfalls of his Aristotelian model (127) – perhaps the clearest critique of Heidegger to appear in Agamben's corpus thus far. It is in this context that Agamben reads onto the record his account of operational time from *The Time That Remains* (126–7) – a move that retrospectively highlights the previous lack of any theory of temporality and history in the previous volumes of the series. Even in the act of consolidating his previous findings, then, he is expanding the scope of his project.

As I note above, Agamben presents Plato's approach as an alternative to – indeed, almost as a pre-emptive critique of – Aristotle's. Where Aristotle treats the presupposition as an immovable principle, Plato handles it precisely *as* a presupposition, that is, as a hypothesis that provides a starting point for an investigation that 'is situated rigorously within language' and hence is able to use 'language in a non-presuppositional, which is to say, non-referential way' (130). This explains the curious fact that 'when it is a question of confronting decisive problems, Plato prefers to have recourse to myth and joking' (130). As in his 1984 essay on Plato, this entails the recognition that the 'thing itself' is not some presupposed object out there, but here he does not make the expected reference to 'sayability', preferring instead to speak in terms of a mute 'contact' between the thing and language (131).

The familiar language of sayability returns, however, toward the end of Part II when it is a question of clarifying the concept of demand. Throughout his discussion, Agamben emphasises the liminal or in-between character of demand, which unsettles the established binaries of Western thought: 'it is at the same time real and not factual, neither simply logical nor completely real' (170). A demand does not force something into existence, because then it would not be demand, but necessity. By the same token, it is not a mere fact, because it contains a virtual or potential element. Where Leibniz – Agamben's primary source for the concept in this chapter – renders demand subordinate to the other ontological categories, Agamben argues that it is not only 'more original than the very distinction between essence and existence, potential and act', but offers the possibility for a new ontological starting point that would place all those categories into question. And it is at this point that he reintroduces the concept of sayability:

> If language and world stand opposite one another without any articulation, what happens between them is a pure demand – namely, a pure *sayability*. *Being is a pure demand held in tension between language and world*. The thing demands its own sayability, and this sayability is the meaning of the word. But in reality there is only the sayability: the word and the thing are only its two fragments. (170)

Something similar happens with the familiar categories of potentiality and act. Whereas Leibniz believed that possibility demands to exist, Agamben argues that the reverse is true: 'the possible does not demand to exist, but rather, it is the real that demands its own possibility' (170). This reversal 'neutralizes and renders inoperative both essence and existence, both potential and act', revealing that these categories 'are only the figures that demand assumes if considered from the point of view of traditional ontology' (170).

At this point, then, Agamben has begun to develop his own distinctive ontological vocabulary and to elaborate the ways that it at once accounts for and resolves the deadlocks in the traditional ontology. Even if some of these notions – most notably Platonic 'sayability' and demand – had been present in earlier texts, this positive articulation is new, marking a step forward in his thought. At the same time, it allows him to settle accounts with Heidegger in an unprecedented way. Up until *The Use of Bodies*, Agamben's approach to Heidegger has tended to be cautious and ambiguous. While his debt to Heidegger is obvious, he also wants to mark his distance, but he does so in ways that are often elliptical and difficult to interpret. In 'Intermezzo II', by contrast, he is finally able to state clearly the limit to Heidegger's thought that was, by the master's own account in the seminars at Le Thor, invisible to him but potentially visible to his students. Though Heidegger's work had pointed Agamben in the direction of a modal ontology in many ways, above all through his prioritisation of potentiality, the pitfall is his tendency to mistake 'demand' for a task or even a destiny – one that Heidegger himself experiences as onerous but impossible to avoid. Agamben even defines the 'fundamental attunement or mood . . . that dominates all of Heidegger's thought' as 'being obstinately consigned to something that just as tenaciously refuses itself, or being consigned to something unassumable' (187). This is what informs Heidegger's understanding of the relation between human and animal life – which is at once read onto the record from *The Open* and significantly recontextualised – in which humanity is a task at which we are continually failing and thus 'the human being is continually in the act of falling back into animality' (188). This means that despite the conceptual fruitfulness of Heidegger's prioritisation of potentiality for Agamben's thought, the way that it functions 'in Heideggerian ontology is indissoluble from the aporia that assigns humanity to the human being as a task that, as such, can always be mistaken for a political task' (188). The limits to Heidegger's thought, then, are what allowed him to be seduced by National Socialism – a tragic demonstration of Agamben's identification of the ontological and the political.

The philosophical life

Compared to the first two-thirds of the book, Part III of *The Use of Bodies*, which promises the long-awaited exposition of 'Form-of-Life', appears almost to be a step backwards. The arrangement of chapters is disjointed, and several of them are very short, giving the appearance of a series of vignettes or reflections rather than the kind of systematic argument that we saw in the previous two parts. Prior to my meeting with Agamben, I suspected that part of the reason for this less elegant organisation is that this section likely brings together materials from the greatest span of time – indeed, that it represents the only significant tranche of texts 'written at the beginning of the investigation, which is to say, almost twenty years ago' that Agamben refers to in the 'Prefatory Note' (UB xiii). While we did not have time to discuss this issue in person, Agamben subsequently confirmed to me via email that the first half of Part III contains the oldest material, some of which was intended for an archaeology of the concept of life that he had planned to include in volume 2 of *Homo Sacer* but never completed.

For whatever reason, Agamben was reluctant to go into further detail on the dating of specific passages, but armed with the confirmation that some of Part III is early, I believe it is possible to make reasonable inferences. For instance, we can say with relative certainty that chapter 2, 'A Life Inseparable from its Form', is a very early text. There are two giveaways here, I think. The first is his reference to Benjamin's 'Theses on the Philosophy of History' as 'more than fifty years old' (209). The text was written in 1940, and while it remains 'more than fifty years old' today, it would surely be more natural for an author writing in in the early 2010s to say that it was 'more than seventy years old'. Hence I conclude that this section was written in the 1990s, an impression that is reinforced by the reference to Nancy's critique of Bataille. Agamben draws on Nancy's *Inoperative Community* in the 1992 essay 'The Messiah and the Sovereign' – his first systematic investigation of the theme – and the 1993 essay 'Form-of-Life', then incorporates his findings into *Homo Sacer* in 1995. After that point, prior to the memoir, Nancy is never heard from again in Agamben's corpus, with the exception of a lament in 'The Friend' that the two were no longer as close as they once were (WA 26). This is as close to intellectual carbon dating as we are likely to get.

If we accept this dating, then it seems likely that chapter 1, 'Life Divided'; chapter 3, 'Living Contemplation'; and chapter 4, 'Life is a Form Generated by Living', are all from around the same period or only slightly later, as all three share important commonalities. The first chapter focuses on the history of the term $z\bar{o}\bar{e}$ in Greek thought, emphasising that it did not have a technical meaning, even in medical contexts, prior to Aristotle's *Politics*, where mere 'living' is distinguished from the politically qualified 'living well'. Going beyond this familiar thesis, Agamben argues that all of Aristotle's divisions of life – including the apparently 'biological' division of the soul into various faculties in *De Anima* – are ultimately political in nature. This leads to a new definition of politics:

> *Politics, as the* ergon *proper to the human, is the practice that is founded on the separation, worked by the* logos, *of otherwise inseparable functions.* Politics here appears as what allows one to treat a human life as if in it sensitive and intellectual life were separable from vegetative life – and thus, since it is impossible in mortals, of legitimately putting it to death. (204)

If the separation of vegetative or nutritive life is the principle of legitimacy of political violence, then overcoming that separation is among the most urgent tasks in developing a form-of-life. By contrast, the next chapter, which we have identified as most likely to be early, emphasises the need to overcome the division between political and intellectual life. Where Greek philosophers had tended to see contemplation as 'a separate and solitary activity', we must instead take up the insights of Averroism, which posited 'the thought of one sole possible intellect common to all human beings', an insight that Dante takes up in his political theory (211). Hence the life of collective thought emerges as the best model of a form-of-life (213).

The third chapter seems to synthesise the two arguments, noting that Plotinus 'attribut[es] contemplation to all living beings, including plants' (215), so that 'what is logical and theoretical' is not some aspect or portion of life, but 'life itself, which is articulated, disseminated, and diversified according to the more or less manifest character . . . of contemplation that is proper to it' (216). This allows Plotinus to grasp life not as a presupposition 'to which determinate qualities come to be added (for example, rational or linguistic being) but as an indivisible whole, which he defines as *eidos zōēs*, form of life' (218). This privileged role for Plotinus may seem strange, given that Agamben had earlier used his famous description of the philosophical life as an 'exile of one alone with one alone' as a byword for the individualistic contemplation he is trying to overcome, but in a later chapter bearing Plotinus's slogan as its title (chapter 6, which cites Erik Peterson and must therefore come from the period around *The Kingdom and the Glory* or later), Agamben seems to attempt to correct himself, arguing that the 'exile' Plotinus refers to needs to be taken in its full political sense. This expulsion from the city is homologous with the 'relation of the ban in which bare life is held', but in the case of the philosopher it 'is laid claimed to and assumed as his own', which opens up a space 'to be together beyond every relation' that Agamben identifies with form-of-life (236). As he points out, this fulfils a long-standing desideratum from *Homo Sacer*, where he asserted 'the necessity of no longer thinking the political-social *factum* in the form of relationship' (236–7).

The short fourth chapter on the place of life in the theology of Marius Victorinus carries the history forward from Plotinus to Christianity. Beyond that, however, it is difficult for me to discern a clear argumentative structure in the remainder of Part III. The fifth chapter is 'Toward an Ontology of Style', which consists of a series of reflections on possible examples of form-of-life – ranging from Plutarch's *Lives* to newspaper personal ads – that seems to interrupt the argumentative flow. And after we return to Plotinus in chapter 6, we get a full chapter that appears to be little more than a detailed set of notes on Wittgenstein's use of the syntagma 'form of life' that Agamben never found a way to properly incorporate into his project. The section concludes with a creative rereading of the Myth of Er from the conclusion of Plato's *Republic*, in which Agamben argues that the mythological account of the afterlife and particularly the souls' opportunity to choose the life they will live when reincarnated is ultimately aimed at encouraging the reader to choose the philosophical life in the present. Thus this section, while it weaves together many of the themes of the book in a compelling way, nevertheless seems to return us to the territory of individual ethics rather than the properly political sphere.

On balance, then, the third part of *The Use of Bodies* does not rise to the level of the rest of the volume. The question then arises of why Agamben would include all this material, particularly the earlier passages that reflect a less rigorous development of his ideas. The stakes here, it seems to me, are ultimately about asserting the unity of the series as a whole. While Agamben has maintained continuity and cohesiveness by means of a series of bipolar structures that operate according to the logic of presupposition, it is nonetheless the case that the later volumes have wandered far afield from the concerns of the original *Homo Sacer*. Most notably, life – especially in the sense of the opposition between *zōē* and *bios* – has faded more or less into the background over the course of volume 2, and even in the first two parts of *The Use of Bodies* itself, it was very much a subordinate concern. By returning to the original themes of *zōē* and *bios*, and particularly by doing so using materials composed at a very early stage, Agamben could be asserting not only that we are still engaged in the same project that began with *Homo Sacer*, but that the project must be unified insofar as *he is ending exactly where he always intended to*. After all, good chunks of the ending were already drafted even as he began!

Alongside this possible gesture of self-assertion, however, there is a tacit acknowledgment that the stakes of *Homo Sacer* were not as clear as they could have been. For instance, the material on the history of the concept of life in Greek thought provides a kind of reply to critics – most famously Jacques Derrida, who devoted portions of *The Beast and the Sovereign* to debunking *Homo Sacer*[7] – who have challenged his reliance on the *zōē/bios* dyad, claiming that the Greek literary corpus does not make such a sharp distinction. If these passages really are from that early period, then it is clear that Agamben knew all along that the linguistic evidence was much more complex and intended all along to deal with the problem at greater length. The *zōē/bios* distinction would thus not be a hard linguistic or conceptual fact so much as a signature – even if he had not yet developed the terminology to make that distinction at this early stage of the project. And 'The Myth of Er', which notes Plato's deviation from the more standard dyad (UB 260ff.), would then reinforce the sense that the literal distinction between these two words was not the basis of his analysis and overcoming of the deeper structure that the dyad points toward – any more than he was claiming that an obscure Roman legal figure somehow 'caused' the structure of sovereignty.

Beyond this indirect commentary – whose legibility depends, of course, on the accuracy of my dating of the passages in question – there is a more obvious sense in which Agamben is still trying to clarify the stakes of *Homo Sacer*. I am speaking, of course, of his direct references to *Homo Sacer*, which in the epilogue take the form of two extended blockquotes (see UB 268). This kind of extended self-quotation is essentially unprecedented in Agamben's entire body of work. He is sparing with explicit references to past works (which he normally cites in whole-book format unless he wants to point the reader to a very detailed philological passage), and so this recourse to directly quoting himself is shocking. At the same time, it is also genuinely helpful, because both passages deal with one of the most puzzling aspects of the original *Homo Sacer*: its enigmatic claim that we need to get past the idea of relation. Agamben had already highlighted that passage in both Part II (144) and Part III (236–7), and this repeated and extended reference seems to be an indication that we are dealing with an idea that he is absolutely determined to clarify, even if it means violating his own sense of propriety by quoting himself. In so doing, he asserts that one of his most radical and important ideas was always present from day one – asserting, once again, the unity of the project – but that it is in danger of being overlooked.

I believe that what is at stake in this self-quotation is one final elaboration of the logic of presupposition, which the opening pages of the epilogue had already asserted to be the series' ultimate object of critique. And as he clarifies here, every relation is ultimately a relation of presupposition, because every relation introduces an artificial division and thus 'constitutes its elements by at the same time presupposing them as unrelated' (270). Hence the task cannot be to find 'new and more effective articulations of the two elements' of whatever instance of the Western machine we are studying, which ultimately amounts to 'playing the two halves of the machine off against one another'. At the same time, neither is it a matter of 'going back to a more originary beginning', because 'philosophical archaeology cannot reach a beginning other than the one that may perhaps result from the deactivation of the machine (in this sense first philosophy is always final philosophy)' (266).

Agamben is thinking, then, of a future, even unprecedented state – and yet he cannot be thinking of revolution, which always activates constitutive power over against the constituted order with which it forms a bipolar system. Instead, he proposes that we need to learn to 'think a purely destituent potential, that is to

say, one that never resolves itself into a constituted power' (268).
Instead of choosing one of the two elements in a relation, destituent potential deposes those elements by exposing precisely the lack
of relation between them – a gesture that actually sets those elements free for a new use. This is why – reading one last concept
from *The Time That Remains* onto the record – Paul can claim that
he is at once rendering the law inoperative and fulfilling it, finding
a new use for the law 'without for that reason constituting another
identity. The messianic (Paul does not know the term "Christian")
does not represent a new and more universal identity but a caesura
that passes through every identity – both that of the Jew and that
of the Gentile' (274). This means that the Pauline *hōs mē* or 'as not'
is an exemplary form of destituent power, insofar as it 'is a deposition without abdication. Living in the form of the "as not" means
rendering destitute all juridical and social ownership, without this
deposition founding a new identity' (274).

Only in this context can we understand the concluding
note on the 'Nocturnal Council' from Plato's *Laws*, which was
appended to the epilogue in the complete Italian edition of the
Homo Sacer series (and in the English translation). The note opens
with an assertion of the inadequacy of the Western political tradition's attempt 'to keep operating in every constituted system two
heterogeneous powers, which in some way mutually limited each
other' (278). While that strategy has produced relative stability
in some circumstances, it inevitably came about that 'one of the
powers had sought to eliminate the other', resulting in unchecked
violence (278). In place of this balance of powers – another form
of relation – Agamben suggests that we

> imagine – something that is not within the scope of this
> book – in some way translating into act the action of a
> destituent potential in a constituted system. It would be
> necessary to think an element that, while remaining hetero-
> geneous to the system, had the capacity to render decisions
> destitute, suspend them, and render them inoperative. (278)

In the context of Plato's *Laws*, at least as Agamben interprets the
text, this element takes the form of an informal committee of power

brokers who meet after dark and hold a kind of veto over the official legal structure. In our setting, particularly given Agamben's continual reference to Benjamin's 'Critique of Violence' throughout the epilogue, something like a general strike that shuts down the system as a way of overriding illegitimate decisions could be what Agamben has in mind.

Whatever the concrete form a 'destituent potential' takes, however, it is certain that it will represent a messianic potentiality – indeed, the *weak* messianic power that the concluding pages of *The Time That Remains* had asserted to represent the secret link between the Letters of Paul and Benjamin's 'Theses' (TTR 138–45). And in a series of short texts published throughout this period – *The Church and the Kingdom*, *The Mystery of Evil*, and *Pilate and Jesus* – Agamben has sought to clarify and refine his distinctively philosophical messianism. Again and again, he rejects the apocalyptic reading of Paul that would call for the destruction and irrevocable overcoming of the figure of this world. In its place, he advocates a messianic stance that would enliven – or render livable – a system that has become nihilistic and death-dealing. In *The Church and the Kingdom*, he seems to envision the possibility of the Church finding a way to 'grasp the historical occasion and recover its messianic vocation'.[8] And in *The Mystery of Evil*, he presents Benedict XVI's nearly unprecedented abdication as pope as a salutary recognition that legality does not always equal legitimacy (though he could have clung to power until death like virtually all his predecessors, he instead willingly gave it up). Agamben suggests this decision was influenced by Benedict's own understanding of the dynamics of history as they appear in the pseudo-Pauline Second Letter to the Thessalonians. Finally, *Pilate and Jesus* stages the encounter between the messiah and the representative of power, which brings the law to a standstill by rendering it incapable of issuing a legal judgment and hence exposing the illegitimacy of its violence.

In none of these cases are we dealing with the exercise of power in a conventional sense. Instead, Agamben seems to have in mind what the Apostle Paul would call a power that 'is made perfect in weakness' (2 Corinthians 12:9). And in what is surely an intentional echo of the correspondence he had already detected between Paul and Benjamin, in the epilogue Agamben puts forth his own version of a weak power: namely, language. Drawing on the Scholastic theologian Duns Scotus's description of language as the *ens debilissimum* or 'weakest being' (UB 270), he argues that overcoming the logic of relation will mean

> engaging in a decisive hand-to-hand confrontation with the weakest of beings that is language. But precisely because its ontological status is weak, language is the most difficult to know and grasp, as Scotus had intuited. The almost invincible force of language is in its weakness, in its remaining unthought and unsaid in what says and in that of which it is said. (271)

And this is why 'philosophy is born in Plato precisely as an attempt to get to the bottom of *logoi* [words], and as such, it has a political character immediately and from the very start' (271). Only once we have truly 'gotten to the bottom of this weakest potential' that is language 'will it be possible to think politics beyond every figure of relation' (272). Here as ever, philosophy and messianism continue to overlap and inform one another, to the point of becoming indistinguishable, united in calling us to grasp what is immediately at hand and yet, precisely for that reason, seems impossibly distant. Nothing could be easier, and hence nothing could be more difficult. This is the paradoxical note – exemplary of what one could almost define as 'fundamental attunement or mood . . . that dominates all of [Agamben's] thought' (187) – with which Agamben takes leave of a life's work that 'cannot be concluded but only abandoned (and perhaps continued by others)' (xiii).

Notes

1. Here I slightly alter my own translation; see the brief discussion below.
2. See Kotsko, *Neoliberalism's Demons*, ch. 2.
3. See 'Paul and the Jewish Alternative' in Dickinson and Kotsko, *Agamben's Coming Philosophy*.
4. See Whyte, *Catastrophe and Redemption*, ch. 5.

5. Kishik, *The Power of Life*, 12.
6. For a critique of this omission in Agamben's earlier work, see Weheliye, *Habeas Viscus*.
7. Derrida, *The Beast and the Sovereign*, vol. 1.
8. Agamben, *Church and the Kingdom*, 41.

5
Late Labours

After publishing the capstone to their decades-long research project, many authors would be tempted to take a break. Not so Agamben – indeed, *The Use of Bodies* was not even the only book he put out in 2014. Alongside it, he published *The Fire and the Tale*, a collection of essays bringing together several pieces from the 2010s along with some new material. And in the year that followed, he put out no less than four books: *Taste*, *Stasis*, *The Adventure*, and *Pulcinella*. As with the contents of *The Fire and the Tale*, these works included a mix of the old and the new, though to a much greater degree. As I noted in my discussion of the text in Chapter 1, *Taste* originally appeared in an Italian reference volume in 1979. The gap between the original drafting of *Stasis* in 2001 and its eventual publication was not so extreme, but still considerable. Why these texts, and why now?

The rationale for publishing these two books at this point, it seems to me, was likely to serve as supplements to *The Use of Bodies*, where Agamben had drawn on the conceptuality of both texts in brief passages. Most striking is his reference to the concept of *stasis* in the opening chapter of Part III. There his topic is Aristotle's notion of autarchy or self-sufficiency as a distinguishing mark of a city, and he proclaims, in italics no less, that '*autarchy, like* stasis, *is a biopolitical operator, which allows or negates the passage from the community of life to the political community, from simple* zōē *to politically qualified life*' (UB 198). Without knowledge of the argument of *Stasis*, this parallel is more confusing than clarifying. Similarly, in the chapter 'Toward an Ontology of

Style', after listing some idiosyncratic tastes (presumably his own) for 'coffee granita, the sea at summertime, this certain shape of lips, this certain smell, but also the paintings of the late Titian', he declares: 'It is necessary to decisively distract tastes from the aesthetic dimension and rediscover their ontological character, in order to find in them something like a new ethical territory' (231). It is difficult to know what to make of this claim without some familiarity with the argument in *Taste*.

Aside from this mopping-up work, however, the direction of Agamben's writing after the banner year of 2014 takes its cue less from *The Use of Bodies* than from *The Fire and the Tale*, which returns to themes related to literature and aesthetics in a more sustained way than his difficult labours on the *Homo Sacer* project had allowed. Thus, although I emphasised in Chapter 3 that many of the essays in *The End of the Poem* were more or less contemporaneous with the gestation of *Homo Sacer*, it is nonetheless the case that that collection represented, at least for that time, a pause in his investigation of poetics. Yet there is another sense in which many of the essays in *The Fire and the Tale* return to his earlier concerns, insofar as they reflect on the personal experience of the artist and, more than that, the quest for something like personal integrity.

Those broadly ethical questions inform both *The Adventure* and *Pulcinella*, along with 2016's *What is Real?*, which investigates the Italian physicist Ettore Majorana's apparent decision to stage his own disappearance. All three works are also personal in another sense, insofar as they return to much earlier themes from Agamben's work. In the case of *The Adventure*, he returns to the medieval love poetry that informed *Stanzas* and *The End of the Poem*, while *What is Real?* goes back even further to the work of Simone Weil – who was the topic of Agamben's doctoral dissertation but is here cited extensively for the first time in his published corpus.[1] For its part, as we will see, *Pulcinella* serves almost as a recapitulation of every phase of Agamben's thought, albeit from a bizarre perspective. This return to earlier themes reflects Agamben's concern to find coherence in his life's work, which means never fully leaving a real intellectual passion – or indeed, a serious intellectual dilemma – behind. We can see the same impulse at work in his memoir, *Autoritratto nello studio* (Self-Portrait in His Studio; 2017), where he returns again and again to his earliest works, reflecting on the friendships and fortuitous discoveries that informed them. By contrast, the works of the *Homo Sacer* period are virtually untouched – in fact, the only significant reference to the first volume, the book that made his name internationally, comes in the context of his discussion of Simone Weil, where he suggests: 'Perhaps the critique of law, which I have never abandoned since the first volume of *Homo Sacer*, has its ultimate root in Weil's essay', namely *La personne e le sacré* (ARS 51).

Yet none of these books is a simple retread. All are experimental and innovative – particularly *Pulcinella*, which rearticulates his key concerns in a completely unexpected way. *The Adventure* reflects the depth of his engagement with Christian theology and also brings the experience of poetry into explicit connection with the concept of anthropogenesis, while including a self-help element that is basically unprecedented. Meanwhile, *What is Real?* represents a startling account of quantum physics. Even the memoir, though admittedly more backward-looking, ends on a surprising note, proclaiming the author's love for grass. Earlier, discussing Aristotle's separation and denigration of vegetative life, he had declared: 'For me plants are a form of life in every sense superior to our own: they live in a perpetual dream, feeding on light' (ARS 143). In that context, the statement seemed to express a wistful regret at humanity's exclusion from the vegetative idyll, but the closing lines clarify that that is not the case: 'Grass', he claims, 'grass is God. In grass – in God – are all those I have loved. Through grass and in grass and as grass I have lived and will live' (167). Certain passages in Part III of *The Use of Bodies* suggest a privilege of vegetative life, but whatever one makes of these statements from the memoir, they at least clarify that those arguments were far from mere thought experiments for Agamben.

The other three major works of this period – *What is Philosophy?* (2017), *Karman* (2018), and *Il Regno e il Giardino* (The Kingdom and the Garden; 2019)[2] – are less overtly personal in the biographical sense, but they reflect the more personal emphasis of his earlier work. Indeed, *What is Philosophy?* returns quite literally to an earlier stage of his thought, as the opening essay,

'Experimentum Vocis' (The Experience of the Voice), 'resumes and develops in a new direction notes I took in the second half of the 1980s' (WP xi). Since the remainder of the volume was 'written over the past two years', this means that *What is Philosophy?* contains materials from a greater chronological range than any of his previous books, even the essay collections. That opening essay returns forcefully to a theme that had lain dormant for many decades – namely, the voice – and the remainder builds on the reading of Plato from 'The Thing Itself', to which Agamben has already returned many times.

By contrast, *Karman* reworks themes and concepts from the *Homo Sacer* project – particularly from the relatively neglected *Sacrament of Language* and *Opus Dei* – into an investigation of the relationship between legal and moral guilt and responsibility. In that context, it develops certain theological themes that *Il Regno e Il Giardino* expands upon, in an investigation of the theme of the Garden of Eden that centres largely on a critique of the doctrine of original sin. Both texts display fresh, and often intricately detailed, research into the theological tradition, and *Karman* in particular is noteworthy for extending its purview beyond the West and into Hindu and Buddhist traditions. For all their new contributions, however, these last three books are concerned more with consolidation than innovation. This is not to call into question their value, however. In fact, I believe that the reader of these three books would walk away with a good sense of what is most promising, as well as most problematic, in Agamben's thought.

This chapter will investigate these late works of Agamben from a perspective that is at once thematic and chronological. I will begin with what is at once his strangest and most substantial work of the period, namely *Pulcinella*, then turn to the other more experimental works (*The Adventure*, and *What is Real?*) before considering the texts with more of an emphasis on consolidation (*What is Philosophy?*, *Karman*, and *Il Regno e Il Giardino*) – forgoing the attempt to give a free-standing account of the memoir, in light of the fact that I have already discussed it at some length at various points in my argument. I will conclude this brief chapter with a discussion of what is certainly his most important publication of this period, namely, the complete *Homo Sacer*. While this

chapter is necessarily incomplete – Agamben will doubtless publish at least two books while mine is in production – my hope is
that a reflection on the implications of his bold gesture of presenting nine books written over the span of twenty years as somehow
'one' book will provide a suitable endpoint for my philological
investigation, while laying the groundwork for my conclusion.

Philosophy as comedy

In the works of 2015, a new theme emerges: namely, aging. This
is understandable, given that Agamben was in his early seventies
by the time he completed the capstone of his life's work. In typical
Agamben fashion, though, he mostly pursues this meditation on
ageing through indirect commentary on two unexpected sources:
Giandomenico Tiepolo in *Pulcinella* and Goethe in *The Adventure*.
More specifically, the two texts comment on works from their
respective figures' old age. As he points out at near both the
beginning and the end of *Pulcinella* (Pu 5, 122), Tiepolo was
70 years old when he completed his last two frescoes of the titular
commedia dell'arte figure and 'decided to dedicate his last labor, the
album of drawings titled *Entertainment for Kids*, to the birth, life,
and adventures of Pulcinella' (10). Given that Agamben uses the
title of the album as part of his own subtitle, his identification
with the figure of Tiepolo – here usually called Giandomenico
to distinguish him from his more famous father, Giambattista – is
perhaps clear enough. Agamben also reinforces it elsewhere, for
instance when he claims that 'whether a priori or a posteriori,
Giandomenico wanted to give his frescoes a unified meaning'
(29), an indirect commentary, perhaps, on the unity, 'whether
a priori or a posteriori', that characterises the diverse works in
the *Homo Sacer* series. Similarly, he points out that Goethe wrote
Urworte (Primal Words), the poem that provides the structure for
The Adventure, as a way of 'reflecting on his life – he is sixty-eight
by then . . .' (A 5). The correspondence is not as exact, but it is
still the case that Agamben has never before flagged the ages of his
sources so emphatically.

Rarer still has been the kind of explicit personal reflection that
opens *Pulcinella*, where we find Agamben lying in his beloved

grass, watching the clouds. Meditating on the course of his life, he says, 'early on I was taken by a desire to search with all my strength whether there were in heaven or on Earth something such that, once I found it, I could eternally enjoy a just and continuous happiness' (Pu 3). That kind of quest normally characterises the contemplative or monastic life, but Agamben found himself incapable of pursuing those paths, since 'my character was foreign to any kind of ascesis and incapable of denying itself the pleasures and the special joy toward which its tastes inclined' (3). Though his disposition inclines toward comedy rather than tragedy, he recognises that some readers may have a hard time recognising that, given that 'the darkness of the times in which I was given to live had constrained me to research that some thought betrayed a rather gloomy soul – which, as my friends know, is clearly untrue. This is why today, having nearly reached my last labor, I would like it not to be toilsome, but cheerful and playful' (4).

This is not to say that his goal is frivolous, however, for he wants to 'show beyond any doubt not only that comedy is more ancient and profound than tragedy – something upon which many already agree – but also that it is closer to philosophy, so close that the two ultimately seem to blur into each other' (4).[3] If the theme is recognisably within the realm of Agamben's concerns with philosophy and literature, though, the form is certainly not. More, perhaps, than any work of Agamben's since *Idea of Prose*, this text defies summary, weaving together accounts of Tiepolo's sketches and paintings with imagined dialogues between Pulcinella and various characters (primarily Giandomenico Tiepolo, but also other *commedia dell'arte* characters – and, bizarrely enough, Leibniz; see 98–9), historical background on the figure of Pulcinella in the context of the *commedia dell'arte*, and a number of thinly veiled references to Agamben's other works. In the English edition, approximately half the pages are taken up with reproductions of Tiepolo's' paintings or drawings, or related works (such as Goya's *The Third of May 1808*, whose execution scene Agamben finds to be similar to one of Tiepolo's depictions of an execution of Pulcinella by firing squad; 67). The format is familiar from *The Unspeakable Girl*, but here it is taken to a new extreme. And aside from the novelty of the staged dialogues, Agamben presents Pulcinella's speech primarily in the Neapolitan local dialect, glossing it in Italian (see 5, fn. 1). On the one hand, this reflects a long-standing interest in the tension between dialects and 'proper' languages,[4] but never before has he directly incorporated dialect materials into his own texts.

Overall, it is difficult to track the status of the various claims and arguments in the text, a problem that is compounded by Agamben's repeated references to the concepts that had guided his previous work. Early on, for instance, he establishes a connection between Plato's love of comedies and mime plays (4) and Giandomenico Tiepolo's historical context to build connections with theological themes. In an era when Venice had hastily surrendered its independence to Napoleon's forces – a situation that surely resonates with Agamben's view of Italian politics in relation to the European Union – Giandomenico must have felt like a historical relic, and hence 'in his eyes Pulcinella is certainly – for better or for worse, in disgrace or in glory – that which survives the end of, if not *the* world, at least *a* world – *his* world: the figure that something assumes when it has seen its time' (11). Yet as Agamben points out, the time of the relic (what we might call the time that remains) is also the time of 'recapitulation' in the theological sense in which Christ is said to have recapitulated all things through his life, death, and resurrection (11). And such moments of recapitulation, Agamben claims, are moments not for tears, but for laughter – more specifically, the laughter of the philosopher (12).

This passage seems to underwrite the recapitulation of Agamben's own work that *Pulcinella* stages, in a strange and almost self-parodic tone. There is virtually no important theme or concept that the figure of Pulcinella fails to evoke or even embody. And he begins with what he had identified in 'Experimentum Linguae' as the heart of his work: 'That language *is*, that the world *is* – this is not something that one can say; one can only laugh or cry about it (and therefore it is not a question of mystical experience but of Pulcinella's secret)' (14). Further on, after a brief dialogue exchange between Giandomenico and Pulcinella, he takes that 'wordplay and misunderstanding' that 'define Pulcinella's relation to language' as reflecting the truth – familiar from his essays on language from the early '80s – that 'language does not serve at all to communicate something; it serves, precisely for this reason, only to provoke language' (17). This, Agamben claims, is what Plato's Seventh Letter meant when it referred to the 'weakness of language': 'To show, within language, an impossibility of communicating and to show that it is funny – this is the essence of comedy' (17). I highlighted the importance of the weakness of language in the concluding pages of *The Use of Bodies* – but who would have ever associated those reflections with laughter or comedy?

Later, Agamben returns to the theme of the relation between humans and animals by referring to 'a constellation, in the Benjaminian sense, between the satyrs and the Pulcinellas', which 'contain a secret index that refers them to each other and makes them inseparable' (32). Here he is referring to the Greek mythological figures who starred in the satyr plays that concluded a sequence of tragedies in Athens, meaning that after the historical action of the tragedy has played out on stage, we see the emergence of 'semi-animal (or at least not properly human) beings. The last humans, in their outdated fashions, leave the scene in a ridiculous minuet and make room for now, unforeseeable actors: satyrs and Pulcinellas' (32). Here, perhaps, is a Greek equivalent to the Jewish manuscript mentioned in *The Open*, where the denizens of the messianic kingdom were shown with animal heads (O 1), but again, the implication is much more clearly comic, as opposed to the grim seriousness that characterised the earlier text. (Or did it? Now I can no longer say with confidence: were we supposed to laugh at the animal heads of the blessed?) In any case, this provides another connection between comedy and philosophy, as Agamben ends the first of the book's four 'acts' by painstakingly recounting the many points where the Platonic dialogues associate Socrates with the satyrs (38–9).

The second 'act' is taken up primarily with a reconstruction of Aristotle's hypothetical definition of comedy, which he promises but never provides in the *Poetics*. Agamben proposes to derive it from his well-known definition of tragedy, which provides the occasion to lay out a genealogy of modern concepts of personhood from tragedy – particularly the tragic mask, as it is the concept of a mask that stands at the etymological root of the term 'person'

(54–5). Drawing a connection with Roman customs surrounding the death mask, he claims that Pulcinella, 'like the *homo sacer*',
has a special relationship with the realm of the dead, but 'in such
an exaggerated way that he jumps entirely beyond death. This is
shown by the fact that it is useless to kill him; if you shoot him or
hang him, he always rises again' (60) – much like a contemporary
cartoon character. In his overcoming of death, Pulcinella is therefore like Christ, and indeed Giandomenico has Pulcinella live out
the stations of the cross in his own strange way.

In the third 'act', Agamben explores the unique nature of
commedia dell'arte characters, who exist somewhere between
impersonal types (like the Everyman of medieval morality plays)
and defined individual characters (like Bugs Bunny). More than
playing the character, the actor embodies it, 'always with the
same mask and costume but each time in totally different circumstances and social conditions' (81). No matter where Pulcinella
appears, however, he always acts in such a way that 'the lowliest
bodily functions are rendered inoperative and shown as such, and
in this way are opened to a new, possible use that appears as the
true and original one' (89) – combining in a single sentence two
of Agamben's key terms. The detailed discussion of the norms of
commedia dell'arte performance gives way, in the fourth and final
'act', to a reading of the Myth of Er, which had also concluded
the main body of the fourth and final 'act' of *Homo Sacer*. Where
in *The Use of Bodies* the myth of reincarnation had served as a
way to think about choosing one's form of life or *bios*, here the
'character' of Pulcinella represents that which exceeds 'a life that
is already packaged . . . which the soul can therefore not live but
only re-live' (103). By contrast, Pulcinella 'lives a life beyond
any *bios* – precisely the life of Pulcinella that Giandomenico's
drawings faithfully present as any and every life' (107) – and here
the translator supplies the Italian equivalent *una vita qualcunque*,
which, in an evocation of the key term from *The Coming Community*, could also be translated as 'whatever life'.

In the first of the concluding 'postils', Agamben builds on this
connection by putting forward Pulcinella as the embodiment of
'form-of-life as a *bios* that is only its own *zōē*' (127), insofar as 'there
is no vegetative life separated from form of life, a *zōē* that can be

distinguished and separated from *bios*' (129). And in the second, the theme of voice makes an unexpected reappearance. Above he had referred to the 'squeaky voice – similar to Donald Duck's – used by puppeteers when they make [Pulcinella] talk' (45) – which I directly quote in part to highlight the strangeness of Agamben making reference to Donald Duck – and in the closing pages of the book he meditates on the kazoo-like device that generates that voice. Pulcinella's voice is not the voice of the puppeteer, who has to go through difficult training to learn to speak intelligibly using the device, and it is also undeniably artificial. Hence he seems to live beyond the presupposition of the voice – or at least that is the conclusion I draw from this odd passage, in which Agamben seems almost to shift into a mode of deliberate self-parody.

Hence, essentially all of Agamben's key problems find their solution in Pulcinella, just as his key concepts find their embodiment in this strange cartoon-like character. It is difficult to know what to make of this book as a positive prescription, because it seems tantamount to declaring that all our problems would be solved if we could find a way to be more like Bugs Bunny. What is going on here? Agamben may have left some hints in the final stages of the *Homo Sacer* series, above all in *The Highest Poverty*, where he declares, 'The perfect comprehension of a phenomenon is its parody' (HP 5). In *The Use of Bodies*, too, a key passage cites Walter Benjamin's dictum that 'shards of messianic time are present in history in possibly infamous and risible forms' (UB 94). Hence this self-parody may not be sheer self-indulgence. Instead, it may be that he chose a cartoon character as the 'hero' of *Homo Sacer* as a way of highlighting how deeply the norms of the 'Western machine' have shaped our expectations and sense of self, such that a truly radical alternative cannot fail to appear absurd. But perhaps the most absurd thing of all would be to prefer this world of ours over a world full of joyful Pulcinellas.

How to find yourself and disappear completely

Already in the first year after completing the *Homo Sacer* series, then, *Pulcinella* rearticulates Agamben's entire intellectual project in a completely unexpected way. The next two works I will be discussing are perhaps not as radical, but they do continue to push his thought in unexpected directions – and as we should expect from Agamben by now, they do so by drawing on some of his deepest intuitions and longest-standing sources. The pairing is admittedly somewhat arbitrary, because on a surface level the two texts – one a study of medieval poetry, the other a combination of a mystery story and a contribution to the philosophy of science – could not be more different. Yet from the perspective of the present investigation, their very diversity is a similarity, insofar as both testify to Agamben's continued creativity. It is as though finishing *The Use of Bodies*, far from exhausting his intellectual energy, freed him to finally get some work done.

At first glance, *The Adventure* seems to be the more accessible of the two, treating themes of personal integrity and love in the context of adventure stories. Yet this short work packs a great deal of Agamben's characteristic erudition into its brief chapters – simply to scan the table of contents, the reader must be familiar with Greek and Provençal. It also represents an extreme example of Agamben's principle, drawn from Benjamin, 'that doctrine may legitimately be exposed only in the form of interpretation' (ST 7). Indeed, it is a commentary on a commentary on a commentary, insofar as it takes its starting point from Goethe's poem *Urworte* (Primal Words), which itself responds to Macrobius's *Saturnalia*. Neither author has played a major role in Agamben's work up to this point, and so it can be difficult to discern his own position in the course of the argument. The ambiguity begins already with the second paragraph, where, after quoting Macrobius's claim 'that four deities preside over the birth of every human being: Daimon, Tyche, Eros, and Ananke (Demon, Chance, Love, and Necessity)' (A 3), Agamben states:

> The life of every human being must pay tribute to these four deities, and should not try to elude or dupe them. Daimon must be honored because we owe him our character and nature; Eros because fecundity and knowledge depend on him; Tyche and Ananke because the art of living also involves a reasonable degree of bowing to what we cannot avoid. The way in which each person relates to these powers defines his or her ethics. (4–5)

Is this a statement of Agamben's own view on the matter, an extrapolation from Macrobius, or both? The problem compounds when Agamben turns to Goethe's appropriation of Macrobius's four deities. Though Goethe 'adds Elpis, or Hope' to the list, the poem *Urworte* 'betrays the superstition to which Goethe devoted his life, namely, the cult of the demon' (5). This is not the evil figure familiar from Christian theology, but instead symbolised Goethe's 'attempt to turn the nexus of his life and work into a destiny' (7–8). This priority affects Goethe's approach to each of the other elements. Hence, while Tyche or chance receives positive treatment insofar as the demon converts chance into destiny, 'Eros appears in a distinctly unfavorable light' (11) as a potential distraction – which reflects Goethe's own personal life, characterised as it was by 'a renunciation of perseverance in love relationships' (10). Overall, Goethe's strategy is aimed at avoiding 'ethical judgment' – a negative goal, one would assume, until Agamben clarifies that 'responsibility is a juridical and not an ethical concept', meaning that the attempt to avoid the responsibility that judgment expresses is 'as alien to ethics as that which would like to assume it' (13). Still, there is something suspicious in Goethe's reliance on what Agamben calls 'the ambiguous power that guarantees success to the individual on condition of renouncing every ethical decision' (14), and the reflections on the ambiguous relationships among Macrobius's four deities (or Goethe's five) seem to indicate that Agamben will not end up favouring either. In fact, over the course of the argument it becomes clear that Agamben's chapter titles – Demon, Aventure, Eros, Event, and Elpis – represent a variation on the theme of Goethe's list.

The next chapter, entitled 'Aventure' (the Provençal term at the root of our 'adventure') begins with a quotation from the medieval poet Chrétien de Troyes that relates a familiar theme: the knight who declares that he is in search of adventure. Agamben's quest here and in the rest of the book, however, is to show us that the theme of adventure is not familiar at all – indeed, that modern culture has lost touch with it altogether. After exploring the etymology of *aventure*, he connects it to the Greek Tyche, which 'designates both chance and destiny', insofar as it designates 'the unexpected event that challenges the knight and a series of facts that will necessarily take place' (24). The most important thing to underline, however, is 'the irresistible involvement of the subject in the adventure that happens to him' (24). This claim may initially seem to be at odds with the fact that, in the medieval sources, 'it is not always easy to distinguish between the event and its transposition into words' (27) – is the adventure the imagined event or the poem that relates it? – but, drawing on a close reading of Marie de France, Agamben argues that the real adventure 'is not an event located in a chronological past, but is always already an event of speech' (32), which means that the truth of the adventure is 'neither the apophatic truth of logic nor historical truth', but 'poetic truth' (33).

This truth is often 'personified by a woman', who represents not the princess who must be rescued, for example, but instead embodies the tale itself 'to the extent that the act of telling and the content of the tale tend to converge' (41). The fact that she can appear in the tale shows that she is not a transcendent entity like the Muse, inspiring the tale from without, but lives and dies with the telling (40). Here Agamben is remaining faithful to one of the true unchanging constants of his thought: if a woman appears in poetry, she is never a real flesh-and-blood woman but represents the poetic experience of language. As I pointed out in Chapter 1, Agamben makes that claim of Dante's Beatrice in 'Comedy' (1978) – an assertion he will repeat later in The Adventure (63) – and he makes similar arguments in multiple essays in The End of The Poem (particularly 'An Enigma Concerning the Basque Woman' [1990] and 'Corn' [1996]), in Nymphs (2003), and in The Unspeakable Girl (2010). What a man truly loves, in Agamben's poetics, is never a woman as such, but only language.

The next two chapters continue to rearticulate the deities in Goethe's list from the perspective of adventure. The chapter on Eros begins by critiquing modern theories of adventure, which tend to contrast the adventure from everyday life as a kind of episode or escape, whether conceived as a torrid love affair in which a man asserts his masculinity or an aestheticisation of existence where one ironically treats life as a work of art. Nothing could be further from the medieval experience, where the knight puts his very self at stake in an adventure that cannot be separated from its artistic retelling. Dante's critique, by contrast, is at once more informed and more incisive, as he refuses to use the term that defined the poetics of his revered predecessors, to which he counterposes the redemptive experience of Christian love. This is true above all of the famous episode of Paolo and Francesca from the *Inferno*, which 'shows that if love remains imprisoned in the field of adventure and the book ('when we read . . .'), it can only be lost' (A 64). Yet if we think that adventure has therefore become somehow questionable, the chapter that follows, in which 'Event' stands in the place of Ananke or Necessity, equates adventure with a number of key concepts from Agamben, most notably the Platonic notion of the 'sayable' (71), the Heideggerian *Ereignis* (of which '"adventure" is the most correct translation'; 81), and – most importantly – the event of anthropogenesis (82). The latter, it seems, is *the* adventure of the title, because 'by becoming human, [the living being] has devoted himself to an adventure that is still in progress and whose outcome is difficult to predict' (82). Here we have the confirmation of Agamben's long-standing intuition from 'Expropriated Manner' (1991) into the 'anthropological change' that accompanies the poetic experience (EP 94).

In the short concluding chapter on Elpis or Hope, Agamben begins speaking more clearly in his own voice, declaring, 'Every human is caught up in the adventure; for this reason, every human deals with Daimon, Eros, Ananke, and Elpis' (85). If we hold fast to adventure in our reckoning with each of the others, it seems, then we will reject the false consolations of destiny and transcendent satisfaction and instead embrace the 'poetic life', which Agamben defines as 'one that, in every adventure, obstinately maintains itself in relation not with an act but with a potential, not with a god but with a demigod' (88, translation altered). From this perspective, love in Dante's sense becomes the greatest temptation, and we must instead hold to hope – not for some external goal that will satisfy us, but for the possibility of being released from the very desire for satisfaction or salvation at all. Here doctrine certainly has been exposed in the form of commentary – a doctrine that can be read as Agamben's indirect manifesto on the life well lived.

Despite its obvious differences in topic and approach, *What is Real?* is ultimately a reflection on the same theme of personal integrity. On the one hand, it is an attempt to solve a mystery that has bedevilled the Italian public for decades – why did Ettore Majorana, one of the nation's most promising physicists, disappear without a trace at the dawn of the Second World War? Rejecting the common theories that Majorana committed suicide or that he was fleeing from the prospect of contributing to the development of the atomic bomb, Agamben proposes, on the basis of Majorana's own writings, that the young physicist was protesting against a fundamental transformation of physics in the era of quantum mechanics:

> while it is not certain that Majorana glimpsed the consequences of the splitting of the atom, it is certainly the case that he clearly saw the implications of a mechanics that renounced every non-probabilistic conception of the real. Science no longer tried to know reality, but – like the statistics of social sciences – only to intervene in it in order to govern it. (WR 14)

Hence Majorana's own disappearance, which is 'an event that is at the same time absolutely real and absolutely improbable' (43), served as a protest against the disappearance of reality and its replacement by the realm of probability.

As I have noted above, this topic provides an opportunity for Agamben to discuss Simone Weil's writings on classical vs. quantum physics from around the same period, which share the same critique he attributes to Majorana. Far from merely returning to familiar territory, however, his investigation also leads him through close readings of Einstein, Bohr, and Schrödinger, as well as the major texts of modern probability theory. He focuses particularly on Pascal, whose infamous 'wager' reveals the real purpose behind calculating probability: 'Statistics is not a science that aims at an experimental knowledge of the real; rather, it is the science that enables us to take decisions in uncertain conditions' (37). All this fresh material initially seems to lead into a boilerplate discussion of Aristotle's distinction between act and potentiality, in which he appears to share with modern statistics and quantum theory the view that 'potency or possibility (*dynamis*) should be considered as a way of being along with actuality (*energeia*)' (37). After laying out the basic terms of Aristotle's theory in a way that is by now quite familiar, Agamben says:

> If we try to define probability in Aristotle's terms, we may say that it is a potential emancipated from its hierarchical subjection to the act. Insofar as it has secured an existence that is independent of its actual realization, such a possibility tends to replace reality and thus to become the object of a science of the accidental – unthinkable for Aristotle – that considers possibility as such, not as a means of knowing the real, but as a way of intervening in it in order to govern it. (40; translation altered)

Though he does not make the explicit connection here, this distinction clearly echoes the two ontologies of *Opus Dei*, where reality corresponds to the ontology of being and probability corresponds to the ontology of having-to-be or command. Already Agamben had claimed that modernity, starting from Kant, begins to supplant the ontology of being with the ontology of command, and here we have the most vivid possible illustration in the most prestigious and foundational of all the natural sciences.

Arguably even more valuable is the clarification of Agamben's own view of potentiality, to which his account of the liberated probability of statistics and quantum theory sounds eerily similar. Returning to an image that proved decisive in Agamben's initial engagement with potentiality in *Idea of Prose*, he claims, 'What happened in modern statistics and quantum physics is that the writing tablet – pure possibility – replaced reality, and knowledge now knows only knowledge itself' (40). Superficially, we could read this as echoing Agamben's own call for a potentiality freed of any relation to actuality and his valorisation of the contemplative life. Yet there is a key difference: far from overcoming the logic of presupposition or relation, this autonomous potentiality pushes it to an extreme by dominating and, in the last analysis, seeking to erase actuality. If in his theory of potentiality, as Agamben put it in

Homo Sacer, 'Aristotle actually bequeathed the paradigm of sovereignty to Western philosophy' (HS 46), the statistical and quantum model seems to echo *State of Exception*'s warning that the collapse of the binary system transforms it 'into a killing machine' (SE 86) – which modern physics would literally create in the form of the atomic bomb, as part of the very conflict in which sovereign emergency powers were pushed to their most destructive limits. Here, however, Agamben does not make those connections explicit, choosing instead to conclude by echoing Majorana's challenge to a scientific regime that has lost all connection with the real – a challenge on which Majorana staked his very life. In that strange gesture of disappearance, then, perhaps we find a paradigm for a scientific experience of adventure.

Variations on a theme

Not all of Agamben's works post-*Use of Bodies* are so experimental and surprising. The memoir does continue in a similar vein, as Agamben uses the keepsakes and photos from his various workspaces over the years as a frame for discussing his intellectual life, mixing text and image in a way reminiscent of the novels of Sebald. The result is a strange autobiography in which the subject himself seems to vanish into the network of friends and books that shaped his thought – and ultimately into the grass. By comparison, the three works to which I now turn – *What is Philosophy?*, *Karman*, and *Il Regno e il Giardino* (The Kingdom and the Garden) – are much more typical of Agamben's output, both in style and content. Indeed, to an uncharitable reader they could initially appear to be little more than a rehash of familiar concepts and themes, particularly *Karman*, which mostly reiterates and extends the arguments of *The Sacrament of Language* and *Opus Dei*. All three make distinctive contributions to Agamben's thought, but given the degree of recapitulation and consolidation at work, I will not be treating them with the same level of detail as the other books I have discussed in this chapter.

The title of *What is Philosophy?* obviously calls to mind Deleuze and Guattari's book on the same subject. I do not believe that Agamben's book is a direct response to Deleuze and Guattari's, but the work seems to be in the spirit of their opening lines: 'The question *what is philosophy?* can perhaps be posed only late in life, with the arrival of old age and the time for speaking concretely.' Only in old age can one finally confront the title question, which amounts to asking, 'What is it I have been doing all my life?' Yet where Deleuze and Guattari hold out the possibility of old age as granting 'a sovereign freedom',[5] Agamben confesses in his foreword that he instead experiences weakness, one that prevents him from attempting to answer the question directly and constrains him to rely on 'those who read . . . in a spirit of friendship' to discern 'an idea of philosophy' (WP xi). In an echo of his remarks in *Pulcinella* about being forced by his times to write on grim topics that do not suit his nature, Agamben continues:

> As has been said, those who find themselves writing in an age that, rightly or wrongly, appears to them to be barbaric, must know that their strength and capacity for expression are not for this reason increased, but rather diminished and depleted. Since he has no other choice, however, and pessimism is alien to his nature – nor does he seem to recall with certainty a better time – the author cannot but rely on those who have experienced the same difficulties – and in that sense, on friends. (xi)

That same foreword notes that, while the first essay, 'Experimentum Vocis', 'resumes and develops in a new direction notes I took in the second half of the 1980s', the majority of the book was 'written over the past two years' – thus in the wake of *The Use of Bodies*. Just as it was only halfway through his great philosophical project that he began to focus in earnest on questions of method, so too does he turn to the question of the meaning of philosophy only after his greatest labour is complete.

Yet Agamben's first concern in this book is with a project that remains decidedly incomplete: the investigation of voice whose abandonment he described in 'Experimentum Linguae'. The essay in its current form – which seems to weave older materials together with new reflections in line with the concerns of the *Homo Sacer* project – thus represents something of a path not taken, a version of Agamben's project that was articulated, as *Language and Death* seemed to anticipate, around the concept of voice. As in the version of the project that we now have, the logic of presupposition is central, and in fact many passages in this opening essay are closely parallel to 'Ontological Apparatus', the chapter on presupposition in Part II of *The Use of Bodies*.[6] Unlike in *Language and Death*, voice is not primarily the presupposition of language – here, as in his mature thought, what language presupposes is extra-linguistic being, which only appears as such from within language. Instead, voice emerges as a way to grasp language in itself, to grasp the moment of anthropogenesis in which 'the primate of the *homo* genus became a speaker' (7).

The way that transition into the realm of language was achieved – at least within 'Western civilization' (7) – was through the articulation of the animal voice into a series of distinct sounds designated by letters. It is this articulation that allows language to be systematised and recognised as such and thus to serve as the foundation for particular political communities. Agamben suggest that the Western linguistic project reaches its outer limits in the construction of Indo-European, which serves as 'something like an absolute *langue* that nobody ever spoke or will ever speak, but constitutes as such the historical and political *a priori* of the West, which guarantees the unity and the reciprocal intelligibility of its many languages and its many peoples' (11). Continuing in the theme of unfinished business, Agamben returns to his early concern with the general science of the human and its ultimate unattainability:

> Linguistics thus became the pilot discipline for the human sciences between the nineteenth and twentieth centuries, and its sudden withering away and foundering in the work of Benveniste coincides with an epochal mutation in the historical destiny of the West. The West, which realized and brought to completion the potentiality it had inscribed in its language, must now open itself to a globalization that simultaneously marks its triumph and its end. (12)

This unexpected reference to globalisation seems like a very different diagnosis of the contemporary condition than those found at various places in the *Homo Sacer* volumes, but the end result is the same: the epochal crisis of the West represents an opportunity to revisit the moment of anthropogenesis 'and try to assume being a speaker anew' (23). The method he proposes is an '*experimentum vocis*, in which humans radically question the role of language in the voice' (23), and the bulk of the essay pursues that agenda by various means. On the one hand, he undercuts the foundations of traditional Western grammar by pointing out that it is 'impossible to clearly separate the elements . . . that the grammatical tradition had identified' (21) – in other words, the articulation of the voice into discrete letter-like sounds is a fiction. And he suggests that Plato's theory of language represents a more productive alternative to the Aristotelian system that has dominated Western thought.

The central essay of the book, entitled 'On the Sayable and the Idea', takes up the contrast between Plato and Aristotle – but leaves aside the theme of voice altogether, as do the other, much shorter essays written fresh for this volume. Instead, Agamben returns to the theme that superseded that of voice in his thought of the 1980s, namely the Platonic Idea or thing itself as the very 'sayability' of language. While his reading of Plato remains essentially unchanged, he deepens his account on two fronts. First, he demonstrates, in vivid detail, that Aristotle's critique of Plato's theory of Ideas is tendentious and misleading. Second, and more importantly, he attempts to construct a minority tradition that remained faithful to Plato's initial insights, starting with the Stoics and continuing through various heretical or otherwise marginal figures in medieval and early modern philosophy. On both fronts, Agamben shows that he is not simply coasting on old research – he delves into figures and fields that he has never touched before, including a 'terminological analysis of Greek geometry' (78). And he concludes by declaring,

> The truth that is expressed in language – and given that we do not have other ways of expressing it, the truth that is at stake for us as speaking humans – is neither a real fact nor an exclusively mental entity, nor a 'world of meanings'; rather, it is an idea, something purely sayable, that radically neutralizes the oppositions mental/real, existent/nonexistent, signifier/signified. This – and nothing else – is the object of philosophy and thought. (89)

This comes as close to an answer to the question of 'what is philosophy?' as the book provides.

Of the remaining essays, two – one on demand and the other on philosophy as a perpetual 'proem' (or preface) to a book that will never be written – dwell primarily on familiar concerns. The concluding appendix on the politics of music breaks new ground, albeit in a strange way. In it, Agamben calls for philosophy to take up the role as Muse to reform the derelict music of our era, in which 'the bad music that today pervades our cities at every moment and in every place is inseparable from the bad politics that governs them' (102). It is difficult to know what to make of this argument, but the obvious connection between the themes of music and voice and the position of the appendix after the short essay on 'proems' suggests that it represents yet another attempt at the unwritten project on voice – one that Agamben's recent seminars, and my discussion with him in Venice, indicate that he continues to pursue in some way.

Where *What is Philosophy?* dwells on the work on language that, as I argued in Chapter 2, opened up the way for Agamben's political work, *Karman* and *Il Regno e il Giardino* both rearticulate the concerns of the latest stages of the *Homo Sacer* project. Yet in a sense, they also reflect an earlier stage in Agamben's thought insofar as both focus on personal experience – specifically, on how the Western machine interpellates the individual by means of the apparatus of guilt. *Karman* focuses on the origins of moral concepts of guilt, which he traces to the juridical realm. The confusion of ethical and legal categories has been a major concern of Agamben's since at least *Remnants of Auschwitz* (1999), but here his intuition is confirmed by a painstaking philological investigation that demonstrates that the legal apparatus presupposes the guilt of the subject and that Christian theological concepts of free will served only to intensify that dynamic of inculpation.

Crucial here is the transition from ancient Greek ethics, which were centred on potentiality and knowledge, and Christian and modern ethics, which were based on the will and intention. And it is above all Augustine who enacts this shift, as Agamben shows in a careful textual study that reveals that his famous dispute with Pelagius was not really over the existence of free will, but on the status of potential. Where Augustine posited the sinfulness of the will, Pelagius – subsequently condemned as a heretic – insisted that human beings retained the potential not to sin (K 51). *Il Regno e il Giardino* takes up and deepens this insight, building on *Karman*'s reading of Augustine by tracing the origins of his concept of original sin – that is, of the inborn guiltiness of every human being. This forms part of a broader archaeology of the concept of paradise, which connects with the experience of anthropogenesis even more literally than usual. While Augustine claims that his doctrine of original sin (which posits that Adam and Eve permanently damaged human nature through their sin in a way that is passed down to all subsequent generations) represents the unanimous teaching of the Church, Agamben shows – through a detailed reading of Augustine's sources and a critique of his construal of the Greek grammar of a crucial verse from Paul – that Augustine was actually breaking with a previous 'exegetical tradition that excluded the transmission of Adam's sin to human nature' (RG 24). And reprising Augustine's debate with Pelagius, Agamben maintains that Augustine's real concern is not philosophical or theological but ecclesiastical, because 'if human nature was capable of not sinning without grace' – as Pelagius maintained – 'then the Church, which dispenses [grace] through its sacraments, would not be necessary' (34).

Much of *Il Regno e il Giardino* investigates minority traditions within Christianity that rejected original sin – not only Pelagius, but also the little-studied early medieval philosopher John Scotus Eriugena (no relation to Duns Scotus) and Dante. Both in their own way reject the doctrine of original sin's attempt 'to attribute to the human will the unheard-of capacity to transform the nature created by God' (32) and instead assert that humanity has access to its original nature and the earthly paradise that symbolises it. He concludes by proposing that the earthly paradise may provide a better political model than the messianic Kingdom at the end of time. In particular, he suggests that it can overcome the problem of the role of the party in the transition to socialism on which 'the Soviet revolution made shipwreck' (117) – a diagnosis that makes an interesting supplement to that found in *Homo Sacer*, where Agamben attributes that shipwreck to a failure to grapple with 'the theory of the state (and in particular the state of exception, which is to say, of the dictatorship of the proletariat as the transitional phase leading to the stateless society)' (HS 12).

By contrast, *Karman* goes beyond the gesture of constructing a minority tradition within the West and ventures into Buddhist traditions, which provide a model of action that overcomes the cycle of guilt and responsibility represented by the title concept (a form of the familiar word 'karma'). This reference is not entirely unprecedented – in *The Kingdom and the Glory*, he had recourse to Sanskrit traditions (cf. KG 225ff.) – but it is surprising in a thinker who has remained so resolutely intra-Western in so much of his work. While in *The Kingdom and the Glory* his engagement was primarily mediated through the work of Marcel Mauss, in *Karman* it is ironically the Indo-European hypothesis, which *What is Philosophy?* had just referred to as the 'the historical and political *a priori* of the West' (WP 11), that provides the path beyond the confines of the Western tradition, insofar as Sanskrit is grouped together with most European languages as part of the Indo-European family. Agamben has previously engaged with other linguistic traditions – primarily Hebrew and Arabic – that are in explicit critical dialogue with the West, but *Karman* represents his first significant presentation of a more or less completely extra-Western tradition of thought, rather than a critical minority tradition within or adjacent to the mainstream Western tradition, as a viable alternative. Hence even in a book that seems like a retread of familiar themes, Agamben is pushing himself into new realms of thought – although likely not a realm in which we should expect creative contributions on par with his readings of Plato, Aristotle, or Augustine.

History and architectonic

Agamben's most significant publication of this period – both in terms of historical importance and sheer physical heft – is the omnibus edition of *Homo Sacer*, which collects all of the existing volumes together as a single massive book. I have already addressed some of the implications of Agamben's architectonic scheme in my discussions of the individual instalments in the series, but here I want to take a step back and respond to the gesture of presenting these materials, so diverse in content, style, and chronology, as somehow a single book.

The first thing to note is that the Italian omnibus edition is not a simple reprint of the existing books. As I have pointed out above, the definitive Italian version includes a supplemental essay on war appended to *Stasis* (which has not yet appeared in English) and a short note on Plato's *Laws* added to the end of *The Use of Bodies* (which does appear in the English translation of UB and hence in the English omnibus edition), along with various small corrections to the text and bibliography (none of which, Agamben assured me via email, are substantive). Since complete editions of the series had already appeared in French and English (in 2016 and 2017, respectively), this choice to augment and otherwise alter the Italian edition counts as a gesture on its own. By rendering the translated editions obsolete, Agamben is forcing future readers to look to his original Italian text for the truly definitive version of the *Homo Sacer* project.

More important from the perspective of my present investigation, however, is the violation of chronology. While the original dates of publication are preserved for the individual volumes – albeit not the dates of composition for the older materials included in *The Use of Bodies* – Agamben is inviting his readers to approach his work in its architectonic order rather than viewing it in terms of its chronological unfolding. In my discussion in previous chapters, I have often highlighted the fact that the volumes were published out of order, but I imagine that it was sometimes difficult for readers to keep track of the overall structure. For ease of reference, then, I have assembled a table that lists the books in their order of publication and then in their architectonic order (Table 5.1). In parentheses after each title, I list, respectively, the original architectonic placement and the year of their original publication (and composition, in the case of *Stasis*).

Table 5.1

Year	Title (original volume)	Volume	Title (year of publication)
1995	*Homo Sacer* (1)	1	*Homo Sacer* (1995)
1999	*Remnants of Auschwitz* (3)	2.1	*State of Exception* (2003)
2003	*State of Exception* (2)	2.2	*Stasis* (2015; drafted 2001)
2007	*The Kingdom and the Glory* (2.2)	2.3	*The Sacrament of Language* (2008)
2008	*The Sacrament of Language* (2.3)	2.4	*The Kingdom and the Glory* (2007)
2011	*The Highest Poverty* (4.1)	2.5	*Opus Dei* (2012)
2012	*Opus Dei* (2.5)	3	*Remnants of Auschwitz* (1999)
2014	*The Use of Bodies* (4.2)	4.1	*The Highest Poverty* (2011)
2015	*Stasis* (2.2)	4.2	*The Use of Bodies* (2014)

When presented in this way, the architectonic order appears to be a thorough scrambling – in fact, aside from volume 1, there is not a single volume whose place in line has not been altered. The most dramatic displacement is of course *Remnants of Auschwitz*, whose designation as volume 3 places it among books published over a decade later. Even where the books are presented in closer to their chronological placement, as in the texts grouped together as volume 2, there are reversals, so that *Stasis* is presented after *State of Exception* and *The Kingdom and the Glory* after *The Sacrament of Language*. In both of these cases, a later work is presented as somehow foundational for one that preceded it. The addition of the essay on war to *Stasis* increases this impression, rendering it almost a series of case studies for instances of the state of exception, when we know in fact that it was the analysis of city and household in *Stasis* that laid the foundation for *State of Exception*'s uncovering of the dynamics of *auctoritas* and *potestas*. And as I noted in my discussion above, by shifting *The Kingdom and the Glory* to come after *The Sacrament of Language*, Agamben implicitly invites us to view the latter's methodological reflections as foundational for the former volume, in which he seems to have developed his methodological approach 'on the fly'. Not only that, but by shifting *The Kingdom and the Glory* to come after it, Agamben also positions *The Sacrament of Language* to serve as a kind of transition point within volume 2 from a focus on politics to an emphasis on religion and theology – and creates the impression that the theological reflections in *Stasis*, which in fact lay dormant until the publication of *The Kingdom and the Glory* many years later, are followed up immediately in *The Sacrament of Language*.

In short, the architectonic organisation of volume 2 serves to cover over some of the seams that would still be showing if the volumes were presented chronologically. This is not to say that his presentation is dishonest – in particular, given that they were written so close together, it seems fair to position the methodological reflections in *The Sacrament of Language* as a lead-in to *The Kingdom and the Glory*, whose complex argumentative strategy did not leave much room for them. The volumes were always meant to fit together, after all, so we should not be surprised to find that they rely on each other (whether explicitly or implicitly), nor should we assume that the order of publication necessarily reflects Agamben's original plan for the project. At the same time, there are nonetheless discontinuities and shifts within the series that the architectonic structure serves to highlight. The place of *Remnants of Auschwitz* is surely the most glaring. While its role in the series seemed clear enough following the publication of *State of Exception*, the expansion of volume 2 pushed the focus further and further from the examination of bare life that had motivated the original *Homo Sacer*, to the point where the interplay of sovereign power and bare life retrospectively became merely one example among others of the broader logic of presupposition. Coming from the other side, volume 4 does begin with a consideration of the Franciscan 'form-of-life', but in a way with no direct connection to the analysis of bare life – a concern that really only returns in the final section of *The Use of Bodies*. Hence the placement of *Remnants of Auschwitz* highlights how much of an outlier it is within the series, an impression that is ironically exacerbated by one of the few signs of apparent continuity: namely, the discussion of Foucault's concept of archaeology (RA 140–4). This methodological approach, which had decisively shaped the preceding three volumes of the series, here appears as more of a side-topic, framing the ethical question of how to testify to the appalling experience of the *Muselmann*. In chronological context, this shift in Agamben's approach represents an obvious case of positive development, but in the architectonic context, it feels like a step backward. Even leaving that value judgment aside, it is clear that *Remnants* is not recognisable as an archaeological investigation in the style that Agamben began carrying out in *The Kingdom and the Glory* and would continue to pursue up through the end of *The Use of Bodies*. What, then, is it doing here? Had Agamben waited until the completion of volume 2 to start volume 3, would he have produced anything even remotely like *Remnants of Auschwitz*?

The jarring effect of *Remnants* brings to mind another strange aspect of the series: the fact that, even in its reshuffled order, the key methodological concepts of archaeology and anthropogenesis do not arrive on the scene until halfway through. Does the articulation of the entire series as a single unit invite us to read retrospectively, treating *Homo Sacer, State of Exception*, and *Stasis* – or, for that matter, *Remnants* – as archaeological investigations *avant la lettre*? The repetition of material from the chapter in *Homo Sacer* on 'The Ambivalence of the Sacred' in the methodological sections of *The Sacrament of Language* may point in that direction – but it could equally be taken as highlighting the difference in context and approach between the two discussions, much as the passage on archaeology in *Remnants* marks development more than continuity.

Overall, then, we can say that by assembling these texts in this order, Agamben invites us to read them together but for the most part does not instruct us on how we are to do so. For every explicit cross-reference – for instance, the reference from *The Highest Poverty* to *Opus Dei*, and from *Opus Dei* back to *The Kingdom and the Glory* – there are whole volumes that are isolated, with no explicit references back to them. This is the case not only for *Stasis* (for obvious reasons of its publication history), but for *The Sacrament of Language* and *Remnants of Auschwitz*. Even in his concluding attempt in 'Toward a Theory of Destituent Potential' to account for the unity of the series, as I have noted, he refers only to three members of the series (*Homo Sacer, State of Exception*, and *The Kingdom and the Glory*), along with one book that falls outside its bounds (*The Open*). At the same time, it is admittedly not Agamben's style to make explicit reference back to previous books – a habit that makes the present study both arduous and necessary – and I have highlighted many places where he appears to be implicitly drawing material from other publications (most notably *The Time That Remains*) into the structure of the series.

I have already mentioned one major exception to Agamben's avoidance of self-reference: his extended quotation from *Homo Sacer* in the epilogue to *The Use of Bodies* (UB 268), which is to my knowledge the sole time that he has quoted himself at such length at any point in his work. Above, I focused on the content of that self-quotation, which was the last in a sequence of references back to Agamben's critique of relation in *Homo Sacer*. Here, I am more concerned with the form. If *Homo Sacer* and *The Use of Bodies* are in some sense part of the 'same' book, then it is a book that quotes itself – though, again, only at this single point. I have frequently used the metaphor of 'reading something onto the record' when describing Agamben's incorporation of previous themes and concepts into the series. What does it mean that he very literally reads *Homo Sacer* volume 1 onto the record of the larger work of which it forms a part?

In his response to a conference paper where I shared an early version of my argument in the present volume, Virgil Brower connected this self-referentiality to a passage from *The Highest Poverty* in which Agamben dwells at length on a monastic rule that mandates that the text of the rule itself be read out loud to the monks during meals. As Agamben points out, this implies that 'there will necessarily be a moment when the reader . . . will read the passage that enjoins him to read the rule every day' (HP 77). This moment is special, Agamben suggests, because

> In reading the other passages of the rule, the reader executes the precept of the reading, but does not actualize what the text enjoins him to do in that moment. In this case, however, the reading and putting into action of the rule coincide without remainder. By reading the rule that prescribes to him the reading of the rule, the reader performatively executes the rule ipso facto. His *lectio* [or reading] realizes, that is to say, the exemplary instance of an enunciation of the rule that coincides with its execution, of an observance that is rendered indiscernible from the command that it obeys. (77)

This passage comes in the context of an examination of the tension in early monasticism between orality and writing, which itself reflects the tension between life and rule that characterised monastic life at its most radical and promising. In this more experimental and less institutionalised phase of monasticism, the written rule continually stages itself as an oral text, transcribing a conversation among exemplary masters – or, in a strange example that Agamben cites on the page before his discussion of the *lectio* (76), the rule can even be pictured as speaking in its own living voice (one last echo, Brower suggested, of the theme of voice).

Whether or not the parallel between the passages is intentional on Agamben's part, it is certainly suggestive. First of all, it helps to clarify what he is *not* doing. The gesture of quoting himself, or producing a text that reads and interprets itself, could be taken as the ultimate attempt to 'lay down the law' – to assert his proprietary authority over the meaning of his work, underwritten by the claim to have had in mind the core foundational idea from the very beginning. This would mean regarding the original *Homo Sacer* as an *archē* in the sense of a command, one that dictates the contents of the remaining volumes while continuing to reign over them throughout. If, by contrast, the gesture is more akin to that of the *lectio* in which commandment and execution become indistinguishable, then the effect would be just the opposite: to put forth the original *Homo Sacer* as an *archē* in Agamben's sense, as the gap that separates the series from any origin and hence exposes it in its contingency. For one could rightly ask: why these studies and not others? Why not an archaeology of law, or of the state as such, or of bureaucracy, or of labour, or of the corporation, or of any of the dozens of other major Western institutional structures that he could have studied? Is this assemblage of texts really 'a rethinking of *all* the categories of our political tradition in light of the relation between sovereign power and bare life' (MWE x, emphasis added), which he promised in the preface to *Means Without End*?

The answer to that final question is: no, of course not. The texts he has assembled are only examples of an investigation that is, in principle, interminable – above all the study that gave rise to the entire project, whose unmasking of the nexus between sovereign power and bare life now appears as but one example among many even in the context of the series that bears its name. A study that aims to overcome relation and the logic of presupposition must direct that critique also at itself, and it does that by renouncing the claim to presuppose itself, to found itself, to command and necessitate itself. In staging the text's reading of itself, then, Agamben consigns his life's work to the weak power of language. It is a gesture in which he renounces any claim to mastery or authority and yet does so in a way that does not insist upon the point. There is nothing stopping us from viewing this self-referentiality as an assertion of mastery or authority, for to attempt to prevent it would be to repeat the mistake of the Franciscan theorists by defining his stance toward his work negatively with respect to the law. Instead, Agamben abandons his work to that ambiguity, in the hope that he will find readers who have eyes to see it not as the definitive statement of a peerless philosophical genius, but as an opening and an invitation – a gesture, in short, not of mastery but of friendship.

Notes

1. When I met with Agamben, I took the opportunity to ask about this dissertation, which is one of the great mysteries of Agamben philology. He claimed that no copy exists – the university archive lost it, and the only other copy would have been among his late mother's belongings, where he did not find it. He did not believe it would be of much value if published.

2. As I complete production for the current volume, I am also working on copy-editing queries and proofs for my translation of *Il Regno e il Giardino* for Seagull Press. The translations provided in this chapter are my own, but may not match up exactly with the final published text.

3. Since I have so often criticised Prozorov's excessive emphasis on continuity, it is only fair to point out that his eye for consistency allowed him to see the centrality of comedy to Agamben's thought before almost any other interpreter – see *Agamben and Politics*, ch. 1.

4. See, for instance, 'The Dream of Language' (1982) from *End of the Poem* and 'Languages and Peoples' (1995) from *Means Without End*. In the years since publishing *The Use of Bodies*, Agamben has also been at work publishing a series of volumes with poetry in various local dialects in Italy, with facing Italian translations.

5. Deleuze and Guattari, *What is Philosophy?*, 1.

6. In email correspondence, Agamben indicated that the corresponding chapter in *The Use of Bodies* 'may' incorporate older material, which might indicate that the borrowing could have proceeded in the opposite direction.

Conclusion: An Archaeology of Agamben

I began this study by observing how remarkably in tune with his times Agamben was in the 1990s and 2000s. My investigation so far has, if anything, highlighted how improbable this feat was, because one of the dominant threads of Agamben's career has been how consistently out of step he has felt with his historical moment. One of his earliest publications, 'The Tree of Language' (1968), laments that the dominant structuralist paradigm is missing something crucial – namely, the individual experience of language – and that the most prominent critique, deconstruction, misses it even more radically. Agamben's attempt to create an alternative paradigm with a 'general science of man' turned out, as he tersely announced in the 1983 postilla to his essay on Warburg (P 101), to be a blind alley. In a 1990 essay, he seems to declare that his effort was obsolete even before he began pursuing it in the 1970s, as the project of a 'general science of the human' had 'reached its apex at the end of the 1960s, dissolved with the political project of the same years' (64). The failure of this project produces even greater alienation, as he declares, 'The severe prose of the world of the 1980s tolerates only positive sciences and, alongside them, a philosophy that is more and more oblivious of its destination' (64–5) – a stance that seems to confirm his identification with the figure of Damascius in the opening pages of *Idea of Prose* (1985).

Though it produced the work that would have the greatest contemporary impact, Agamben's shift toward politics at the end of the Cold War was also out of step with his times. For Agamben, the Cold War dichotomy was so obviously unworthy of serious intellectual consideration that he barely deigned to mention politics explicitly in the early decades of his work. Now, amid the triumphalism that proclaimed liberal democratic capitalism the permanent winner of that false conflict, Agamben began charting an alternate course. In *The Coming Community* (1990), he tries to imagine a form of politics subtracted from *all* existing identities, an intuition that he will continue to shape and refine until it reaches its mature form in his secular reworking of the Pauline *hōs mē* or 'as not'. At a time when the brutality of the Yugoslav wars seemed to most contemporary observers to be a resurgence of an anachronistic atavism, Agamben took it as evidence of the fundamental dynamic of Western politics – a dynamic that had only intensified in modernity. Later, when the hegemony of global capitalism seemed most unassailable, Agamben exposed the theological impostures of the economic model of world governance, which promises freedom but delivers only a more inescapable form of bondage.

In a world order that had reached its supposedly final form in the system of sovereign nation-states competing within a single world market, Agamben identified the nation-state as ultimately productive of nothing but death and destruction and the economy as a system of nihilistic control that saps life of all meaning. This diagnosis leads him to make this bracing declaration in 2009, which is to say at the end of the decade that brought him to international prominence: 'I say the following with words carefully weighed: nowhere on earth is a legitimate power to be found; even the powerful are convinced of their own illegitimacy.'[1] In other words, Agamben's urgent contemporary relevance was accompanied, if anything, by an even more emphatic rejection of the mainstream consensus of his time than in his earlier work. His opposition to the contemporary world is so absolute that it is very difficult to imagine an alternative that he would find acceptable, leading Jessica Whyte to suggest that Agamben's greatest value as a political theorist is that the exaggerated negativity of his critique – which casts a harsh light on even the apparently positive aspects of the Western political tradition, such as democracy and human rights – leaves no room for nostalgia or easy answers.[2]

Hence we are not dealing with a situation where the times finally caught up to the system that Agamben had been consistently elaborating for decades. Indeed, the case is just the opposite – and yet the contemporary appeal of *The Coming Community*, *Homo Sacer*, *The Open*, *State of Exception*, and *The Kingdom and the Glory* seems undeniable. How is this possible? In a seminar delivered in the wake of this period, Agamben reflected on this question, albeit in his characteristically indirect way. Entitled 'What is Contemporary?' (2008), it draws on the authority of Barthes and Nietzsche to declare, apparently paradoxically, that contemporariness and untimeliness necessarily go together:

> Those who are truly contemporary, who belong to their time, are those who neither perfectly coincide with it nor adjust themselves to its demands. They are thus in this sense irrelevant [*inattuale*, or non-contemporary]. But precisely because of this condition, precisely through this disconnection and this anachronism, they are more capable than others of perceiving and grasping their own time. (WA 40)

This distance does not imply a transcendent objectivity but is its own form of embeddedness in one's era: 'An intelligent man can despise his time, while knowing that he nevertheless irrevocably belongs to it, that he cannot escape his own time' (41). And this implies that those who are apparently most contemporary actually fail to be contemporary at all: 'Those who coincide too well with the epoch, those who are perfectly tied to it in every respect, are not contemporaries, precisely because they do not manage to see it; they are not able to firmly hold their gaze on it' (41). Here we might think of a figure like Francis Fukuyama, whose infamous meditations on the end of history are chronologically contemporary with Agamben's reflections in *The Coming Community*. Yet Fukuyama's very identification with the triumphalism of the post-Cold War era rendered him almost instantaneously irrelevant and out-of-date, whereas Agamben's book still feels fresh and even urgent.

The advantage of the true contemporary is that he 'firmly holds his gaze on his own time so as to perceive not its light, but rather its darkness' (44). This darkness is not a mere void or absence. Instead, it is akin to the darkness we see when we close our eyes and our brain activates certain cells that 'produce the particular kind of vision that we call darkness' (44). On a grander scale, Agamben relates it to the dark patches in the night sky, which represent 'light that, though traveling toward us, cannot reach us, since the galaxies from which the light originates move away from us at a velocity greater than the speed of light' (46). Leaving aside the scientific veracity of that claim, the point of the image is that the contemporary is one who manages to 'perceive, in the darkness of the present, this light that strives to reach us but cannot' (46). Thus the contemporary relates not so much to the actual (whose cognates in Romance languages can be synonymous with 'contemporary') as with the potential, not with the inert reality of their era but with the demand that, 'working within chronological time, urges, presses, and transforms it' (47). This demand corresponds in some way with the *archē* or origin, leading Agamben to declare, 'Only he who perceives the indices and signatures of the archaic in the most modern and recent can be contemporary' (50). As we would expect, however, this *archē* does not designate a chronological past so much as a 'proximity to the origin that nowhere pulses with more force than in the present' (50). It is not a matter of recapturing the past but of finding that which 'remains unlived' in past eras and which, somewhat like the stellar light that can never catch up to us, 'is incessantly sucked back toward the origin, without being able to reach it' (51).

I have repeatedly emphasised that Agamben's archaeological method is not about finding the *archē* in the sense of the command that would force everything necessarily to turn out the way it did. Instead, he seeks to expose the gap that separates our tradition from the origin, thereby rendering it groundless and contingent – and opening it up to a new future. That future is not new in the sense of being radically discontinuous and unprecedented, however, but in the sense of picking up the alternate histories that define the present moment that seeks so doggedly to foreclose them. If the works of the 2010s have been less straightforwardly contemporary than their predecessors, they have been increasingly contemporary in this more rigorous

sense of attempting to reopen the past and make it live again –
sometimes positively and sometimes negatively.

We can see both sides of his approach in the dyad of *The Highest
Poverty* and *Opus Dei*. The former seeks to render the debate over
the Franciscans' claim to live without property a living controversy
for us today, goading us to pick up where they left off and develop
a theory of use that would no longer be defined, even negatively,
in terms of the law. For its part, the latter's complex genealogy of
modern concepts of moral duty – which culminates in a contemporary culture in which it is increasingly impossible to imagine a
moral exhortation other than 'do your job!' – highlights the strange
and wayward path that got us to our present moment, exposing its
contingency. The point of the theological reference, which surely
accounts in large part for the comparative unpopularity of this stage
of Agamben's work among American academics in particular, is not
a mania for tracing everything back to a theological origin, but to
use that unexpected (and, from a secular perspective, deeply undesirable) history to jar the reader into recognising the contingency of
the present and awaken awareness of the demand to stop allowing
this particular *archē* to command us.

Not all forms of non-contemporaneity are created equal, of
course. For all the benefits of anachronism, Agamben sometimes
appears to be out of step with his time in ways that are undesirable
or counterproductive. Though my project in this book did not
lead me to foreground these concerns, I have indicated two areas
where I see serious lacunae in his thought: the absence of any consideration of racialisation and his tendency to treat women never as
concrete women but always as figures for something else (usually
language). More broadly, his resolutely intra-Western perspective –
underwritten by the Indo-European hypothesis – raises questions
about the applicability of his work in other contexts, even granting
that the globalisation of Western political and economic structures
has rendered the conceptual deadlocks of the Western tradition
'everyone's problem'.

When I asked him about these gaps, Agamben responded that
when he approaches a thinker, he prefers to focus on what they
have done rather than what they have not done – and he pointed
out, fairly, that he has done quite a bit. Hence it seems unlikely

that he will overcome these limitations in his work on his own. But if I am right in claiming that he is offering up his labours, not as the definitive statement of a master, but as an invitation to carry them on in a spirit of friendship, then it perhaps falls to the younger generation of scholars who are attracted to his style of thought to deepen his analyses by connecting them to questions of race, gender, and the critique of Western hegemony.

*   *   *

How should we characterise Agamben's style of thought? I can think of many generalisations – a tendency toward sweeping world-historical declarations, a reliance on philology and etymology, an eye for where traditional disciplinary scholars' reach exceeds their grasp, a preference for brevity and allusiveness over explicit large-scale argumentative structures – but none that describe all his major works without exception. Even if we speak only of a sense of the 'atmosphere' of Agamben's writing, which becomes familiar to readers without necessarily being clearly articulable, it is surprisingly hard to generalise. Does *Man Without Content* really 'feel' like *Creation and Anarchy*? My experience that it very much does not is part of what drove me to undertake the reading project that resulted in this book. For that matter, does *Homo Sacer* 'feel' like *The Use of Bodies*? In the tranches of early material in Part III, the answer is sometimes yes – but that only highlights how much Agamben's tone and approach has evolved from the concentrated urgency of *Homo Sacer* to the patient philological exposition that characterises much of *The Use of Bodies*. And to pick an especially extreme example: does *Pulcinella* 'feel' like *any* other work by Agamben?

If I seem to be shifting back and forth between the style of his prose and the style of his thought, it is because the two seem to be closely intertwined in Agamben's work. His writing is not a dispensable vehicle for the underlying ideas, but an essential element in a philosophical corpus that strives always to have a poetic element. In fact, in the 'Prefatory Note' to *The Use of Bodies*, he implicitly calls into question which aspect of his work is really primary by characterising the *Homo Sacer* series as 'an investigation

that, like every work of poetry and of thought, cannot be concluded but only abandoned' (UB xiii).

Hence it is fitting that in two important chapters, 'The Inappropriable' (Part I) and 'Toward an Ontology of Style' (Part III),
Agamben explicitly addresses the question of style. In the latter,
he makes a case for the ontological importance of style:

> In Western thought, the problem of form-of-life has emerged
> as an ethical problem (*ethos*, the mode of life of an individual
> or group) or an aesthetic problem (the style by which the
> author leaves his mark on the work). Only if we restore it
> to the ontological dimension will the problem of style and
> mode of life be able to find its just formulation. (UB 233)

His example of how this works is at once poetic and philosophical,
as he here hearkens back to Averroism and its notion of a single
intellect shared by all of humanity and, in an implicit reference to
Stanzas, points to 'Averroistic poets, like Cavalcanti and Dante',
as those who most thoroughly reckoned with the 'problem of the
conjunction (*copulatio*) between the singular individual and the one
intellect' (233). By contrast, the discussion in 'The Inappropriable'
is much more grounded in the idea of artistic style as it is com-
monly understood. In the course of his discussion of language as an
example of inappropriability, he points out that poets experience
this dynamic most intensely, torn as they are between the impulse
to forcefully appropriate language and make it their own and the
recognition that one has been expropriated by a source of poetry
that remains irreducibly external (the Muse). The poetic act is thus
'a bipolar gesture, which each time renders external what it must
unfailingly appropriate' (86). Agamben connects this dynamic to the
tension between style (what is most particular and idiosyncratic to
an artist) and manner (what is most stereotyped and conventional).
For the poet, then, as for every speaker, language as inappropriable
'defines a field of polar forces, held between idiosyncrasy and stereotype, the excessively proper and the most complete externality'
(87). Yet it is not enough to map style and manner onto the dyad
of appropriation and expropriation, because the tension between

them ultimately means that 'style is disappropriating appropriation (a sublime negligence, forgetting oneself in the proper), manner an appropriating disappropriation (a presenting oneself or remembering oneself in the improper)' (87). And this dynamic, he claims, is crucial for understanding his key concept of 'use', which marks out 'the field of tension whose poles are style and manner, appropriation and expropriation' (87).

In the description of style as 'forgetting oneself in the proper', one can perhaps hear an echo of Agamben's claim that *Idea of Prose* is 'the work in which I recognize myself more than in all the others, perhaps because in it I succeeded in forgetting myself' (ARS 69). As for manner as 'remembering oneself in the improper', we can perhaps think of his distinctive way of navigating realms of scholarship that fall outside his own 'proper' expertise. It is in the latter case that the danger of repetition and stereotype is most acute, as Agamben's archaeological works can sometimes appear to follow a formula: a telling gap in the scholarly literature, an etymological investigation, a tracing of the history of a certain word, the identification of a crucial minority tradition within the tradition. This broad formula could describe both his genealogy of economy and archaeology of glory in *The Kingdom and the Glory*, his archaeology of the oath in *The Sacrament of Language*, of office in *Opus Dei*, of ontology in Part II of *The Use of Bodies*, of life in Part III, of crime and guilt in *Karman*, and of paradise in *Il Regno e il Giardino*. If these later works are less read and less commented upon, it may not be solely because of the off-putting theological and philological material, but from a sense of having seen and done all this before.

This question of repetition becomes all the more acute when we recognise that the discussion of style and manner in 'The Inappropriable' is taken almost word-for-word from the 1991 essay 'Expropriated Manner' (EP 97–8), to which I have returned several times.[3] I have suggested above that this essay represents his first engagement, albeit *avant la lettre*, with the problem of 'anthropogenesis', and here we can see that it is among his earliest explorations of the concept of use. What are we to make, though, of this unmarked *re*-use of material from such a distant period of his career, prior even to the first volume of *Homo Sacer*?

This is not the only example of repetition in the latest phase of his work. I noted above that Agamben seems to re-use passages across different works most often in the formative stage of his political thought, but the period surrounding *The Use of Bodies* evinces nearly as much borrowing among works. I have already discussed the re-use of unpublished material in *What is Philosophy?*, which also overlaps at many places with the chapter 'Ontological Apparatus' from *The Use of Bodies*. And while word-for-word repetition is not as frequent in *Karman*, there is nonetheless much in that book that could be found in a similar form in *The Sacrament of Language* and *Opus Dei*. More broadly, Agamben seems ever more drawn to the themes and concepts of his early work, returning again and again to the unfinished labour of the pre-*Homo Sacer* period. If his archaeological method creates the danger of an overly formulaic approach, this persistent return to his earliest work lends his later output an increasingly self-referential and even self-enclosed character.

Yet that same period has also seen the emergence of some of the most surprising and idiosyncratic works in Agamben's corpus: above all *Pulcinella*, but also *The Adventure* and *What is Real?* And the return to unfinished early material – the drafts that became 'Experimentum Vocis' in *What is Philosophy?* and the series of older notebooks that are informing his return to the theme of voice in a planned future work – is accompanied by fresh ongoing research, as the close readings of Augustine in *Karman* and *Il Regno e il Giardino* attest. What we are seeing, then, is not so much the emergence of a 'late style' as an intensification of the tension between style and manner in Agamben's own work – between the stereotyped formula and the bold experiment, between returning to familiar paths and charting new territory. And as in his analysis of style and manner, there is no simple opposition between the two poles. While his fresh research often appears in the context of seemingly formulaic archaeological investigations, his reengagement with older problems functions to expose the contingency of his intellectual trajectory. If he does ultimately write a book on voice, it will not be the same book he would have written in the late '80s, just as 'Experimentum Vocis' – which includes many themes from late stages of the *Homo Sacer* project that are unattested in earlier work – is surely not the same essay he would have published had he completed the draft at the time.

I claimed in the introduction that the continuity of Agamben's work is never pre-given, but must constantly be won. Nothing could demonstrate that more clearly than the gesture of returning to earlier themes and rearticulating them in light of what he has achieved in the *Homo Sacer* series. If Agamben's work demonstrated the kind of systematic cohesion that so many commentators have attributed to it, this return would be simply redundant. There would be no need for a version of the project on voice that reflects the insights of *Homo Sacer*, for instance, because *Language and Death*, with its fleeting reference to the *homo sacer* figure, would *already be* what Agamben is trying to accomplish now. This is not to say that what Agamben did in *Language and Death* is incompatible with what he did in *Homo Sacer*, only to point out that bringing them together takes work. The way they fit together is not obvious, nor is what will result from the combination. The attempt to do so on Agamben's part is self-referential, but in such a way that it does not presuppose that he already knows the 'self' to which he is referring. In his attempt to rediscover what he was seeking those many years ago, he is finding something – and someone – new. That is what it means to live a life, without presupposing either a stable subject underlying it or a transcendent master unfailingly guiding it.

*   *   *

What remains, then, to those of us who have been living with Agamben? How are we to make the best use of this vast and varied body of work? In closing, I would like to suggest that we should use it just as Agamben does – as the contingent and inappropriable body of work that it is. We should aim to uncover in his writings the same *Entwicklungsfähigkeit* or capacity for development that he seeks in the work of the authors he loves, pushing the text beyond its limits until 'the difference between what belongs to the author of a work and what is attributable to the interpreter becomes as essential as it is difficult to grasp' (ST 8). That, I believe, is what he is doing with his own past writings as he ceaselessly rearticulates and recontextualises them, traveling down the paths not taken in his own career and taking them in directions he never could have anticipated. Does the resulting work belong to his early period or his later period? I have opted for the latter in this book for purely logistical reasons, but the answer is: neither and both.

This attitude toward his own work is in keeping with his broader effort to bring to light the paths not taken in a given scholar's investigation, in the tradition of Western thought, in the very event of anthropogenesis itself. What is his archaeological method, for instance, but an attempt to re-join the alternate history where the 'general science of the human' did not run aground in the work of Benveniste? What is *The Use of Bodies* but an attempt to imagine a world where the Aristotelian ontological apparatus had not set the terms of philosophical – and therefore political – thought for millennia to come? From that perspective, the gesture of imagining what his project on voice could have looked like if he had known then what he knows now shows that he does not exclude himself from scrutiny or presuppose himself as a stable reference point that passes sovereign judgment on the way that things should have been. Instead, he seeks to dwell in his own potentiality, which his work renders ultimately indistinguishable from the potentiality of the tradition that has shaped him in such a way that he wants to reshape it.

Hence one way to make use of Agamben's work is to explore those alternate histories. In some cases, that will mean focusing on what he did not do. What would it look like if Agamben's analysis of the production of bare life had taken seriously the experiences of racialisation and chattel slavery?[4] What would it look like if Agamben had grappled more extensively with questions of gender and sexuality in his analyses of the *Dolce Stil Novo* poets – or of monasticism, for that matter? How would Agamben's style of thought fare outside the confines of the West (or the Indo-European language group)? Those alternate histories could also take a more intra-textual dimension. Instead of seeking to demonstrate that an earlier work anticipates a later one, one could view the earlier formulation as a path not taken, which might have opened up more productive possibilities than Agamben's own mature reflections. There is particularly rich material in the experimental essays from *Means Without End*: what if Agamben really had centred his political thought on surveillance, for example, or 'the task of managing *the survival of humanity in an uninhabitable world*' (ME 87)?

Ultimately, these two approaches are correlative, as they converge at the point where 'the difference between what belongs to the author of a work and what is attributable to the interpreter becomes as essential as it is difficult to grasp' (ST 8), or in other words, where Agamben is treated no longer as an intellectual master but as a friend. My goal in this book has been to lay the groundwork for such an approach to Agamben by presenting him, not as a machine that has generated a philosophical system, but as a living thinker who has spent his life continually discovering himself and his tradition anew – and who invites us to go and do likewise.

Notes

1. Agamben, *The Church and the Kingdom*, 40.
2. Whyte, *Catastrophe and Redemption*, 21–3.
3. In the parallel passage in *Creation and Anarchy* (CA 38–50), in fact, there is even more material copied from 'Expropriated Manner', including a discussion of Goethe's 'late style', which became at once deeply idiosyncratic and stereotyped.
4. Weheliye's *Habaeas Viscus* is an indispensable starting point for any such investigation – see my discussion in *The Prince of This World*, particularly 167 and 191–2.

Bibliography

Abbott, Mathew. *The Figure of This World: Agamben and the Question of Political Ontology*. Edinburgh: Edinburgh University Press, 2014.

Agamben, Giorgio. *The Church and the Kingdom*. Trans. Leland de la Durantaye. New York: Seagull, 2012.

Agamben, Giorgio. *The Fire and the Tale*. Trans. Lorenzo Chiesa. Stanford: Stanford University Press, 2017.

Agamben, Giorgio. *The Mystery of Evil: Benedict XVI and the End of Days*. Trans. Adam Kotsko. Stanford: Stanford University Press, 2017.

Agamben, Giorgio. *Nymphs*. Trans. Amanda Minervini. New York: Seagull, 2013.

Agamben, Giorgio. *Pilate and Jesus*. Trans. Adam Kotsko. Stanford: Stanford University Press, 2015.

Agamben, Giorgio. *Taste*. Trans. Cooper Francis. New York: Seagull Books, 2017.

Arendt, Hannah. *The Human Condition*. 2nd edn. Chicago: University of Chicago Press, 1958.

Attell, Kevin. *Giorgio Agamben: Beyond the Threshold of Deconstruction*. New York: Fordham University Press, 2015.

Badiou, Alain. *Saint Paul: The Foundation of Universalism*. Trans. Ray Brassier. Stanford: Stanford University Press, 2003.

Benveniste, Émile. *Dictionary of Indo-European Culture and Society*. Trans. Elizabeth Palmer. Chicago: HAU, 2016.

Colebrook, Claire, and Jason Maxwell, *Agamben*. Cambridge: Polity, 2016.

Colilli, Paul. *Agamben and the Signature of Astrology: Spheres of Potentiality*. New York: Lexington, 2015.

De Boever, Arne. *Plastic Sovereignties: Agamben and the Politics of Aesthetics*. Edinburgh: Edinburgh University Press, 2016.

Debord, Guy. *Society of the Spectacle*. Detroit: Black & Red, 2005.

Deleuze, Gilles, and Félix Guattari. *What is Philosophy?* Trans. Hugh Tomlinson and Graham Burchell. New York: Columbia University Press, 1994.

Derrida, Jacques. *The Beast and the Sovereign*. Vol. 1. Trans. Geoffrey Bennington. Chicago: University of Chicago Press, 2009.

Dickinson, Colby. *Agamben and Theology*. New York: T&T Clark, 2011.

Dickinson, Colby, and Adam Kotsko. *Agamben's Coming Philosophy: Finding a New Use for Theology*. New York: Rowman & Littlefield International, 2015.

Durantaye, Leland de la. *Giorgio Agamben: A Critical Introduction*. Stanford: Stanford University Press, 2009.

Hegel, G. W. F. *The Phenomenology of Spirit*. Trans. A. V. Miller. New York: Oxford University Press, 1977.

Heidegger, Martin. *Being and Time*. Trans. John Macquarrie and Edward Robinson. New York: Harper Perennial, 2008.

Heidegger, Martin. *The Fundamental Concepts of Metaphysics: World, Finitude, Solitude*. Trans. William McNeill and Nicholas Walker. Bloomington: Indiana University Press, 2001.

Kantorowicz, Ernst. *The King's Two Bodies: A Study in Medieval Political Theology*. Princeton, NJ: Princeton University Press, 2016.

Kishik, David. *The Power of Life: Agamben and the Coming Politics*. Stanford: Stanford University Press, 2012.

Kotsko, Adam. *Neoliberalism's Demons: On the Political Theology of Late Capital*. Stanford: Stanford University Press, 2018.

Kotsko, Adam. *The Prince of This World*. Stanford: Stanford University Press, 2016.

Mills, Catherine. *The Philosophy of Agamben*. Ithaca: McGill-Queen's University Press, 2008.

Nancy, Jean-Luc. *The Inoperative Community*. Ed. Peter Connor. Trans. Peter Connor, Lisa Garbus, Michael Holland, and Simona Sawhney. Minneapolis: University of Minnesota Press, 1991.

Norris, Andrew, ed. *Politics, Metaphysics, and Death: Essays on Giorgio Agamben's Homo Sacer.* Durham, NC: Duke University Press, 2005.

Peterson, Erik. *Theological Tractates.* Trans. Michael J. Hollerich. Stanford: Stanford University Press, 2011.

Prozorov, Sergei. *Agamben and Politics.* Edinburgh: Edinburgh University Press, 2014.

Ross, Alison, ed. *The Agamben Effect (South Atlantic Quarterly).* Durham, NC: Duke University Press, 2008.

Salzani, Carlo. *Introduzione a Giorgio Agamben.* Genoa: il melangolo, 2013.

Schmitt, Carl. *Political Theology: Four Chapters on the Concept of Sovereignty.* Trans. George Schwab. Chicago: University of Chicago Press, 2006.

Taubes, Jacob. *The Political Theology of Paul.* Ed. Aleia Assmann and Jan Assmann. Trans. Dana Hollander. Stanford: Stanford University Press, 2004.

Watkin, William. *Agamben and Indifference: A Critical Overview.* New York: Rowman & Littlefield International, 2014

Watkin, William. *The Literary Agamben: Adventures in Logopoiesis.* New York: Continuum, 2010.

Weheliye, Alexander G. *Habeas Viscus: Racializing Assemblages, Biopolitics, and Black Feminist Theories of the Human.* Durham, NC: Duke University Press, 2014.

Whyte, Jessica. *Catastrophe and Redemption: The Political Thought of Giorgio Agamben.* Albany: SUNY Press, 2013.

Index